AA100
The Arts Past and Present

Book 4
Place and Leisure

Edited by Deborah Brunton

This publication forms part of the Open University course AA100 *The Arts Past and Present*. Details of this and other Open University courses can be obtained from the Student Registration and Enquiry Service, The Open University, PO Box 197, Milton Keynes, MK7 6BJ, United Kingdom: tel. +44 (0)870 333 4340, email general-enquiries@open.ac.uk

Alternatively, you may visit the Open University website at http://www.open.ac.uk where you can learn more about the wide range of courses and packs offered at all levels by The Open University.

To purchase a selection of Open University course materials visit http://www.ouw.co.uk, or contact Open University Worldwide, Michael Young Building, Walton Hall, Milton Keynes, MK7 6AA, United Kingdom for a brochure. Tel. +44 (0)1908 858785; fax +44 (0)1908 858787; email ouwenq@open.ac.uk

The Open University
Walton Hall, Milton Keynes
MK7 6AA

First published 2008

Edited and designed by The Open University.

Typeset in India by Alden Prepress Services, Chennai.

Printed in Malta by Gutenberg Press Limited.

ISBN 9780749217037

1.1

MIX
Paper from responsible sources
FSC
www.fsc.org   FSC® C022612

The paper used for this book is FSC-certified and totally chlorine-free. FSC (the Forest Stewardship Council) is an international network to promote responsible management of the world's forests.

Contents

Tom Gilfillan, *Cheap holiday tickets to Saltcoats, the finest tidal lake on the Firth of Clyde*, railway poster produced by London, Midland and Scottish Railway (LMS), 1935. National Railway Museum, York, 1989-7115. Photo: © Science and Society Picture Library/NRM – Pictorial Collection.

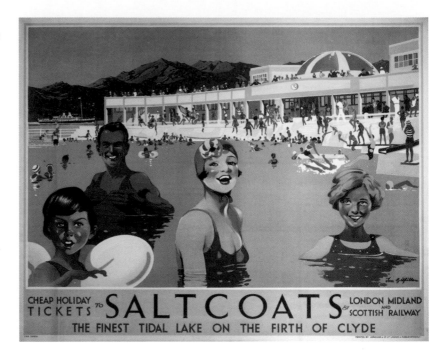

INTRODUCTION

Deborah Brunton

After the complexities of *Cultural Encounters*, the themes of this book – place and leisure – seem much less academic, simpler and more familiar. Almost everyone thinks of leisure as the free time we spend in evenings, weekends and holidays. If you were asked what is the purpose of leisure, you might well say that it is for 'unwinding' – relaxing our minds and bodies to recover from the stresses of the rest of life. The idea of place is equally familiar. On this course you've already learned about events in different geographical places – in Britain, Ireland, Greece and Benin, for example – and about various places associated with particular activities, such as theatres, museums and churches.

By now, you may be wondering why we chose such commonplace ideas as place and leisure as the themes for this book. Will you learn anything new from them? Will it be worth applying all your hard-won study skills to considering them? We selected the themes for the book for two reasons. First, we chose them *because* they are familiar. This gives you a route into the themes, which should make your studies more approachable and enjoyable. We hope that this book will give you insights and make you think again about how and where you spend your work and leisure time. The second reason is that (as you discovered in Book 1 on *Reputations*) familiar and apparently straightforward concepts can be much more complex when studied in depth.

This book gradually takes you into the complexities of our themes. In the first chapter, philosophers Jon Pike and Carolyn Price ask: what is the purpose of leisure? Jon raises some fundamental questions. How does leisure relate to work? And can we have too much leisure? Carolyn describes how Greek philosophers thought about the best way to spend our precious leisure time. (You will be pleased to discover that study and rational conversation were considered to be excellent uses of leisure.)

The second chapter turns to the theme of place, and of places with multiple uses and identities. Graham Harvey and Marion Bowman look at three sites – Stonehenge/Avebury, Glastonbury and Milton Keynes – and ask why they are seen as 'sacred' by different groups. At the centre of this chapter is the question of whether sacredness is inherent. Does this involve something in the natural features of the landscape, or is it constructed by past and present generations?

The rest of the book looks at the relationship between place and leisure and why some places have been seen as particularly appropriate for leisure. In Chapter 3 Paula James and Janet Huskinson use classical literature and archaeology to explore how Roman villas – large country houses – reflected their owners' ideas of how best to spend their leisure time. These villas were designed to make the most of natural landscapes – peaceful, rural surroundings – but had added facilities to turn them into ideal sites for relaxing, reading, talking and dining.

The last part of the book takes you to another place strongly associated with leisure – the seaside. Though requiring all your study skills, this part is intended to end *The Arts Past and Present* on a lighter note. As the Greeks claimed, studying is part of leisure. Here the format of the book changes. Instead of one long chapter, this part of the book consists of seven short sections, each written from the perspective of a different subject. Together with interactive DVD ROM material, they explore the history of the seaside holiday – from when it first became fashionable in the late eighteenth century, through the tranquil seaside pleasures of the nineteenth century when activities were based around the natural features of the beach, the sea and the surrounding countryside, to the louder, more energetic pastimes of the twentieth century carried on at funfairs, dance halls and swimming pools. At the same time, these sections explore a number of themes. Four broadly historical sections explore why leisure at the seaside changed over time, looking at how entertainments were aimed at different classes of visitors; what people wore and what they did on the beach; how technology created new ways of having fun (and the possibility of foreign travel); and how concerns with health were reflected in seaside leisure. Overall, they demonstrate how time spent at the seaside, though portrayed as being completely different from the rest of life, in fact reflected wider concerns and issues. The three remaining sections explore how the seaside has been represented – in scenes of relaxation, as the site of violent confrontations between Mods and Rockers, and in the Blackpool of the 1990s where it became the setting for exploring cultural and generational tensions.

This book gives you an opportunity to utilise all the study skills you have developed during *The Arts Past and Present* – in reading, note taking, and analysing texts and images. It also requires new skills. You have already combined material from different disciplines when studying the art of Benin in Book 3, but the study of the seaside requires this approach on a much bigger scale, giving you a taster of interdisciplinary study. In addition, here you are given a chance to shape your own study – the opportunity to skim and select the materials which most interest you. In the seaside section you'll also have an opportunity to use documentary films as a historical source and to view a feature film as a representation of different cultures. There is also an emphasis in this book on using electronic materials such as interactive DVD ROMs.

As you approach the end of *The Arts Past and Present*, it's time to sit back and think about what you've achieved. A week has been set aside for you to reflect on the subjects you've studied and think about what you might do in the future. Take the opportunity to decide which topics have appealed to you, which subjects have made you want to find out more, and which you have struggled with (and understanding why you have struggled is helpful in determining what to do in the future). To help you, there are materials on the course website giving insights into studying at a more advanced level. As this is the last book of the course, it does not have an Afterword. The next steps for you are the courses you will take after *The Arts Past and Present*.

1 LEISURE AND THE PURPOSE OF LIFE

Jon Pike and Carolyn Price

MATERIALS YOU WILL NEED

- Audio CD: Selling the Experience Machine

AIMS

This chapter will:

- introduce you to a range of philosophical questions and arguments about the nature and importance of leisure
- show how philosophers use 'thought experiments' to test philosophical claims
- explore some connections between different types of philosophical question.

1.1   LEISURE, LAZINESS AND FEELING GOOD
Jon Pike

What is leisure?

What is leisure? Perhaps the answer seems obvious: leisure is the time left over from work and other chores. To define leisure in this way is to define it negatively, as the absence of something: to be at leisure is not to be at work. But is this the right way to define leisure?

One limitation of this definition is that it does not say what counts as work. We might start with the thought that work is what people are paid to do, but this seems much too narrow. People can be forced to work without pay. Others may undertake voluntary work – working in a charity shop, for example. Household chores and some aspects of childcare are also naturally thought of as kinds of work, even when they are unpaid. So is there another way to distinguish between work and leisure?

Activity   Look at the following list of activities, and try to sort them into work activities and leisure activities. Is this a straightforward task? (In each case, try to imagine different reasons someone might have for engaging in the activity.)

- lying on a beach
- mending a car
- eating a meal
- going for a run.

Discussion   On the face of it, lying on a beach looks like a straightforward example of a leisure activity. That seems right if I'm lying on a beach for the sake of it – just to relax and soak up the sun. But suppose that my job is to lie on a beach, perhaps because I'm being paid to model beachwear. In this case, lying on a beach is a kind of work. Similarly, if you imagine someone mending a car, you might assume that he or she is at work. But some people mend cars in their leisure time, for their own enjoyment or satisfaction. Eating a meal or going for a run seem to be leisure activities if they are done for their own sake, but if I'm eating just to get food inside me, or exercising just to lose some weight, I might well think of these activities as chores. So there seems to be no simple way to divide the activities on the list into leisure activities and work activities. Whether I'm doing something as work or as leisure seems to depend on my reasons for doing it.

This suggests an alternative way of thinking about the distinction between work and leisure – one that appeals to the difference between doing something as a means to an end and doing something for its own sake. There are many things that I do with some further end in mind. I eat a sandwich to sustain me during a long meeting; I attend the meeting to get some funding for a project; I work on the project because it is what I need to do to get a pay rise. When so much of what people do is simply a means to an end, life can sometimes seem like a laundry list of jobs to be done. But leisure activities seem to be

Figure 1.1 'Relaxing at the seaside'. Photographed by Michael Howard. Photo: © Michael Howard/Alamy. Are these people at leisure? What if they are being paid to model beachwear?

different, and importantly so: when someone is at leisure, he or she is pursuing activities for their own sake, because they are worth doing just in themselves.

So another possible answer to the question 'What is leisure?' is that leisure is time spent on activities for their own sake. Lazily lying on a beach or busily mending a car might both be leisure activities, if they are done for their own sake. If we were to define leisure in this way, we would be defining it positively – as time spent on a particular kind of activity. I am not going to endorse this positive conception of leisure here; instead, I shall leave it for you to think about as you work through this chapter. As you will see, though, it is an idea that has had an important role in philosophical thinking about leisure, and we shall explore it further in what follows.

Philosophy and leisure

As we have already seen, a particular activity can be pursued for a variety of reasons. Hence what is work for one person can be leisure for another, and the ways in which people spend their leisure can change over time. Later in this book you will encounter some material on the social history of leisure, exploring how leisure has been organised and used at different times. In this chapter, we are going to look at some philosophical questions about leisure. We shall consider how different philosophers have defined leisure, and we shall explore some more concrete issues about its purpose and value. What is the point of leisure? How much leisure is needed to ensure a good life? What should people do with their leisure time? Perhaps surprisingly, these issues lead on to some fundamental questions about the nature and purpose of human lives. The aim here is not to answer these more fundamental questions, but rather to understand how they connect with some quite practical issues about the way in which people spend their time.

In this chapter we shall consider the views of four different philosophers. To set the scene, we begin by looking at an excerpt from *The Right to be Lazy* – a tract by the nineteenth-century thinker Paul Lafargue (see Figure 1.2), in which he argues passionately for the importance of leisure. We then go on to look at a **thought experiment** devised by the contemporary philosopher Robert Nozick, which raises some questions about how people should spend their leisure time. Your main task here will be to reflect on an audio discussion of the experiment. Then, in Section 1.2, Carolyn Price will investigate what two ancient Greek philosophers, Aristotle and Epicurus, have to say about the value of leisure and the purpose of human life.

Note that we are not taking these authors in chronological order. This might strike you as surprising. But there are different ways of reading texts, and different purposes that we have in mind when we read them. If we were constructing a history of ideas about leisure, it might be a serious mistake to abandon a chronological approach. Here, however, our aim is to use these texts in order to explore some issues about leisure. And so it makes sense to order them in a way that reflects the issues that they address, rather than discussing them chronologically.

Paul Lafargue on 'the murderous passion for work'

Paul Lafargue wrote *The Right to be Lazy* as a contribution to a debate about the nature of work in a rapidly developing and industrialising society. It is a short work – a political pamphlet designed to stir workers to protest against long working hours and capitalist exploitation. Because it has this intent, it does not have the tight logical structure that you might expect from a piece of philosophical writing. But philosophical ideas can be found in all sorts of places, including political tracts. Lafargue has something to say about what leisure is and about its value – and he says it with some gusto.

In the excerpts presented here, Lafargue considers the harmful effects of work on both working people (the proletariat) and capitalists. You might also notice his reference to technological advance (the 'liberating machine').

Born in Cuba, **Paul Lafargue** (1842–1911) moved as a child to Europe, where he became active in the French workers' movement. He married Laura Marx, the daughter of Karl, and introduced the views of Marx to the French labour movement. He was forced to flee from France after the Paris Commune (a brief revolutionary government) of 1871, which ended with the killing of an estimated 30,000 **communards**. In 1882 he returned, and became leader of the Parti Ouvrier Français (French Workers' Party). He took part in many strikes and demonstrations, and was frequently imprisoned. In 1911 he and Laura committed suicide, disappointed by the absence of the political breakthrough that they had hoped for.

Figure 1.2   Paul Lafargue, French workers' leader, *c*.1900. Unknown photographer. Photo: Frédéric Longuet Collection/akg-images.

Activity   Study Reading 1.1 and then answer the following questions:

1   What, according to Lafargue, is the value of leisure?

2   What does he take to be the harmful effects of the 'love of work'?

Discussion   1   Lafargue makes a connection between leisure and freedom. When people are at leisure, he suggests, they are free to flourish, both physically and mentally. Although he puts a great deal of emphasis on fun and feasting, he also suggests that leisure leaves room for intellectual development. He asserts that the greatest achievements of humankind have been products of leisure, not of work.

2   Lafargue's main point seems to be that work is dehumanising: people addicted to work live cramped and unhealthy lives, unable to realise their full potential as human beings. He adds the idea that over-production fuels excessive consumption. Capitalists, far from

benefiting from the labours of the proletariat, waste their lives in unhealthy and pointless indulgence. Lafargue portrays a society chasing its own tail, trapped in a damaging cycle of overwork and over-consumption.

As the title of his tract suggests, the aim of Lafargue's argument is to show that people have a right to be lazy. But it is not clear that he says enough to support such a strong conclusion. To say that I have a right to something goes beyond saying that it would be good for me to have it. It implies that other people ought to allow me to have it, and, in some cases, that they have a duty to supply it. For example, to say that children have a right to education is not just to say that education would be good for them. It implies that other people should not stop them from being educated, and perhaps that parents or governments have a duty to provide an education for them. Conversely, to say that it would be good for me to be able to use my neighbour's lawnmower does not imply that I have a right to use it. Lafargue does provide some reasons for us to think that a life of leisure would be good for us. But he would need to do a bit more work to establish that we have a *right* to such a life.

Nevertheless, Lafargue does provide some strong reasons as to why leisure is of crucial importance in human lives. Underlying his argument is the idea that leisure frees people to live as human beings are supposed to live. The notion of the 'noble savage' uncorrupted by 'the dogma of work' is supposed to represent what a human being would be, and should be, without the dehumanising influence of the love of work. For Lafargue, then, the value of leisure is not simply that it is good for people's health or that it gives them time to do a little philosophy, but that it gives them the freedom to be human. For this reason, he argues that people should have as much leisure as possible. He recommends that people should restrict their working day to three hours – the minimum necessary, he thinks, to provide for a good life.

Lafargue seems to define leisure primarily in a negative way – as freedom from work. But what should people do with this freedom? On this, Lafargue is non-committal. On the one hand, he claims that leisure produces great intellectual achievements; on the other hand, he praises past generations who used their leisure simply 'to taste the joys of earth'. One important theme in his discussion, though, is that a full life does not require high levels of material wealth. His warnings about the damaging effects of over-consumption are echoed by contemporary concerns about consumerism and excess – it would not be hard to update his portraits of over-stuffed gourmands and martyrs to fashion. Still, you may have noticed some ambiguity in Lafargue's attacks on excess: he lampoons the greedy capitalist crammed with capons and truffles, while waxing lyrical about the 'sublime gargantuan stomachs' of yesteryear.

Another important theme in Lafargue's discussion is the relationship between leisure and technology. As he notes, the ancient Greeks tended to assume that extensive leisure was possible for only a minority of the population. This is because slaves were needed to satisfy the basic needs – food, clothing, and so on – of everyday life. (He is exaggerating, though, when he suggests that slaves did all the work.) In contrast, Lafargue holds that technological advance means that a life of leisure is possible for everyone. As he points out, however, technology has yet to free people from the need to work long hours. This, he suggests, is due to the relationship between capitalists and workers; his argument is part of a broader critique of capitalist society.

But Lafargue's concerns also reflect specific ways in which his society was changing in the nineteenth century. In fact, over time, technological change did produce an increase in leisure and paid holidays for working people. Clearly, though, the liberating effect of technology has not been nearly as great as Lafargue thought it could be, and the relationship between technology, work and leisure continues to be an issue today. Polemical and utopian though it is, *The Right to be Lazy* poses some genuine questions about the ways in which economic and technological change can – and should – affect people's lives.

The experience machine

One of Lafargue's key points is that leisure is valuable because it gives people the freedom to choose how to spend their time. But what should we do with this freedom? Are some ways of using leisure more valuable than others? In this section, I shall introduce this question by looking at a thought experiment designed by the philosopher Robert Nozick (see Nozick, 1974).

> Robert Nozick (1938–2002) was a prominent American philosopher, best known for his work in political philosophy.

A thought experiment is an exercise in hypothetical, or 'what if ...?', thinking. A thought experiment invites you to think about a hypothetical – often fantastical – situation and to consider its consequences. People sometimes engage in thought experiments just for fun ('What if you won the lottery tomorrow ...?'; 'What if you could travel back in time ...?'). But philosophers sometimes use thought experiments to test philosophical claims. As with arguments by analogy, using a thought experiment requires some imagination and judgement, as well as analytical skills. Indeed, they are not easy to handle, and some philosophers have real doubts about how much faith we can put in the results. But Nozick's experiment is one of the most well constructed – and influential – that philosophers have devised.

Arguments by analogy are discussed in Book 3, Chapter 3.

The claim that Nozick's thought experiment is designed to test might be expressed like this:

> Nothing else matters to us, other than how our lives feel from the inside.

If this claim were true, it would have important implications for our discussion of leisure: it would imply that the best way to spend your leisure is in pursuit of things that make you feel good – things that will provide you with pleasant experiences. On the face of it, this looks like a pretty plausible claim. After all, many of the ways in which people do choose to spend their leisure – eating nice food, soaking up the sun, relaxing with friends – seem to be valuable simply because they feel good. So perhaps the value of leisure is that it leaves people free to choose to spend their time in ways that make them feel good.

To test this claim, Nozick tries to describe a situation in which people are free, if they choose, to spend their whole life enjoying pleasant experiences. He imagines that people are able to do this by plugging themselves into an 'experience machine' – a piece of virtual-reality technology. If the claim above is true, people should be willing to plug themselves into the machine. Conversely, if people are not willing to plug themselves in, that suggests that the claim is false: there is something that they care about apart from feeling good.

Nozick's experiment might remind you of scenarios presented in science fiction films such as *Total Recall* (1990) and *The Matrix* (1999). Indeed, with the advent of virtual-reality technology, Nozick's experiment seems rather less fantastical than it did when he first described it in 1974. Nevertheless, the possibility that he describes is certainly extreme, and (at the time I write this) beyond the reach of current technology. The point of Nozick's example is not to pose a real practical question, but to allow us to focus as precisely as possible on the claim that he wants to test.

Activity   Turn to Reading 1.2, and then answer the following questions. Jot down your answers, no matter how undeveloped, so you can refer to them later.

1   Suppose there was an experience machine available to you. Would you plug in?

2   How might you justify your decision to someone who disagreed with you?

Now listen to the Audio CD 'Selling the Experience Machine'. In this discussion Carolyn Price, in the guise of a sales representative, tries to persuade me to plug into an experience machine, while I put the case for refusing. You might notice one or two changes that we've made to Nozick's description of the machine's workings: the changes are just for the sake of simplicity, and do not affect the philosophical point.

You might wish to listen to the whole discussion once and then go through it again more slowly, jotting down some notes. This should take you about 30 minutes in all. As you listen, try to identify the reasons I give for refusing to plug in, and try to decide whether or not you agree with any of them. Do your own initial thoughts about the experiment echo any of the points made during this discussion? Has listening to it encouraged you to change your mind?

In Section 1.2 Carolyn Price will continue our investigation by exploring what Aristotle and Epicurus have to say about the nature and value of leisure. Working through this material will offer you an opportunity to think further about the issues raised by the experience machine. As you will see, the views of these two philosophers suggest rather different conclusions about the attractions of plugging in.

1.2   ARISTOTLE AND EPICURUS ON LEISURE
Carolyn Price

Philosophical jigsaws

As Lafargue points out, ancient societies were far from egalitarian. The wealthiest citizens were able to spend much of their time at leisure, a privilege made possible by the labour of slaves and poorer citizens. This did not mean that wealthy aristocrats never worked: a large proportion of their time would have been taken up with family matters, business affairs, and military and political duties. Nevertheless, for the most privileged members of ancient society at least, questions about the value of leisure and how leisure should be spent were far from academic.

How did Aristotle and Epicurus approach these questions? You saw earlier that, in arguing for the right to be lazy, Lafargue makes an appeal to what human beings really are – what it means to be human. So Lafargue sees a connection between these two questions:

> Question 1: How should people spend their time?

> Question 2: What is it to be human?

Like Lafargue, Aristotle and Epicurus assume that the answer to the first of these questions depends on the answer to the second. However, you might notice that these are questions of rather different kinds. The first concerns what people ought to do: it is about morality or **ethics**. But the second question concerns how things actually are: it involves **metaphysics**. (Metaphysics is a branch of philosophy which is concerned with what kinds of thing there are in the world.)

In studying philosophy, it is often helpful to be aware of the way in which different kinds of philosophical question interconnect. Understanding the views of a particular philosopher can be like solving a jigsaw: as you put the jigsaw together and begin to see the whole picture, it becomes much easier to make sense of the individual pieces. In the rest of this chapter one of my aims is to bring out this aspect of studying philosophy, by considering how Aristotle and Epicurus connect the two questions above. This will involve giving some close attention to their arguments, but it will also involve taking a step back, to get a broader overview of how their theories fit together.

Aristotle: leisure as the aim of life

Aristotle (384–322 BCE) was born in the kingdom of Macedonia. As a young man he travelled to Athens, where he became a student at Plato's Academy. He became one of Plato's favourite students and a trenchant critic of his teacher's ideas. After Plato's death he returned to Macedonia, becoming tutor to the young prince Alexander the Great. Aristotle eventually returned to Athens and set up his own school at the Lyceum, a gymnasium located outside the city walls. The Lyceum also came to be called the Peripatetic School, supposedly due to Aristotle's habit of discussing philosophy while strolling around the shaded walkways (*peripateoi*) surrounding the building.

Figure 1.3   Bust of Aristotle, fourth century BCE, marble. Kunsthistorisches Museum, Vienna.

I shall begin by considering the views of the Greek philosopher Aristotle (see Figure 1.3). In what follows, we shall examine extracts from two of Aristotle's works: the *Politics* and the *Nicomachean Ethics*. The *Nicomachean Ethics* is a set of writings on ethical issues compiled by Aristotle's son, Nicomachus. In these writings, Aristotle's main concern is to discover the ultimate aim or objective of human life. In the *Politics*, he considers how states should be organised to allow some citizens to achieve this objective.

What, then, is the ultimate objective of human life? Aristotle answers this question in several different ways, all of which he takes to be compatible with each other. His principal answer is that the objective of human life is happiness or well-being. (The Greek word is ***eudaimonia***.) But he also sometimes suggests that it is leisure – or, more precisely, leisure well spent (*Politics*, 1337b). So, for Aristotle, leisure and well-being are intimately connected: living well involves having plenty of leisure, and using it in the best possible way. Hence Aristotle agrees with Lafargue about the central importance of leisure in human life.

But why does Aristotle think that the ultimate objective of human life is to make good use of leisure? There are two assumptions that underlie this claim. First, Aristotle assumes that the aim of human life is not to acquire certain things or to achieve a certain state of mind, but to engage in certain kinds of activity. (I shall say a little more about this later in the chapter.) As he points out, if these activities are to constitute the *ultimate* aim of human life, they must be pursued for their own sake, not just as a means to some further end. For example, he dismisses the idea that the ultimate objective is to make money: making money, he thinks, is valuable only as a means to further ends (*Nicomachean Ethics*, 1096b). For Aristotle, then, discovering the ultimate aim of human life is a matter of finding out which activities are worth pursuing for their own sake.

Second, Aristotle holds that any activity that is pursued wholly for its own sake is, by definition, a leisure activity. In other words, Aristotle endorses the positive conception of leisure mentioned in section 1.1. For Aristotle, leisure is not simply the time that is left over once work and chores have been done; rather, it is the pursuit of activities that we value for their own sake.

So Aristotle makes two claims:

> Premise 1: To know the ultimate objective of human life is to know which activities are worth pursuing for their own sake.

> Premise 2: Activities that are pursued wholly for their own sake are leisure activities.

Putting these two premises together, it follows that:

> Conclusion: To know the ultimate objective of human life is to know which leisure activities are worth pursuing.

So, for Aristotle, choosing how to spend one's leisure is not simply a matter of taste or convenience: it is an issue of profound ethical importance.

Leisure and play

When people think of leisure, they often think of time spent relaxing or having fun – enjoying a good film, playing football, messing about on a beach. And indeed, many people regard the time that they spend at work as justified precisely because it allows them to enjoy various kinds of recreation or entertainment in their spare time. So is the ultimate objective of human life just to play and have fun?

Activity

Work through Reading 1.3, and then answer the following questions:

1 How does Aristotle characterise the relationship between work and leisure in this passage?

2 What does Aristotle take to be the value of play?

3 What does this imply about the relationship between leisure and play?

Discussion

1 According to Aristotle, leisure is the foundation and the objective of all that we do. It implies living happily and well, and is valued for its own sake. In contrast, work is a means to an end. We put up with the trouble and exertion involved in work so that we can have leisure.

2 Aristotle denies that play is valuable in itself: rather, it is valuable only as a means to an end. Its function is to enable people to relax when they are tired from work. He draws an analogy between play and medicine: both of these, he suggests, are supposed to help people to recover their strength.

3 This implies that play shouldn't be thought of as a leisure activity. A leisure activity is something that we do just for its own sake, but play is properly pursued only as a cure for fatigue.

Aristotle's argument, then, rests on two premises:

Premise 1: A leisure activity is an activity that is valued for its own sake.

Premise 2: Play should be valued only as a means to an end.

He concludes that playing and having fun are not properly regarded as leisure activities. Instead, play should be compared to convalescing after an illness – as a necessary concession to human frailty, not as an end in itself. Its proper purpose is to prepare people for work. Leisure, by contrast, is not a preparation for work; rather, the purpose of work is to create the conditions under which people can enjoy leisure.

Aristotle knows that, in taking this line, he is challenging majority opinion. Most people, he says, work in order to play. But Aristotle does not believe that this kind of issue can be settled by consulting majority opinion. Instead, he suggests, we should consider how excellent or virtuous people choose to spend their leisure. Underlying this claim is the thought that excellent or virtuous people are the people who know what is really valuable in life. The point is similar to the one that Nicias makes in Plato's *Laches* when he suggests that courage is a kind of knowledge possessed by only a few people. I shall say a little more about why Aristotle took this view later on.

You read extracts from the Laches *in Book 2, Chapter 1.*

How, then, should people use their leisure? Rather than trying to answer this directly, Aristotle approaches the issue by asking a rather different question: what is it to be an excellent human being? Aristotle thinks that excellent people are those who excel at certain activities – not just any old activities, but the very best activities that a human being *can* pursue. So if we know what it is that excellent human beings are good at doing, we will know which activities are best or most worthwhile. But what is it that excellent people are good at doing? In the *Nicomachean Ethics*, Aristotle tries to answer this question using an argument that has become known as the 'function argument'. We shall now look at this argument in some detail.

The function argument

I have mentioned the idea that there are certain *aims* or *objectives* that people pursue. In the function argument, Aristotle introduces a slightly different idea: the idea that human beings have a *function*. But what is the difference between a function and an aim?

I have been using the term 'aim' to refer to what someone wants or is trying to achieve. For example, one of my aims is to visit Egypt. In contrast, a function is a task that someone or something is supposed to do, regardless of whether or not he, she or it wants to do it. For instance, a tin-opener has the function to open tins because it has been manufactured to perform that task. As a lecturer at The Open University, one of my functions is to write course materials – that is what I am employed to do. Luckily, writing course materials is also an aim of mine – it is something that I want to do.

You might think that a function and a job are not quite the same thing. In particular, I can give up being a lecturer, but a tin-opener cannot stop being a tin-opener. But Aristotle talks about functions and jobs in a similar way, so I am going to ignore this distinction here. Still, it is worth bearing in mind that, according to Aristotle's account, a person can have many functions. For example, someone might have one function as a university lecturer, another as a parent, and yet another as an amateur birdwatcher. And to these, Aristotle thinks, we can add the function that he or she has just as a human being.

Activity   This activity is designed to test whether you're clear about the distinction between a function and an aim. Which of the following sentences refer to functions and which to aims?

1   A striker is supposed to score goals.

2   Alison wants to spend a day in London.

3   Ben's dearest wish is to score a goal for his club.

4   The Thames Barrier is there to prevent London flooding.

Discussion   Sentences 1 and 4 refer to functions; 2 and 3 refer to aims.

In the function argument, Aristotle tries to establish what it is to be an excellent human being.

Activity   Work through Reading 1.4 slowly and carefully. Don't worry if there are some claims that strike you as strange, or even obviously false: at this point you are just trying to understand how the argument is meant to work. When you have read the extract, answer the following questions:

1   What, according to Aristotle, is the function of a human being?

2   Why does Aristotle reject the idea that the function of a human being might be feeding, growing or sense-perception?

3   How does Aristotle think that knowing the function of a human being will help us to decide what it is to be an excellent human being?

Discussion   1   Aristotle suggests that the function of a human being is to engage in activities that involve the exercise of reason.

2   Aristotle suggests that the function of a human being can't be feeding, growing or sense-perception because these are activities that we share with other living things. He assumes that the human function must be one that distinguishes human beings from all other living things.

3   Aristotle suggests that, for everything that has a function, success or excellence is a matter of performing that function well. For example, an excellent kite is one that flies well, an excellent pastry chef is someone who excels at making pastry, and so on. As we have seen, the function of a human being is to engage in activities that involve the exercise of reason. It follows that to be an excellent human being is to excel at rational activities.

The function argument, then, can be set out as follows:

> **Summary of the function argument**
>
> *Premise 1*: The function of a human being is to engage in rational activities.
>
> *Premise 2*: For everything that has a function, excellence is a matter of excelling at that function.
>
> *Conclusion*: So, an excellent human being is someone who excels at rational activities.

Leisure, study and politics

For Aristotle, then, it is the ability to reason that makes us human. It is when we use reason that we realise our true nature as human beings. Aristotle takes this to show that rational activities are the best activities that a human can pursue: when people are exercising their reason, they are realising their full potential as human beings. The most valuable activities of all will be those that involve exercising reason not for the sake of some further end, but as something precious in itself. Hence the best way to use one's leisure is to devote it to activities of this kind. But what kinds of activity does Aristotle have in mind?

In fact, Aristotle finds only one kind of activity that fits the bill. He suggests that the best way to use one's leisure is in the study of philosophy and science. What Aristotle has in mind, though, is not the kind of study that students and researchers tend to engage in. Typically, students and researchers spend their time inquiring into a subject in order to understand it. Inquiry, Aristotle thinks, is a means to an end – a way of getting knowledge or understanding. But he suggests that there is another kind of intellectual activity that is pursued purely for its own sake: once inquirers have discovered some philosophical or scientific truths, they will be able to reflect on them, to understand them and to appreciate the connections between them. When people engage in this kind of intellectual reflection, Aristotle argues, they are wholly at leisure, exercising reason for its own sake and realising human nature at its highest and best (*Nicomachean Ethics*, 1177b). Hence intellectual reflection, pursued at leisure, is the ultimate objective and the 'crowning glory' of the best human lives (Broadie, 1991, p. 418).

The task of politics, Aristotle thinks, is to create a peaceful and well-ordered society, in which some people at least will have plenty of leisure (*Politics*, 1334a). In fact, Aristotle suggests that political activity is itself a form of rational activity, because it involves making rational decisions about what to do. Hence he allows that it is worth pursuing in its own right. Indeed, for much of the *Nicomachean Ethics* Aristotle seems to be assuming that the people he is discussing are citizens who are active in public life. But a life wholly dedicated to politics, he suggests, would be happy only in a 'secondary' way (*Nicomachean Ethics*, 1178a). This is because political activity is pursued primarily for the sake of further ends – whether for personal glory or the public good. Primarily, then, it is a form of work, though it is work of a particularly important kind.

Unlike Lafargue, Aristotle does not suggest that everyone should have plenty of leisure. This is because he thinks that most people are incapable of pursuing a life aimed at intellectual and rational activity. Children, he supposes, have not yet learned how to use reason properly; whereas women are capable of making rational choices, but are poor at acting on them (*Politics*, 1260a). And in a notorious defence of slavery, he argues that some people are 'natural slaves', who are unable to make good rational choices at all (*Politics*, 1254a–5b). Finally, of those men who are capable of using their reason to the fullest extent, some do not receive the kind of education that will allow them to do so (*Nicomachean Ethics*, 1179b). According to Aristotle, then, only a small number of people will be able to live the best kind of life and to make the fullest use of their leisure.

Aristotle's views on women and slavery can be criticised, both on scientific and on philosophical grounds. His assumption that there is a natural hierarchy among human beings is rejected not only by

Liberal philosophers are discussed in Book 3, Chapter 3.

Lafargue, but also by the liberal philosophers whose ideas you have encountered elsewhere. However, Aristotle's broader views about leisure do not depend on his hierarchical view of human nature. It would be quite possible to accept what he has to say about the importance of leisure and about the value of intellectual activity in human life, without accepting his views about the capacities of women or the existence of 'natural slaves'. Even so, Aristotle's account does seem to imply that many people will not have the opportunity to lead a happy and fulfilling life. This will be possible only for people who have the right capacities and education, and access to plenty of leisure.

Why does Aristotle think that human beings have a function?

Look back at the section above on 'The function argument'. Were there any claims that Aristotle makes, as I set them out in that section, which you found puzzling or implausible?

One claim which you might have found puzzling is that human beings have a function. This notion might not seem odd if you believe that human beings have been created by God. If human beings are God's creations, then it makes sense to suppose that they might have been created for some purpose. But Aristotle does not suppose that God has conferred a function on human beings. Rather, his claim emerges from a theory about what it is to be alive (Irwin, 1980). Exploring this idea will enable us to see more clearly how Aristotle connects the ethical claim that leisure is best devoted to rational activities with a metaphysical claim about what kind of thing a human being is.

You read about humoural medicine in Book 3, Chapter 5.

What is the difference between a living thing and something that is not alive? Some ancient thinkers suggested that what is distinctive of living things has to do with what they are made of. You are already familiar with the idea, crucial to humoural medicine, that life depends on a balance of basic elements – the hot, the cold, the wet and the dry – and that when this balance is disrupted the living organism becomes ill, and perhaps dies. Aristotle accepted this account of what living things are made of, and why they become ill and die. But, as he makes clear in a work called *De Anima* (*On the Soul*), he thought that this was not the right way to capture the difference between living and non-living things. The significant difference between a live plant and a dead one, he suggests, is not what they are made of, but what they *do*. For a plant, to live is to take in food and grow. Animals feed and grow too, but they also perceive what is going on around them and react to it. Human beings have a further ability: the ability to reason about what they perceive and about what they should do. According to Aristotle, as we have seen, it is the capacity to reason that is the distinctive and highest human capacity (*De Anima*, 414b).

Furthermore, Aristotle holds not only that living things do these things, but that it is their function or purpose to do so. For example, he states that the function of a plant is to feed and to grow. This is not to say that plants *want* to feed and grow, but rather that it is not simply an accident that they behave in this way. By feeding and growing, plants are able to carry on feeding and growing and to produce more plants that will continue to feed and grow in the future. Similarly, human beings use their reason in ways that help them to go on living as rational, intelligent beings, and to bring up children who will become rational, intelligent beings too. So, Aristotle thinks, reason is not just an ability that humans have: it is the function or purpose of human life (*De Anima*, 415b).

There are several objections that might be made to the function argument – and in particular to Premise 1 (the claim that the function of a human being is to engage in rational activities). I shall mention just two objections here, but you may be able to think of others:

1   I suggested earlier that some people are likely to find the claim that human beings have a function rather puzzling. In this section, I have tried to explain how this claim emerges from Aristotle's views about the nature of living things. Nevertheless, it is not obvious that those views are correct. As we shall see, Epicurus presents a serious challenge to the claim that living things have functions or purposes.

2   Is Aristotle right to put so much emphasis on what distinguishes human beings from other animals? Aristotle assumes that what is important in human lives is very different from what is important in the lives of other animals. As we shall also see, Epicurus denies that the distinction between human beings and other animals is as significant as Aristotle thinks.

What I particularly want to emphasise, however, is the pivotal role that the function argument plays in Aristotle's theory. It is this argument that allows Aristotle to link a metaphysical claim about what a human being is with an ethical claim about the value of a certain kind of leisure activity. Understanding the function argument allows us to see how these pieces of the jigsaw fit together.

Indeed, understanding the function argument will allow us to fit another of Aristotle's claims into the jigsaw. This is the claim – mentioned in the section on 'Leisure and play' above – that it is the choices of excellent people which reflect what is truly valuable in life. According to the function argument, excellent people are people who are excellent at reasoning. And so it makes sense to suppose that excellent people are in the best position to make rational choices about how to live and make use of leisure (*Nicomachean Ethics*, 1113b).

These claims can be fitted into a grid, like the one in Table 1.1.

Table 1.1   Aristotle's views

Question	Aristotle's answer
What is a human being?	A living being, whose special function is to reason.
What is the value of leisure?	Used properly, leisure enables people to realise human nature at its best.
What is the best way to use one's leisure?	In an activity that involves the exercise of reason for its own sake – that is, intellectual reflection.
Who is in the best position to judge how leisure should be used?	Excellent people (that is, people who are excellent at reasoning).

Activity   This activity will help you to review this discussion of Aristotle. Aristotle would certainly not have advised you to plug yourself into an experience machine. Thinking back over the whole of this discussion, try to pinpoint exactly why Aristotle would have taken this view.

Discussion   As Jon Pike points out in the Audio CD 'Selling the Experience Machine', once you are plugged into the machine, you won't know how things are in the real world. So you won't be able to engage in the intellectual activity that Aristotle takes to be the ultimate aim of human life.

More fundamentally, Aristotle holds that the aim of human life is not to enjoy experiences of certain kinds but to *do* certain kinds of things. The machine provides experiences, but it allows you to do next to nothing. Plugged into the machine, all you can do is take in food and grow. According to Aristotle, someone in this position is leading the life of a plant. So Aristotle would certainly agree with Jon Pike when he complains, 'I wouldn't be a person anymore ... I'd just be a cabbage'.

Epicurus: at ease in the Garden

Epicurus (341–270 BCE) was born on the island of Samos, but in his mid-thirties he moved to Athens, where he set up his own school known as 'The Garden' (see Figure 1.5). There he gathered a small group of devotees. After his death, his philosophical views attracted many followers among both Greeks and Romans, including the Roman poets Horace and Lucretius.

Like Aristotle, Epicurus (see Figure 1.4) set out to describe the ultimate objective of human life. But his account contrasts with Aristotle's in several ways. One important difference is that Epicurus thought that this objective could be achieved by anyone, regardless of gender or social class. As a result, he thought that it was of paramount importance to explain his philosophical views to a wide audience. Although he did write long, scholarly treatises, he also presented his philosophical theories in easily digestible form, publishing short letters and collections of maxims to be learned by heart. His followers found other ways to publicise Epicurean doctrines. For example, the Roman poet Lucretius presented **Epicureanism** in a long poem entitled *De Rerum Natura* (*On the Nature of Things*). These writings aimed to get Epicureanism across to a wide audience, reflecting Epicurus' philosophical belief that the best life is possible for all.

Figure 1.4   Bust of Epicurus, Musei Capitolini, Rome. © Photo, Scala, Florence.

My aim in what follows is not to give you a comprehensive account of Epicurean ethics, but to point up some key points of difference between Aristotle's views and those of Epicurus and his followers. In particular, I shall suggest that the disagreement between Aristotle and Epicurus starts not with their ethical theory, but with what they take a human being to be. Earlier, I summarised Aristotle's views in Table 1.1. Table 1.2 now adds an extra column, to contain Epicurus' views. As you work through the remaining sections of this chapter, fill in the empty column in this table.

Figure 1.5   The Schools of Athens. This map of Athens shows the location of Epicurus' school, known as 'The Garden', just outside the city walls. It also shows Plato's Academy nearby and, across the city, Aristotle's Lyceum. In the heart of the city is the Agora, the city's main marketplace and the hub of its political and social life. To one side of the Agora stands the Stoa Poikile ('Painted Colonnade'), home to another school of philosophers, the Stoics.

Table 1.2 Epicurus' views

Question	Aristotle's answer	Epicurus' answer
What is a human being?	A living being, whose special function is to reason.	
What is the value of leisure?	Used properly, leisure enables people to realise human nature at its best.	
What is the best way to use one's leisure?	In an activity that involves the exercise of reason for its own sake – that is, intellectual reflection.	
Who is in the best position to judge how leisure should be used?	Excellent people (that is, people who are excellent at reasoning).	

Tranquillity and the simple life

I shall begin this section by considering how Epicurus characterised the objective of human life. Once we are clear about this, it will be easier to identify what he took to be the value of leisure, and what kinds of leisure activities he thought people ought to pursue.

Activity Reading 1.5 is taken from Epicurus' *Letter to Menoeceus*. This is a summary of Epicurus' ethical doctrines, presented in a short letter addressed to one of his followers. Read this extract now, and then answer the following questions:

1   What does Epicurus take to be the objective of human life?

2   According to Epicurus, why do we need to exercise reason or judgement in our lives?

Discussion 1   Epicurus suggests that the objective of human life is pleasure. He identifies pleasure with a state of tranquillity – a body free from pain and a mind free from anxiety.

2   Epicurus does not think that we should pursue all pleasures or avoid all pains, but that we should do whatever will bring the most pleasure in the long run. We need to exercise reason or judgement in deciding which pleasures to pursue.

Already we can see a stark contrast between Epicurus' ethical views and those of Aristotle. According to Epicurus, the objective of human life is not reason but pleasure, which he conceives as a state of mental and physical tranquillity. (The Greek word is ***ataraxia***.) Reason or judgement is required in order to attain this aim, but it is not valuable for its own sake.

How can we achieve this state of tranquillity? First, Epicurus suggests, we need to avoid likely sources of annoyance or danger. As a result, he rejects Aristotle's views about the value of political activity.

Activity

The Epicurean attitude to politics is nicely summarised by the poet Lucretius in a passage reproduced here as Reading 1.6. Read this extract now. What does Lucretius have to say about the desire to take part in politics?

Discussion

Lucretius suggests that the desire to take part in politics rests on a mistaken belief – the belief that wealth and status will secure a comfortable life. If we look around us, he suggests, we will soon realise that political activity brings nothing but trouble and danger. A comfortable life can be secured only by living quietly and at leisure.

> Titus Lucretius Carus (*c*.99–55 BCE) was a Roman poet. His only known work is *De Rerum Natura*. Nothing is known about his life.

Epicurus, then, agrees that leisure has a crucial role to play in human life. But his reasons for taking this view are very different from Aristotle's. As we have seen, Aristotle values leisure as an end in itself. Used properly, he argues, leisure enables people to achieve the very best of which they are capable. In contrast, Epicurus values leisure only as a means to an end; and he conceives it not as an opportunity to reach for the stars, but as a safe and comfortable haven in a dangerous and uncomfortable world.

What kinds of pleasure should people pursue, once they are safely at leisure? Epicurus emphasises the value of simple pleasures: a modest meal or a conversation with friends (*Vatican Sayings*, 66). He also recommends certain kinds of intellectual activity – not for their own sake, as Aristotle does, but as sources of pleasure. Philosophical activity is particularly important, both because it is enjoyable (Epicurus thinks) and because it can help to counteract mistaken beliefs that create anxiety and frustration in people's lives (*Vatican Sayings*, *27*). Above all, he argues, the key to tranquillity lies in knowing that pleasure can be found in simple things. Once people recognise this, they will realise that pleasure is easy to secure; and so they will be able to stop worrying about the future and enjoy what they have. Again, the contrast with Aristotle is plain to see: while Aristotle directs us to aim at the highest things that a human being can achieve, Epicurus' strategy is to avoid risk and learn to desire only things that are within our reach.

Hence Epicurus does not suggest that leisure should be spent in feasting, as Lafargue sometimes seems to do. Too much feasting leads to indigestion, after all. But his main concern is that people who indulge in luxuries often begin to believe that they cannot live without them, risking anxiety and disappointment (*Vatican Sayings*, 59).

Epicurus needed to take special care to emphasise this aspect of his theory. As he complains in the *Letter to Menoeceus*, he was sometimes misrepresented as recommending a life of excess and debauchery. This misunderstanding of his doctrines persisted for many centuries, and is reflected in the use of the word 'Epicure' to mean someone devoted to sensual pleasures. Figure 1.6, for example, illustrates how the term

Figure 1.6   Thomas Rowlandson, *The Disappointed Epicures*, published by William Holland, 1790, etching, 34 x 50 cm. Private collection. Private collection/The Bridgeman Art Library.

'Epicure' was understood in eighteenth-century England: the cartoonist Thomas Rowlandson's uproarious 'Epicures' are grievously disappointed when a badly aimed champagne cork overturns a dish of delicacies. You might contrast this image with the portrayal of the 'philosopher's garden' by Antal Strohmayer (Figure 1.7). Although Strohmayer's image is highly idealised, it provides a more accurate depiction of the sober life of leisure that Epicurus recommended to his followers.

Pause now to answer the second and third questions in Table 1.2 above.

Activity   How might Epicurus have advised someone who is considering whether to plug him or herself into an experience machine?

Discussion   This question isn't altogether straightforward to answer. On the one hand, life plugged into an experience machine would be very different from the pleasurable life as Epicurus describes it. On the other hand, Epicurus holds that the things that make up that life – simple food, friendship and philosophy – have no value in themselves. Like the salesperson in the Audio

Figure 1.7 Antal Strohmayer, *The Philosopher's Garden*, 1834, oil on canvas. Private collection. Private collection, Archives Charmet/ The Bridgeman Art Library.

CD 'Selling the Experience Machine', Epicurus asserts that what ultimately matters is the character of our experiences. The experience machine guarantees to provide the most pleasurable set of experiences that it is possible to have. Hence an Epicurean might well conclude that plugging in would be the wisest thing to do.

Perhaps you agreed with Jon Pike when he rejected the salesperson's offer. If so, you have a reason to resist Epicurus' claim that pleasure is the ultimate objective of human life. Conversely, you might be sympathetic to Epicurus' claim that if you feel good on the inside, you have everything you need in life. If so, you have a reason to question the arguments that Jon Pike deployed in answer to the salesperson.

Life without purpose

How does Epicurus argue for the claim that pleasure is the objective of human life? Like Aristotle, Epicurus bases his ethical claims on a metaphysical theory – a theory about what a human being is. By seeing how his metaphysical views differ from Aristotle's, we can better understand why he rejects Aristotle's account of what is valuable in life. As you read this section, try to fill in the remaining boxes in Table 1.2 above.

Epicurus denies that human beings have a function. He believes that everything that exists is made up of 'atoms' – minute, indivisible particles of various shapes that come together to form complex objects, including living things. He argues that living things were originally produced as atoms banged into each other in random ways (*Letter to Herodotus*, 73–4). Some of these chance creations were better at surviving than others, and these are the ones whose descendants are living today. None of this, Epicurus thinks, implies that living creatures behave in certain ways *in order to* carry on living or to produce descendants. They just do behave in those ways – and, as a result, they survive and reproduce (Lucretius, *De Rerum Natura*, 5: 837–77). Whether or not there are functions in nature is still a highly controversial issue among biologists and philosophers, so I am not going to try to settle this issue here. But I do think that Aristotle faces a serious challenge from Epicurus on this point. If living beings have not been created by God, it is at least tempting to think that they do not have any purpose or function. They simply are as they are.

If human beings do not have a function, as Epicurus argues, does it make sense to suppose that there is some particular thing that people ought to aim for? It might be thought that if human beings are just collections of atoms, it does not matter how they spend their time: one pursuit will be just as good as another. But Epicurus does not take this line: he thinks that people ought to aim at pleasure. How does he support this claim?

Activity

Reading 1.7 is taken from *De Finibus* (*On Ends*), a discussion of ethics by the Roman politician and philosopher Cicero. Cicero wasn't sympathetic to Epicurean philosophy, but he did give an accurate presentation of some Epicurean arguments. Study the reading, and then answer the following questions:

Marcus Tullius Cicero (106–43 BCE) was a Roman statesman, lawyer and philosopher. He wrote a number of philosophical works, and played a key role in introducing the main principles of Greek philosophy to Rome.

1   According to Cicero, what reason does Epicurus give for his claim that the aim of life is pleasure?

2   What differences can you find between the way in which Epicurus tries to identify the objective of life and Aristotle's approach?

Discussion

1   According to Cicero, Epicurus states that pleasure is the aim of life because it is what every animal *does*, in fact, want.

2   I can find three ways in which Epicurus' approach differs from Aristotle's:

(a)   Epicurus tries to settle the issue by considering what human beings (and other animals) actually want, rather than by considering what it is appropriate for them to want, in accordance with their function. Since, he thinks, people just do want pleasure, the only question that remains is how to get it.

(b)   Epicurus makes no distinction between human beings and other animals: he takes it that every sentient creature has exactly the same aim. In making this assumption, Epicurus is rejecting

Aristotle's assumption that there is a significant difference between human beings and other animals.

(c) Epicurus supports his argument by appealing to the 'innocent and sound' judgement of a young animal – including, presumably, young children. Aristotle holds that only excellent people are able to make rational judgements about what is important in life. In contrast, Epicurus suggests that the judgements made by animals and children are likely to be correct, because they have not been corrupted by the mistaken beliefs that cause so much unhappiness among adult human beings.

You should now be able to complete Table 1.2 above by contrasting Aristotle's views with those of Epicurus. Pause to do that now, before checking my version in Table 1.3.

Table 1.3 Completed table

Question	Aristotle's answer	Epicurus' answer
What is a human being?	A living being, whose special function is to reason.	A random collection of atoms, which desires pleasure.
What is the value of leisure?	Used properly, leisure enables people to realise human nature at its best.	It is a means to pleasure – a sanctuary from the hassles and hazards of public life.
What is the best way to use one's leisure?	In an activity that involves the exercise of reason for its own sake – that is, intellectual reflection.	In simple pleasures that produce a healthy body and a tranquil mind.
Who is in the best position to judge how leisure should be used?	Excellent people (that is, people who are excellent at reasoning).	Children, animals, and followers of Epicurus.

Like Aristotle's function argument, the Epicurean argument is open to some challenges. I shall mention two:

1   Is Epicurus right to assume that what all sentient beings want is just to be free from pain and anxiety? For example, many animals appear to care about their offspring, and some seem to be just curious.

2   Epicurus rejects Aristotle's claim that there are significant differences between human beings and other animals, and between adults and children. But it is not obvious that he is right about this. So, even if Epicurus is right to say that non-human animals and children aim only at pleasure, he still needs to defend the claim that adult human beings aim only at pleasure too. As you have seen, Nozick's thought experiment provides one way to test this claim.

CONCLUSION
Carolyn Price

Lafargue, Aristotle and Epicurus all agree that leisure is of crucial importance in human life. The value of leisure, they think, is that it enables people to flourish as human beings. And so the best lives will contain as much leisure as possible.

Despite this broad consensus, this chapter has found some significant disagreements between these three philosophers about the nature and value of leisure. Epicurus and Lafargue both define leisure in a negative way – as time spent away from the demands of work or the dangers of public life. For them, leisure is a space in which people are free to live as they please. In contrast, Aristotle defines leisure in a positive way, as the pursuit of activities valued for their own sake. Leisure at its best, he thinks, constitutes the ultimate objective of human life.

But perhaps the most conspicuous disagreement concerns how leisure should be spent. For both Aristotle and Epicurus, this is an issue of pressing importance. Aristotle argues that intellectual reflection is the supreme leisure activity and the crowning achievement of human life. Only a few people, he thinks, are able to spend their leisure in this way. In contrast, Epicurus holds that leisure is best spent pursuing simple pleasures; and, like Lafargue, he thinks that the benefits of leisure can be enjoyed by all.

As we have seen, this ethical disagreement is rooted in a metaphysical dispute – a dispute about what a human being is. According to Aristotle, human beings are defined by their capacity to reason. He argues that reason is the function of human life, and ought to be its aim. For Epicurus, by contrast, human life has no purpose. A human being is just a collection of atoms that happens to be averse to pain and distress.

Along the way, we have met some challenges and objections to these accounts. For example, I have suggested that Epicurus' conception of a purposeless world presents a serious challenge to Aristotle's suggestion that living things have functions. Again, Epicurus' claim that people aim only at pleasure or tranquillity is open to question. (Your reaction to Nozick's thought experiment may help you to decide what you think about this.) Certainly, it does not seem that any of these philosophers has wholly succeeded in defending his position. Nevertheless, as you continue through this book you may wish to look out for some of the ways in which the ideas discussed here continued to influence conceptions of leisure in both the ancient and the modern world – from the tranquillity and seclusion of the Roman villa to the intellectual challenge of judging a brass-band competition at the Victorian seaside.

REFERENCES

Aristotle (1985) *Nicomachean Ethics* (trans. T.H. Irwin), Indianapolis, IN, Hackett.

Aristotle (1986) *De Anima* (trans. H. Lawson-Tancred), London, Penguin.

Aristotle, (1995) *Politics* (trans. E. Barker, revised R.F. Stalley), Oxford, Oxford University Press.

Broadie, S. (1991) *Ethics with Aristotle*, Oxford, Oxford University Press.

Epicurus (1995a) *Letter to Herodotus* (trans. C. Bailey, R.D. Hicks and J.C.A. Gaskin) in Gaskin (1995).

Epicurus (1995b) *Letter to Menoeceus* (trans. C. Bailey, R.D. Hicks and J.C.A. Gaskin) in Gaskin (1995).

Epicurus (1995c) *Vatican Sayings* (trans. C. Bailey, R.D. Hicks and J.C.A. Gaskin) in Gaskin (1995).

Gaskin, J. (ed.) (1995) *The Epicurean Philosophers*, London, Everyman.

Irwin, T.H. (1980) 'The metaphysical and psychological basis of Aristotle's ethics' in Rorty, A. (ed.) *Essays on Aristotle's Ethics*, Berkeley, CA, University of California Press.

Lafargue, P. (2002 [1883]) *The Right to be Lazy and Other Studies* (trans. C.H. Kerr), Amsterdam, Fredonia Press.

Lucretius (1975) *De Rerum Natura* (trans. W.H.D. Rouse, revised M. Smith), Loeb Classical Library, Cambridge, MA, Harvard University Press.

Nozick, R. (1974) *Anarchy, State and Utopia*, Cambridge, MA/Oxford, Basic Books/Blackwell.

FURTHER READING

For an accessible introduction to Aristotle's philosophy, see Barnes, J. (2000) *Aristotle: A Very Short Introduction*, Oxford, Oxford University Press.

Slightly more challenging is Ackrill, J.J. (1981) *Aristotle the Philosopher*, Oxford, Oxford University Press.

As well as the work edited by Gaskin (see above), a useful collection of Epicurean writings is Inwood, B. and Gerson, L. (1984) *The Epicurus Reader: Selected Writings and Testimonia*, Indianapolis, IN, Hackett.

For accessible introductions to Epicurus' philosophy, you might try Rist, J. (1977) *Epicurus: An Introduction*, Cambridge, Cambridge University Press; and Sharples, R. W. (1996) *Stoics, Epicureans and Sceptics*, London, Routledge.

For a contemporary introduction to issues concerning happiness and the purpose of life, see Baggini, J. (2004) *What's It All About: Philosophy and the Meaning of Life*, Oxford, Oxford University Press.

For a more wide-ranging introduction to ethics, including some discussion of the issues addressed in this chapter, you might try Blackburn, S. (2001) *Being Good: A Very Short Introduction to Ethics*, Oxford, Oxford University Press.

RESOURCES

Reading 1.1   # The right to be lazy

A strange delusion possesses the working classes of the nations where capitalist civilization holds its sway. This delusion drags in its train the individual and social woes which for two centuries have tortured sad humanity. This delusion is the love of work, the furious passion for work, pushed even to the exhaustion of the vital force of the individual and his progeny. [...]

In capitalist society work is the cause of all intellectual degeneracy, of all organic deformity. Compare the thorough-bred in Rothschild's stables, served by a retinue of bipeds, with the heavy brute of the Norman farms which plows the earth, carts the manure, hauls the crops. Look at the noble savage whom the missionaries of trade and the traders of religion have not yet corrupted with Christianity, syphilis and the dogma of work, and then look at our miserable slaves of machines. [...]

> The **Rothschilds** were a banking family, famed for their wealth, who built up a large financial business across Europe in the nineteenth century.

The Greeks in their era of greatness had only contempt for work: their slaves alone were permitted to labor: the free man knew only exercises for the body and mind. And so it was in this era that men like Aristotle, Phidias, Aristophanes moved and breathed among the people. [...] The philosophers of antiquity taught contempt for work, that degradation of the free man, the poets sang of idleness, that gift from the Gods [...]

> **Phidias** (*c.*480–430 BCE) was a celebrated Greek sculptor.

[T]he proletariat [...] has let itself be perverted by the dogma of work. Rude and terrible has been its punishment. All its individual and social woes are born of its passion for work. [...]

> **Aristophanes** (*c.*456–*c.*386 BCE) was an equally celebrated writer of comedies.

These individual and social miseries, however great and innumerable they may be, however eternal they appear, will vanish like hyenas and jackals at the approach of the lion, when the proletariat shall say 'I will'. But to arrive at the realization of its strength the proletariat must [...] return to its natural instincts, it must proclaim the Rights of Laziness. [...] It must accustom itself to working but three hours a day, reserving the rest of the day and night for leisure and feasting. [...]

A Greek poet of Cicero's time, Antiparos, [...] sang of the invention of the water-mill (for grinding grain), which was to free the slave women and bring back the Golden Age. [...] Alas! The leisure which the pagan poet announced has not come. The blind, perverse and murderous passion for work transforms the liberating machine into an instrument for the enslavement of free men. Its productiveness impoverishes them. [...]

That the competition of man and the machine might have free course, the proletarians have abolished wise laws which limited the labor of the artisans of the ancient guilds; they have suppressed the holidays. Because the producers of that time worked but five days out of seven, are we to believe the stories told by lying economists, that they lived on nothing but air and fresh water? Not so, they had leisure to taste the joys of earth, to make love and to frolic, to banquet joyously in honor of the jovial god of idleness. [...] Where, O, where, are the sublime gargantuan stomachs of those days; where are the sublime brains encircling all human thought? We have indeed grown puny and degenerate. [...]

The abstinence to which the productive class condemns itself obliges the capitalists to devote themselves to the over-consumption of the products turned out so riotously by the laborers. At the beginning of capitalist production a century or two ago, the capitalist was a steady man of reasonable and peaceable habits. He contented himself with one wife or thereabouts. He drank only when he was thirsty and ate only when he was hungry. He left to the lords and ladies of the court the noble virtues of debauchery. Today every son of the newly rich makes it incumbent upon himself to cultivate the disease for which quicksilver is a specific [syphilis] in order to justify the labors imposed upon the workmen in quicksilver mines; every capitalist crams himself with capons stuffed with truffles and with the choicest brands of wine in order to encourage the breeders of blooded poultry and the growers of Bordelais. [...] The women of fashion live a life of martyrdom, in trying on and showing off the fairy-like toilets which the seamstresses die in making. [...]

If, uprooting from its heart the vice which dominates it and degrades its nature, the working class were to arise in its terrible strength, not to demand [...] the Right to Work which is but the right to misery, but to forge a brazen law forbidding any man to work more than three hours a day, the earth, the old earth, trembling with joy would feel a new universe leaping within her.

Source: Lafargue (2002 [1883]), pp. 9–56 (footnotes omitted).

Reading 1.2   **The experience machine**

Suppose there were an experience machine that would give you any experience you desired. Superduper neuropsychologists could stimulate your brain so that you would think and feel you were writing a great novel, or making a friend, or reading an interesting book. All the time you would be floating in a tank, with electrodes attached to your brain. Should you plug into this machine for life, preprogramming your life's experiences? If you are worried about missing out on desirable experiences, we can suppose that business enterprises have researched thoroughly the lives of many others. You can pick and choose from their large library or smorgasbord of such experiences, selecting your life's experiences for, say, the next two years. After two years have passed, you will have ten minutes or ten hours out of the tank to select the experiences of your *next* two years. Of course, while in the tank you won't know that you're there; you'll think it's all actually happening. Others can also plug in to have the experiences they want, so there's no need to stay unplugged to serve them. (Ignore problems such as who will service the machines if everyone plugs in.) Would you plug in? *What else can matter to us, other than how our lives feel from the inside?*

Source: Nozick (1974), pp. 42–3.

Reading 1.3   **Work, leisure and play**

As has often been said, our very nature demands not only that we should work well, but also that we should make good use of our leisure. For, let me emphasise once again, leisure is the foundation of all that we do. Both leisure and work are necessary, but leisure is to be preferred to work, and is its aim.

So we need to consider what we should do with our leisure. We should not spend it in play, for then it would follow that play is the objective of our lives. That is certainly not the case. Rather, play is needed by those who are hard at work and who need to rest from their labours, for the point of playing is to rest. Work involves labour and exertion, and so we should make room for play at the right times, applying it as a kind of medicine. For its effect on the mind is a sort of relaxation, and the pleasure it gives provides rest.

But leisure in itself seems to imply pleasure and happiness and life at its very best. This is what comes not to people who are working, but to people who are at leisure; for when people are at work they are striving for something which they have yet to achieve, but happiness is an end in itself.

Source: Aristotle, *Politics* 1337b30–8a7, translated by Carolyn Price.

Reading 1.4   **The function argument**

But perhaps we shall find a more precise account if we first determine the function of a human being. For the same thing applies to a flautist or a sculptor or any kind of craftsman, and in general anything that has a function or an action to perform [...]: what counts as its being good or its doing well depends on what its function is. And it will be just the same for human beings, if they have a function. [...]

What then might the human function be? Simply living seems to be something that we share with plants. But what we are looking for is something distinctively human. So we can disregard a life of feeding and growing. After that might come sense-perception, but we seem to share that with horses and cows and every other kind of animal. What remains is the exercise of reason. [...] So the function of a human being is to engage in activities that use or are governed by reason.

Now suppose that someone has a function – a lyre-player, for example. We will ascribe the same sort of function to him whether he is just an ordinary player or a really good one; and it is the same in every case.

[...] For the function of a lyre-player is to play the lyre, and the function of a really good lyre-player is to play it well. Now, we are claiming that the function of a human being is to live in a certain way – that is, to engage in activities and actions that involve the exercise of reason. It follows that the function of a really good man is to exercise his reason in ways that are good and admirable.

Source: Aristotle, *Nicomachean Ethics* 1097b22–8a20, translated by Carolyn Price.

Reading 1.5   ## Pleasure and the simple life

[H]ealth for the body and tranquillity for the mind [...] are the objectives of a life of blessedness. For the end of all we do is to be free from pain and fear, and when once we have attained this, all turmoil of mind is dispersed and the living creature does not have to wonder as if in search of something missing, nor look for anything to complete the good of mind and body. [...]

In this way, regard pleasure as the beginning and end of a blessed life. For we recognize pleasure as the primary and natural desire, and we return to it in all our judgements of the good, taking the feeling of pleasure as our guide.

But given that pleasure is the primary and natural good, we do not choose every and any pleasure, but often pass by many if they are outweighed by the discomforts they bring. And similarly we consider pain superior to pleasures when submission to the pains for a significant time brings a greater pleasure as a consequence. Thus every pleasure, because it is naturally akin to us, is good, but not every pleasure is fit to be chosen – just as all pain is an evil and yet not all is to be avoided. It is by comparison and by looking at the advantages and disadvantages, that all these things must be judged. [...]

And again we regard independence of external things [wealth and possessions] as a great good, not so that in all cases we may enjoy only a few things, but in order to be contented with little if we have little, being honestly persuaded that they have the sweetest pleasure in luxury who least need it. [...] To become accustomed [...] to simple and inexpensive foods gives us all we need for health [...] and when at intervals we approach luxuries we are in a better condition to enjoy them. [...]

When we say that pleasure is the objective, we do not mean the pleasures of the profligate or the pleasures of sensuality, as we are understood to do by some through ignorance, prejudice, or wilful misinterpretation. By 'pleasure' we mean the absence of pain in the body and of turmoil in the mind.

Source: Epicurus, *Letter to Menoeceus*, in Gaskin (1995), pp. 44–5.

Reading 1.6   ## On staying out of politics

Yet should you wish to steer your life by sound
reason, the greatest of man's riches is
to live on a little, level-headedly,
since little is seldom lacking. And yet men
have always wanted to be rich and famous,
that their good fortune should endure on sure
foundations, and to spend their lives in wealth
and peace. It isn't going to happen, since
the struggle to climb the height of honour makes
the route itself unsafe, and even from
the summit, Envy like a thunderbolt
capriciously strikes the climbers down with scorn
to grisly Tartarus. It's therefore much
the best simply to hold your place in peace
than to hanker after power and the rule
of kingdoms. Let them wear themselves away
pointlessly, sweat blood struggling along
ambition's narrow track, since all their knowledge
is second hand and they hearken to hearsay
instead of paying heed to their own senses.

In Roman mythology, Tartarus was a deep pit in the underworld, in which the souls of evil-doers were confined.

Source: Lucretius, *De Rerum Natura*, Book 5, 1118–36, adapted and translated by Richard Danson Brown. (See also the prose translation by W.H.D. Rouse (1924), revised by M. Smith (1975), Loeb Classical Library, Cambridge, MA, Harvard University Press, pp. 466–7.)

Reading 1.7   ## Pleasure as a natural aim

[A]s soon as every animal is born, it seeks after pleasure and rejoices in it as the greatest good, while it rejects pain as the greatest bad and, as far as possible, avoids it; and it does this when it is not yet corrupted, on the innocent and sound judgement of nature itself. Hence he [Epicurus] says there is no need to prove or discuss why pleasure should be pursued and pain avoided. He thinks these matters are sensed just like the heat of fire, the whiteness of snow and the sweetness of honey, none of which needs confirmation by elaborate arguments; it is enough to point them out.

Source: Cicero, *On Ends*, I, 30, in Long, A.A. and Sedley, D.N. (1987) *The Hellenistic Philosophers*, vol. 1: *Translations of the Principal Sources with Philosophical Commentary*, Cambridge, Cambridge University Press, p. 20.

2 SACRED SPACE AND LANDSCAPE

Graham Harvey and Marion Bowman

MATERIALS YOU WILL NEED

- DVD Video: Sacred Space and Landscape
- Illustration Book

AIMS

This chapter will:

- introduce you to sacred places and the different ways in which they are treated and understood
- encourage you to think about what makes some places 'sacred' for some people
- further develop consideration of ways of studying places of religious importance
- suggest some ways in which religions play significant and sometimes unexpected roles in the contemporary world.

INTRODUCTION

This chapter contributes to the study of place and leisure by focusing attention on places that are important to various religious groups and individuals. You may be surprised to find a chapter dealing with religion in a book where place, leisure, travel and tourism are the main themes. However, travel and religion have been connected for thousands of years through pilgrimage, and travelling with a spiritual purpose is something that continues on a considerable scale to this day. Indeed, pilgrimage, or what some people prefer to describe as spiritual tourism, increased significantly throughout the latter part of the twentieth century, aided in part by the increasing ease with which it is possible to travel and the increased leisure time enjoyed by many. Because people travelling to sacred places have the same needs as other tourists (e.g. places to eat and to stay, and souvenirs of their trip), many traditional pilgrimage centres have engendered complex service industries. Indeed, the line between tourism and pilgrimage can often be hard to draw. As the anthropologist Simon Coleman and art historian John Elsner point out in introducing their book about pilgrimage:

> The most famous instigator of mass leisure travel was Thomas Cook, himself a Baptist minister and social reformer, who specialised in arranging morally uplifting tours. Some of these actually involved journeys to the Holy Land itself, making explicit the association between pilgrimage and tourism.

(Coleman and Elsner, 1995, p. 214)

The British tour guide **Thomas Cook** (1808–1892) established the travel agency that still bears his name today.

Religion and leisure are also linked not only in space but in time too: many national holidays originated in religious holy days, and many people spend at least some of their leisure time visiting places that can be defined as 'sacred'. In this course you have already been introduced to debates about sacred sites, such as St Chad's Cathedral, Birmingham, while the widespread interest in historical and/or heritage sites is covered in the discussions of Newgrange and Roman villas. In this chapter we invite you to consider some of the multiple views, commitments, understandings and passions that people bring to particular places that they (or others) consider as 'sacred' and/or as 'heritage', 'leisure', 'work' or 'home'.

We will concentrate on three locations in England which are, in a variety of ways and for various reasons, regarded as sacred. These are the combined World Heritage Site of Stonehenge and Avebury; Glastonbury; and Milton Keynes. For some people two of these landscapes are primarily sacred places, but many others visit them out of archaeological or historical interest. The third place is essentially a modern town, conventionally regarded as a venue for shopping, leisure, work and study (of course!) but which has an underlying 'sacred geometry' at its centre that is of great importance to some

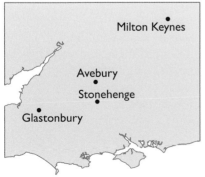

Figure 2.1   Map showing the locations of Avebury, Glastonbury, Stonehenge and Milton Keynes.

people. In fact, just as work and shopping are part of what happens in all three sites, so too notions of what is sacred are also significant in various ways in all three.

After some consideration about what 'sacred' might mean, we go on to discuss these sites, providing some descriptive orientation that will be richly enhanced by viewing the DVD Video 'Sacred Space and Landscape', where you will view these locations and encounter some of the people engaging with them. It will be helpful to keep in mind that our focus is as much on the places as on the people.

Earlier in this course you were introduced to the understanding that religion is something that people do, and something that structures people's lives (i.e. it is not only about beliefs). Religion may involve rituals or ideas that seem unlikely or even ridiculous to outsiders, but it is part of the job of the academic study of religion to explain how people see the world and what informs how they act in it. Even if one does not embrace a particular world view personally, it is important to understand how it functions in the lives of others. Awareness of diverse perspectives and experiences is as vital here as it was when you previously considered multiple answers to the question 'Who is the Dalai Lama?' Similarly, here we are asking questions that resonate strongly with those asked elsewhere in this book. For example, earlier you examined the nature of leisure, authentic experience and the 'best life' from a philosophical angle, noting that different views exist. And later you will look at the popularity of villas as venues for leisure, from Roman times to today, placing this alongside the plain fact that in order for some people to have leisure others must labour. A beach, a villa or Stonehenge may be quite different places to different people. In all these chapters you are asked to examine particular phenomena from different angles, thus gaining and applying skills of importance in academic study and in reaching a full appreciation of the world around you.

2.1   WHAT MAKES A PLACE SACRED?

If you think of a sacred place, what or where would you immediately envisage? Would an urban location, such as Jerusalem, Makah (Mecca) or Varanasi (Benares), spring to mind? Or would you think of a natural feature like a river or a mountain? Might you see in your mind's eye a significant religious building, such as a temple, church or mosque? Maybe your thoughts would even turn to a sports stadium? Or you might think of your home, or some place within your home, or somewhere you once lived.

Sacred places may be natural landscape features or human constructions; inside or outside; ancient or modern. Their sacredness may be widely recognised and agreed upon, or acknowledged only by particular groups or individuals. The sacredness or special nature of a place may be connected with the presence of a particular person or divine figure, with a significant event, or with something about the location or natural feature itself.

Before considering what makes particular places sacred to particular people, especially those who belong to particular religions, more general questions have to be asked. In addition to defining the nature of sacred places – what makes them different from ordinary places – it is important to be clear that some of the differences between definitions emerge from hotly contested differences of understanding about academic approaches to the topic.

Activity   In this activity you are asked to read extracts from the works of scholars interested in defining what makes some places (and people, objects, animals and events) sacred rather than profane or ordinary.

As you read the extracts, pay particular attention to claims about who or what makes places sacred. At the end of the activity, you should be able to summarise a range of interpretations of the word 'sacred' and understand some of the differences of opinion and approach to the topic among scholars of religions.

The first two extracts are from the work of an influential but increasingly controversial historian of religion, Mircea Eliade:

> Whatever the historical context in which he is placed, homo religiosus [the ideal religious person] believes that there is an absolute reality, the sacred, which transcends this world but manifests itself in this world, thereby sanctifying it and making it real.
>
> (Eliade, 1961, p. 202)

> Man becomes aware of the sacred because it manifests itself, shows itself, as something wholly different from the profane. To designate the *act of manifestation* of the sacred, we have proposed the term *hierophany*. It is a fitting term, because it does not imply anything further; it expresses no more than is implicit in its etymological content, i.e., that *something sacred shows itself* to us. It could be said that the history of religion – from the most primitive to the most highly developed – is constituted by a great number of hierophanies, by manifestations of sacred realities. From the most elementary hierophany – e.g. manifestation of the sacred in some ordinary object, a stone or a tree – to the supreme hierophany (which, for a Christian, is the incarnation of God in Jesus Christ) there is no solution of continuity. In each case we are confronted by the same mysterious act – the manifestation of something of a wholly different order, a reality that does not belong to our world, in objects that are an integral part of our natural 'profane' world.
>
> (Eliade, 1961, p. 11)

Succinctly opposing Eliade's view, the next extract is from Kim Knott's book *The Location of Religion: A Spatial Analysis*:

> Nothing is inherently sacred, but things, places, persons, and events are attributed with that quality by societies, groups, or individuals according to their own cultural context.
>
> (Knott, 2005, p. 221)

A more extensive presentation of this view is found in the following extract from a book about American sacred spaces which draws attention to the inherently contested nature of all sacred spaces:

> Sacred space may be set apart, but not in the absolute, heterogeneous sense that Eliade insisted upon. Against all the efforts of religious actors, sacred space is inevitably entangled with the entrepreneurial, the social, the political, and other 'profane' forces. In fact, [...] a space or place is often experienced as most sacred by those who perceive it at risk of being desecrated by the very forces – economic, social, and political – that made its consecration possible in the first place. In one way or another, [we seek to] set to rest the Eliadian notion that the sacred is necessarily the opposite of the profane or absolutely separate from the profane. [...]
>
> [The] assertion that the sacred irrupts or manifests is a mystification that obscures the symbolic labor that goes into making space sacred. It erases all the hard work that goes into choosing, setting aside, consecrating, venerating, protecting, defending, and redefining sacred places. This mystification is even more seriously misleading, however, when it covers up the symbolic violence of domination or exclusion that is frequently involved in the making of sacred space. Sacred places have been exploited by dominant political and economic interests, and they have been reclaimed and even desecrated by those who have been dominated or excluded, all in the context of often violent contests over power and purity.
>
> (Chidester and Linenthal, 1995, p. 17)

Discussion The most obvious difference between these various definitions of sacred is that Eliade asserts that 'the sacred' reveals itself, while Knott, Chidester and Linenthal insist that sacrality is always the product of human efforts. While all the authors recognise that sacred places (or people, animals, objects or events) are somehow separate from other places, i.e. those identified as ordinary or profane, Knott, and Chidester and Linenthal make it absolutely clear that they think sacredness is made, not found. Rituals in particular make places sacred. The word 'sacred' indicates the deliberate separating or setting apart by particular people of whatever is thereafter labelled sacred. People make places sacred by separating them off from other places, perhaps initially with rituals and thereafter by acting in different (perhaps 'sacred') ways within them.

Knott offers the strongest statement ('Nothing is inherently sacred') in opposition to Eliade's view. Chidester and Linenthal's extract adds the recognition that because the labour of defining what is sacred always excludes everything else it is a process entangled in powerful social, political and economic interests. In the part of their work that follows the extract above, they go on to cite the example of Jerusalem: at one and the same time a sacred city and a place of conflict. Stonehenge and Avebury, Glastonbury, and Milton Keynes do not provide such stark illustrations of what Chidester and Linenthal call 'violent contests over power and purity', but they are venues of disagreement and diversity.

Some aspects of these disagreements are mentioned on the DVD Video, which we will come to in a while.

The brevity of these extracts may mask another angle that is worth noting here. Underlying these divergent definitions of 'sacred' is the question of the status of religious explanations. Eliade proffers religious definitions (sacred places manifest themselves), while the other authors insist that this begs the question. Religious explanations are what academic research sets out to discuss; they do not form the answers. When Chidester and Linenthal write about 'mystification' they are accusing Eliade of presenting a *religious* belief rather than an *academic* argument. Much of Eliade's work promotes his own religious world view. It neither respects the different views of people he claims to be discussing, nor does it interrogate these claims from a non-religious perspective. Eliade encourages others to become 'homo religiosus' rather than aiding them to engage critically with the actual data presented by diverse religious and cultural phenomena. When we turn, as we do shortly, to the question of the religious significance of Stonehenge and Avebury, Glastonbury, and at least parts of Milton Keynes, our task must involve an attempt to understand what different religious people do and think, but it must not stop there. We shall attend to the contested and multiple understandings of places that some people consider sacred, while others proffer different views. By examining what 'sacred' means to a range of groups and individuals we shall gain a better understanding of the material and ideological construction of places as aspects of the formation, maintenance and contestation of identities performed in relation to those places.

We shall note that some religious people might agree with Eliade's claims, especially the notion that sacred places are revealed not made, found not formed. They are 'sacred' because of something inherent in themselves, not because people make them sacred. Yet we shall see that other people not only accept that some places are set aside as sacred, sometimes with considerable expenditure of effort, but also value the diversity of opinions about them as somehow indicating that they are special, at least. Others may doubt the sacredness of particular places which, nonetheless, they greatly value as places to visit for a range of meaningful purposes, including leisure, the acquisition of knowledge, commerce and employment.

2.2   STONEHENGE AND AVEBURY

Activity   Look at the maps, photographs and illustrations of Stonehenge and Avebury
(Figures 2.2–5 and Plates 4.2.1–2 in the Illustration Book) and jot down your
impressions and responses. If you have visited either or both places you
could add a brief summary of your memories.

Discussion   Your impressions and responses to these places are as valid as anyone else's.
They are part of the data about the multiple understandings and reactions to
places that can be labelled 'sacred places'. At the end of this chapter we shall
invite you to reflect further on your notes about all the places discussed here.

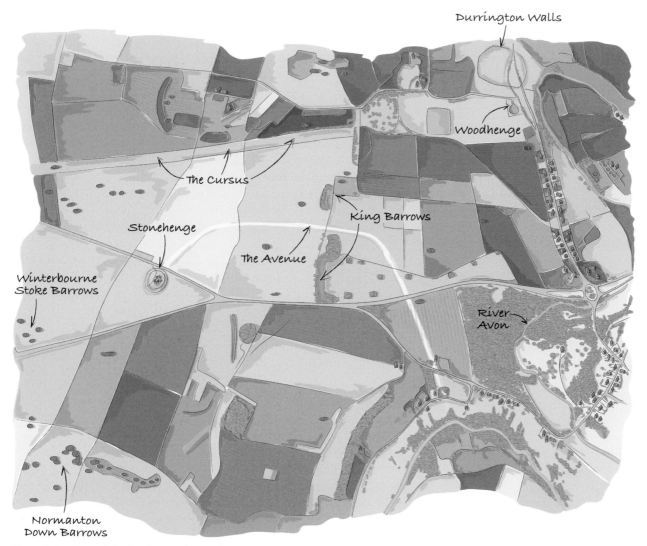

Figure 2.2   Map of the landscape of Stonehenge.

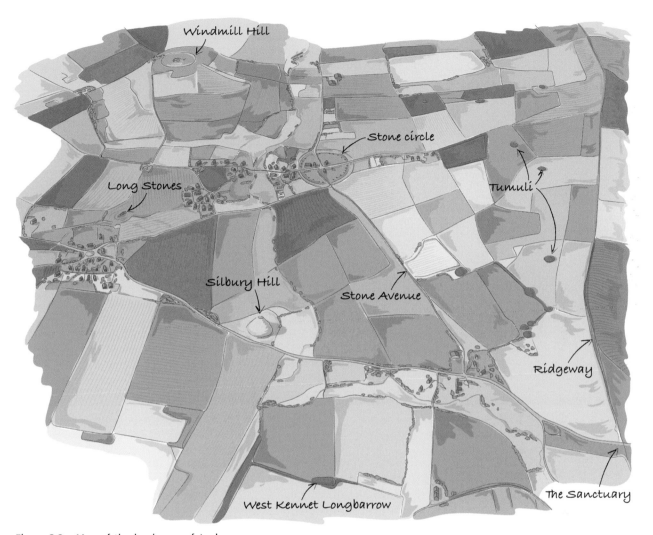

Figure 2.3 Map of the landscape of Avebury.

UNESCO (the United Nations Educational, Scientific, and Cultural Organization) has registered Stonehenge and Avebury as a combined World Heritage Site. They are described thus:

> Stonehenge and Avebury, in Wiltshire, are among the most famous groups of megaliths in the world. The two sanctuaries consist of circles of menhirs arranged in a pattern whose astronomical significance is still being explored. These holy places and the nearby Neolithic sites are an incomparable testimony to prehistoric times.

(UNESCO, 1998–2008)

After your consideration of the problem of adopting religious explanations, it may strike you as peculiar that UNESCO uses

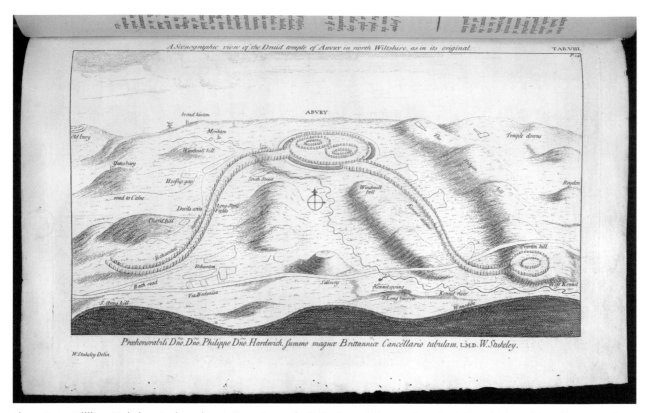

Figure 2.4   William Stukeley, *Avebury (Great Stone Serpent)*, 1743. From *Adbury a Temple of the British Druids, with some others described, etc.* 1743, London. British Library, London. Shelfmark: G.6042.(2.). Photo: © by permission of the British Library.

religious language ('sanctuaries' and 'holy') here. In fact, UNESCO's listing of sacred sites elsewhere follows a similar practice of respecting the views of religious insiders. In the case of Stonehenge and Avebury, it also uses the language of archaeology ('**megaliths**', '**menhirs**', 'neolithic' and 'prehistoric'). Perhaps 'sanctuary' has a double reference here, as the term is not only synonymous with 'temple' but was, according to the antiquarian and eyewitness William Stukeley (1687–1765), also the name given by local people to two concentric circles of standing stones at the end of an avenue leading to and from the larger Avebury circles, until its destruction in the winter of 1724. The UNESCO text also hints at the contested issue of the possible 'astronomical significance' of the pattern of standing stones. But it begins and ends on a celebratory note that chimes with the notion that these are famous parts of a global heritage shared by all humanity. The majority of visitors to these sites come as tourists, but it is undoubtedly the case that among the many reasons for visiting (not least, an interest in ancient cultures and heritage, and the aesthetic appeal of the sites) a general sense that these are or were sacred places is significant. In the wider context in which tourism accounts for a significant portion of contemporary leisure (catered for by an expanding industry) places of religious interest are common venues for encounters between religiously committed and more broadly interested or curious visitors.

Figure 2.5   William Blake, plate 100 from *Jerusalem* (Bentley Copy E), 1804–20, etching with pen, watercolour and gold on paper, 15 x 22 cm. Yale Center for British Art, Paul Mellon Collection, USA/The Bridgeman Art Library.

(Many of the tour buses that stop at Stonehenge also take groups to Salisbury to visit its cathedral on the same day.) Some of those who manage places like Stonehenge and Avebury find it difficult to cater for all potential visitors.

It is hard, perhaps even impossible, to offer short descriptions of Stonehenge and Avebury without including interpretations that may not be acceptable to everyone interested in them. Once you have said that they are arrangements of standing stones within roughly circular banks and ditches, and that they are located near other interesting and often enigmatic features (especially burial mounds, and other landscape features including Silbury Hill, at Avebury – the largest artificial mound in Europe), everything else may be contested. To say that these are prehistoric monuments may be to suggest that they are *only* of archaeological interest, or that current archaeological theories about the origins of a place should somehow determine its current meanings. To say that Stonehenge has an entrance – marked by outlying standing stones and an avenue – that points to the sunrise on the summer solstice may be to privilege only one possible interpretation of the site as a focus for midsummer rituals. Both contemporary **Druids** and heritage managers use the terms 'archaeological monument' and 'sacred place' in describing Stonehenge and Avebury, variously valuing the intersection between the ancient and present-day celebration of *something* at Stonehenge. Even talking about 'standing stones' invites further debate: for everyone who sees the stones as inanimate rock (inert matter), there are others for whom the stones are living and active participants in sacred ceremonies.

Much of this diversity of opinion is expressed humorously in the following extract from *Bollocks to Alton Towers: Uncommonly British Days Out* (an alternative and sometimes irreverent guide to less well-known British 'attractions'):

> For Britons, stone circles are a vital link with the prehistory of our islands. Without them we'd have no idea what our ancestors were up to before Roman and French invaders started insisting we write it all down. And, despite the hordes of well-meaning hippies who've claimed these ancient stones as their own, you don't have to believe in ley lines or be dressed as a druid to get tingles up your spine at a Neolithic monument.
>
> It doesn't matter whether these things were spiritual batteries, calendars, temples or Britain's earliest fish-and-chip shops, whatever they were, your great great great great great grandparents cared about them enough to use every ounce of their willpower and ingenuity to move lots of enormous stones into important-looking shapes. That's an incredible thought. If you can get a kick out of the sheer force of will it must have taken to build York Minster, you can get a kick out of a stone circle.
>
> These monuments express mankind's relationship to our environment, staking a place out between the earth and the sky (and whatever the builders thought might be beyond), which makes what has been done to Stonehenge a national and historical insult.
>
> (Hazeley et al., 2006, p. 223)

The authors go on to vilify those responsible for the roads and tourist-industry paraphernalia that, they claim, justify their assessment of Stonehenge and lead to their encouragement to visit Avebury instead. Clearly their claims that 'it doesn't matter' what Stonehenge was, and their criticisms of what it does now, are opinions not shared by everyone who values the place. Many people (whether archaeologists or UFO enthusiasts) think it is of vital importance to know what Stonehenge was or is. In short, almost every statement about Stonehenge and Avebury invites contest and endorses polemics.

Activity	Now turn to the DVD Video 'Sacred Space and Landscape' and watch the film about Stonehenge and Avebury. Take note of the variety of activities engaged in by people visiting the sites and what the interviewees claim about these places. How do they compare with either Eliade's or with his critics' understandings of 'sacred place'?
Discussion	In the film, significant numbers of people are shown celebrating seasonal and cosmic events that appear to be of religious significance to them. Most obviously, the celebration of the summer solstice attracts large gatherings. Some people have felt such a strong attraction to the place that they have moved to Avebury. Some participants stand out because they wear unusual rather than everyday costume. Others perform acts that may appear peculiar to some observers. A group who object to the display of human remains in Avebury's museum, calling for the reburial of ancestral remains, are included as one example of a difference of opinion about the past.

Sometimes it is hard to tell whether someone is dressed distinctively (e.g. wearing a blanket) for a religious purpose or because of the weather. Perhaps the notion of religion can dovetail with practical concerns like keeping warm and at the same time legitimise wearing a costume that makes someone distinctive (or reveals them to be so). Similarly, there have been heated debates about whether the solstice celebrations constitute a spiritual gathering or a party, with some seeing these interpretations as necessarily opposed to each other, and others asserting that carnival-like events are inherently sacred. Some of the costumes you can see in the film are almost certainly indicative of a carnivalesque approach to the solstice celebrations, or at least of a playful use of stereotypical images of Druids and wizards. In addition to the various people who are engaging in rituals or parties, the film also shows a number of people who might be described as tourists: people whose purpose in visiting these sites may be identical to their interest in any other archaeological or historical place. Security officials of various kinds and employees of the relevant heritage management groups (English Heritage at Stonehenge, the National Trust at Avebury) are also made visible by their costumes, actions and ways of talking about the sites.

In the film you can also hear some claims that support the opinion that places are found to be sacred, and that they attract people because of some inherent sacrality or spirituality that is there whether or not people visit. In other words, people encounter sacredness here. Other people contest this claim and assert that the actions of particular people, perhaps especially the more ritualised actions, actively make Stonehenge and Avebury sacred. While these claims may match those of either Eliade or his critics, you should continue to ponder whether it is sufficient to accept either assertion or whether alternative explanations should be found.

Pagans and Druids

The more familiarity you gain with people (individuals and groups) who celebrate at particular sacred places, the better you will understand what they do and why they do it. In this chapter we are mostly interested in the places and what makes them sacred for some people. However, a brief introduction to some of the religious movements involved will aid your appreciation of what happens in these places.

It may be sufficient to note here that **Pagans** identify their religion as a 'nature religion': the celebration of life in this world rather than an attempt to reach heaven or gain enlightenment. Their celebration of solstices at Stonehenge and Avebury are part of a wider celebration of the ever-changing life-cycles of the earth and all its inhabitants. (See the image of the 'Wheel of the year', Plate 4.2.3.)

John Wood the Elder (1704–1754) was the architect and planner responsible for much of the Georgian style of the city of Bath in the south-west of England.

The term 'Druid' is derived from ancient Roman literature, referring to some kind of religious–political leaders who held sway up until the Roman invasion of north-west Europe. For example, Julius Caesar says in his campaign histories that the Druids 'preside over sacred things, have the charge of public and private sacrifices, and explain their religion' (*Gallic Wars* 6:13). In the eighteenth century not only were the Druids credited with the building of Stonehenge and Avebury, but this now-discredited notion inspired the architect John Wood the Elder, in his designs for the Crescent and Circus at Bath (see Figure 2.6). He based the dimensions for the Circus on rather idiosyncratic measurements of and theories about Stonehenge and the stone circles at nearby Stanton Drew. The poet and visionary William Blake (1757–1827) identified Britain as bounded by 'Albion's Ancient Druid Rocky Shore' and wrote of Druids as proponents of a 'Natural religion' who erected 'a stupendous Building on the Plain of Salisbury' (Blake, 1979 [1804], pp. 649, 701).

Figure 2.6   Aerial view of the Circus in Bath. Photographed by Trevor Smithers. Photo: © Trevor Smithers ARPS/Alamy.

Many people throughout history have claimed to be heirs of the Druids, reviving their wisdom and ceremonies. The twentieth century saw experiments in reconstructing pagan Druidry by various groups and individuals in Britain and elsewhere. Many of these new Druids gravitated towards Avebury, Stonehenge and other megalithic sites in order to celebrate seasonal festivals, venerate deities and conduct rites of passage (child namings, marriages and memorial services).

Precisely because Pagan and Druidic sacred places are other people's archaeological monuments or tourist venues, few Druids or Pagans forget or ignore alternative – and dominant – interpretations of these places. Especially at Stonehenge, the power dynamics are evident even when the authorities (in this case the organisation English Heritage, which also labels this a sacred place) strictly control entry. In other words, contemporary Druids offer explanations that might fit both with Eliade's idea that sacred places reveal themselves and with Knott, and Chidester and Linenthal's insistence that people set aside places as sacred.

2.3 GLASTONBURY

Activity As you did with Stonehenge and Avebury, look at the photographs and illustrations of Glastonbury (Figure 2.7 and Plates 4.2.4–7). Then jot down your impressions and responses, and summarise your memories if you have visited the town.

Discussion Once again, at the end of this chapter we will invite you to reflect further on your notes about all the places we are discussing here.

While many people are attracted to Stonehenge and Avebury primarily on account of their great stone structures (often ignoring the larger landscape with its complex remains of ancient settlements, sacred sites and burials), it is mainly natural phenomena that attract attention and myth-making in Glastonbury, and different parts of Glastonbury attract different people.

Glastonbury could be described as a multivalent location (a place having many meanings). In conventional terms, it is a small town (population *c.*9000) in rural Somerset. It is probably best known as the venue of an annual performing arts festival (actually held on farmland near Pilton, seven miles from Glastonbury) that attracts large numbers of people with a remarkable array of different motivations and interests. However, our focus is the town itself, because of the attraction it exerts on a variety of spiritual seekers and scholars on account of the many myths that surround it and the myriad claims made for it (Bowman, 1993, 2000, 2005; Ivakhiv, 2001). In popularly accepted chronological order, some believe that Glastonbury was a significant prehistoric centre of Goddess worship, an idea confirmed for present-day devotees by figures of the Goddess they feel they can

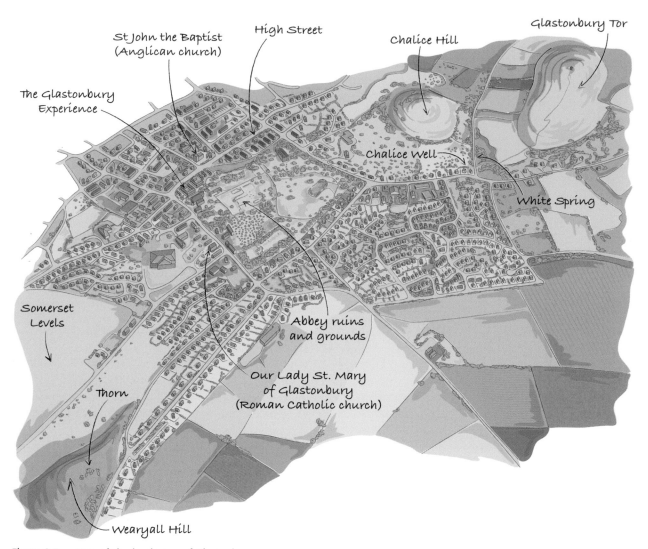

Figure 2.7   Map of the landscape of Glastonbury.

discern in the very landscape of Glastonbury (Jones, 2000). For others, Glastonbury's significance lies in the claim that it was the site of a great Druidic university, a centre of learning to which people flocked from all over Europe and beyond. There are also those who assert that in Glastonbury the Druids had anticipated the coming of Christianity, and that here the transition from the old religion to the new was smooth.

For many Christians, past and present, Glastonbury's status has rested on it being the so-called cradle of English Christianity, the point at which Christianity took root in England. Some claim that Joseph of Arimathea (the person who provided a tomb for Jesus, according to the Gospel of St John, 19: 38–42) brought Christianity to Britain and built the first church in the British Isles at Glastonbury. They say that after Jesus' crucifixion Joseph arrived in Glastonbury with a staff which he thrust into the ground at Wearyall Hill. The staff took root and became the Glastonbury Thorn, a tree which flowers twice a year, in spring and around Christmas. Each year this legend is celebrated in the Holy Thorn Ceremony and a sprig of the Christmas flowering thorn is sent to the British monarch. (Offshoots of the thorn have been planted in Milton Keynes, among other places.) Joseph is also reputed to have brought with him the chalice used at the Last Supper, the Holy Grail, although in some versions of the legend he brought containers holding the blood and possibly the sweat of Jesus.

You read works by William Blake in Book 2, Chapter 2.

Even more significantly, many believe that Jesus himself came to Glastonbury with Joseph, and furthermore that he may have spent some time living there before he commenced his ministry. The words of William Blake –

> And did those feet in ancient time
> Walk upon England's mountains green?
> And was the holy Lamb of God
> On England's pleasant pastures seen?

(Blake, preface to *Milton*, 1804–08)

– are widely thought to express this belief. More recently, the Northern Irish musician Van Morrison's song 'Summertime in England' (1980) contains the line 'Did you ever hear about Jesus walkin', Jesus walkin' down by Avalon?', demonstrating the continuing currency of this idea.

Traditionally (though questionably) connected with Celtic saints such as Patrick, Bridget, Columba and David (see Carley, 1996, pp. 99–112), Glastonbury is regarded by some people as a bastion of Celtic Christianity, suggesting that here was a more nature-orientated, egalitarian, spiritually intuitive form of Christianity than the Roman version which many of them consider was later imposed upon it. Some claim this early Christian form was shaped by the insights and esoteric knowledge incorporated from Druids who became Christians.

Van Morrison's lyric also touches on Arthurian mythology. King Arthur, probably a sixth-century Celtic leader, is well known in relation to numerous legends about his followers, the Knights of the Round Table (its roundness denoted equality), who were dedicated to the quest for the Holy Grail (this is never specifically described but is widely thought to be the chalice used by Jesus at the Last Supper). Most of the literary Arthurian myths date from the twelfth century or later, and there are many local legends connecting Arthur with places in Wales and the west country. Glastonbury has been identified with the Isle of Avalon, the place where Arthur was taken for healing after his last battle and where, according to popular tradition, he lies sleeping, waiting to return at a time of great national emergency. This Arthurian connection, apparently reinforced when the monks of

Glastonbury allegedly found the bodies of Arthur and his wife Guinevere in the abbey grounds in the twelfth century, was for some further confirmed by the 1920s 'rediscovery' of the 'Glastonbury Zodiac'. By looking at maps and studying topography, artist and sculptor Katharine Maltwood (1964) claimed to discern a huge planisphere or zodiac, ten miles in diameter, in the landscape around Glastonbury. Some see in the Glastonbury Zodiac the original and 'true' Round Table of Arthurian myth.

From the 1970s onwards Glastonbury gained a reputation as a centre for hippies, New Age Travellers and people seeking alternative lifestyles and spiritual experiences – most prominently, but not only, in the context of the Festival. Regarded as the epicentre of the New Age in England, Glastonbury is now seen by some as having significance in terms of ley lines (lines of alleged earth energy), and indeed as a node where ley lines converge: an important centre of earth energies. In global terms, Glastonbury is regarded as the 'heart chakra' of planet Earth, or, as one Glastonbury resident puts it, 'the beginning of where the spiritual energy comes into the physical plane'. In the wake of numerous reports of UFO sightings and crop circles in the area, some feel that it is also an important communication point for extra-terrestrial contact.

Mention Glastonbury to some people and they will immediately picture the Tor, a curiously contoured and conical hill that seems to stand alone above the flat Somerset levels. At the foot of the Tor is the Chalice Well, sacred to some for its association with the Holy Grail (its red waters said to represent the blood of Jesus shed for humanity), while others insist it is the menstrual flow of the Goddess. Wearyall Hill is of interest to many Christians as the site of Joseph of Arimathea's arrival in Glastonbury, while for others it is significant as one of the two fish making the sign of Pisces on the Glastonbury Zodiac. On the hill is the Glastonbury Thorn – to some, Joseph's staff miraculously rooted in the ground and flowering at Christmas; to others, a remnant of pre-Christian tree veneration. At the heart of the town are the ruins of the abbey, brutally dissolved at the time of the Reformation in the 1530s, which remain the focus of Christian devotion and are also significant to others who detect powerful energy lines and traces of sacred geometry there.

A geological metaphor may help explain Glastonbury's contemporary multiplicity of meaning. Sedimentary rock is normally stacked in horizontal layers, but sometimes pressure forces it to fold in such a way that the earliest layers stand vertically alongside more recent layers. In Glastonbury, while there is a popularly perceived 'layering' of events and religions (patriarchy replacing matriarchy; Christianity replacing Paganism; the New Age replacing the old), it is also as if all the different 'pasts' stand together in the present. In effect, Glastonbury is not one place but many; it is a place of parallel pasts and presents. Not surprisingly, we find that these different claims and visions sometimes complement, frequently interact and on occasion compete with each other (see Ivakhiv, 2001; Bowman, 2004).

Activity

Now turn to the DVD Video 'Sacred Space and Landscape' and watch the film about Glastonbury. Particularly note the ways in which different people or groups act in or speak about the same sites in different ways. In which ways does sacredness seem to be constructed, experienced or contested? What different views of Glastonbury are expressed and in which ways do they differ?

Is it possible to completely disentangle religious and secular activities and/or motivations?

Discussion

Glastonbury exerts an attraction on a wide variety of pilgrims and spiritual tourists – many of whom are shown in the film, especially participants in contrasting pilgrimages. In particular, the interviewees reveal that Glastonbury is a contested site: a single place that looks completely different to different people. Nonetheless, it certainly seems that the place is perceived to reveal itself as sacred to many people. Even if Glastonbury boasts at least two springs, two lots of trees and two hills (each either attracting different people or generating different interpretations), various landscape features here are often seen to have an inherent sacredness. Yet again, however, the variety of interpretations suggests that visitors and residents are constructing sacred places with reference to different world views from those of their neighbours or competitors.

The film clearly shows that Glastonbury has many shops (and thus workers) supporting or benefiting from its religiously inspired visitors. The availability of leisure time enables people to make their visits, but many choose to live in Glastonbury permanently for religious reasons. A wider community of tourists visit the same sites but, perhaps, do so without seeking life-changing or world-view-confirming experiences. Perhaps the distinction between 'purposeful' and 'purposeless' activities (made in Chapter 1) is useful here as a way of distinguishing religion from leisure to some degree. But it is likely that you will have decided that it is not possible to entirely separate the two.

Two extreme views of sacred sites might help to explain Glastonbury's attractiveness: these might be characterised as the 'empty vessel' versus the 'cornucopia' approach. Anthropologists John Eade and Michael Sallnow claim:

> The power of a shrine [...] derives in large part from its character almost as a religious void, a ritual space capable of accommodating diverse meanings and practices.[...] This, in the final analysis, is what confers upon a major shrine its essential universalistic character: its capacity to absorb and reflect a multiplicity of religious discourses, to be able to offer a variety of clients what each of them desires.[...] The sacred centre, then, in this perspective, appears as a vessel into which pilgrims devoutly pour their hopes, prayers and aspirations.

(Eade and Sallnow, 2000, p. 15)

At the other end of the spectrum is the view of the late Anthony Roberts (an alternative publisher and earth mysteries writer):

> ✳ The holy ground of Glastonbury holds many strange secrets. They are heavily festooned with the rich (often gaudy) accoutrements of myth and magic, but they all resolve themselves around a uniformly synergic nexus. This is that the Glastonbury terrain, with its physical and meta-physical alchemies, is a vast orrery [model of the solar system] and teaching environment for revealing (and enhancing) all that is spiritual in the nature of mankind.
>
> (Roberts, 1992, p. 18)

Eade and Sallnow's assessment of what makes a sacred centre echoes Knott's assertion that nothing is inherently sacred and that places 'are attributed with that quality by societies, groups, or individuals according to their own cultural context' (Knott, 2005, p. 221). However, Roberts (like many others) has a more 'Eliadian' view of Glastonbury, seeing there 'the manifestation of something of a wholly different order, a reality that does not belong to our world' (Eliade, ✳ 1961, p. 11). The sacred is perceived as inherent in and revealing itself through the 'holy ground of Glastonbury', but although people may feel that the landscape can communicate, clearly it tells a number of different stories. The presence and practices of different kinds of Christianity (most obviously, Roman Catholic, Anglican and Orthodox, but also high church and evangelical) at Glastonbury and its abbey – both now and in the past – resonate with the discussion earlier in this course. Seemingly monolithic structures and circumscribed landscapes serve distinct and even dramatically opposing interests and agendas.

From a landscape that some consider inherently sacred, let us now turn to the self-conscious creation of a sacred landscape.

2.4   MILTON KEYNES

Activity   Now look at the photographs and illustrations of Milton Keynes (Figures 2.8–9 and Plate 4.2.8). Then jot down your impressions and responses, and summarise your memories if you have visited the town.

Discussion   At the end of this chapter we will invite you to reflect further on your notes about all the places we are discussing here.

The new town of Milton Keynes (conceived in 1967 and still growing) is rarely, if ever, included in anyone's list of sacred places. Many people only ever associate the town with the (in)famous concrete cows that decorate one public space, or with seemingly endless roundabouts on the roads that divide the town into grids. Of course, the presence of The Open University and more than one sports stadium might

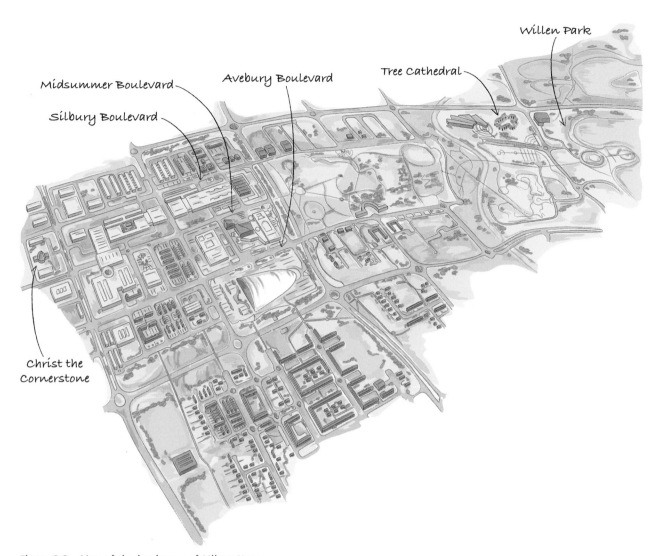

Willen Park

Tree Cathedral

Midsummer Boulevard

Avebury Boulevard

Silbury Boulevard

Christ the
Cornerstone

Figure 2.8 Map of the landscape of Milton Keynes.

contribute to some more positive and exalted assessments of Milton Keynes' sacrality or profanity! However, attributing sacrality to the central district, predominantly shops and business premises, may be considered quite bizarre, but some people have done so. The absence (as yet) of a cathedral means that by popularly accepted conventions in the UK Milton Keynes is not yet a city. There are some old churches, once the centre of villages that are now enveloped in larger developments or districts, and some new religious buildings (e.g. the ecumenical church of Christ the Cornerstone, and a Buddhist complex by Willen Lake). Nonetheless, it may not be immediately apparent that there is anything distinctive about the town. The street names in the central district provide the first major clue: Midsummer Boulevard is paralleled by Avebury Boulevard and Silbury Boulevard. These at least suggest a connection between Milton Keynes and the ancient ritual landscape of Avebury. Like Stonehenge, Midsummer Boulevard is, as its name suggests, aligned towards the sunrise on Midsummer Day, the summer solstice (around 21 June).

The basic layout of Milton Keynes is a grid formed of ten horizontal (roughly west–east) roads and eleven vertical (roughly north–south) roads, seemingly exemplifying a modernist planning for efficiency (Clapson et al., 1998). The religious landscape of the town seems to be either an accident (parish churches in existing villages just happen to exist within the grid squares), or an additional urban functionality (gathering places include pubs and clubs, so a few new religious buildings aid sociality) or even a planned celebration of modern pluralism and/or multiculturalism (the centre's most visible church is ecumenical rather than denominational, while various seemingly religious constructions in nearby parklands are made accessible and acceptable by being linked as multicultural 'art').

Nothing so far suggests that anyone planning the town was attempting to design a new sacred place, let alone a new holy city. However, the alignment of Midsummer Boulevard, which might elsewhere have been called the High Street, established not just a wider geographical but also a cosmic position for Milton Keynes. It links the central district to a relationship between the earth and the sun as marked by sunrise on the longest day of the year – just like Stonehenge. References to the sacred places of Avebury and Stonehenge are made not only by the street names but also by the planting of yew trees and bright flowers in the roundabouts, echoing the shape of the ancient standing stones and the brightness of sacred sunrises. An unfulfilled plan to construct a mound reminiscent of Silbury Hill (see Figure 2.9) would have added another link.

The architects of Milton Keynes' midsummer alignment and of the links with Wiltshire's ancient sacred places were at least partly inspired by the work of John Michell, an influential writer in alternative or esoteric circles since the 1960s. Beginning with his book *The View over Atlantis* (1973), Michell has promoted the argument that ancient buildings, cities and landscapes were engineered to promote cosmic and civic harmony, and that these ideas are relevant and possible today. He has, for example, argued that in prehistoric times there was a worldwide common cultural heritage whose origins he traces to the mythical civilisation of Atlantis (the loss of which is told in Plato's *Timaeus*, 24e–5e). Michell has presented evidence that sophisticated prehistoric engineering techniques can be discerned in the Great Pyramid in Egypt, in ley lines and in the Glastonbury

For an explanation of the standard references to Plato's works, see the Resources section of Book 2, Chapter 1.

Figure 2.9   Early plan for Belvedere Park (including the unrealised Silbury Hill).
Photographed by John Donat. John Donat/RIBA Library Photographs Collection. Image
supplied by Milton Keynes City Discovery Centre.

Zodiac. Michell's ideas on sacred geometry have also been influential.
He says, for example, that:

> Glastonbury Abbey was laid out according to the same plan as at
> Stonehenge and that its builders, Christian geomancers, heirs to
> the ancient magic tradition, invoked the solar power by
> constructing their church by numbers and by reference to the
> geographical position of the earlier monument.

(Michell, 1973, p. 131)

Geomancers are people who
practise the art of divination by
reference to numbers and to the
configurations of sites.

He also asserts that the

> geometrical structure [of Stonehenge, the Great Pyramid in Egypt and the Pyramid of the Sun in Mexico], consisting of figures related to each other both in proportion and in number, is an example of the cosmic scheme or holy city, complied by the philosophers of the ancient world.

> (Michell, 1973, p. 134)

This gives us a clue as to what the centre of Milton Keynes might be about.

Certainly the main planners of the town were committed to designing a thoroughly modern city, rationally laid out for cars and commerce. However, those responsible for the central district made considerable efforts to 'inject a feeling that there is meaning here' and wished to 'create a sense of place' that citizens of the town would celebrate and enhance. (These statements by Tim Mars, an ex-resident of the town and a member of the Civic Trust, are expanded upon in the film about Milton Keynes on the DVD Video.) In fact, if you look again at the map of the town (Figure 2.8) you can see that the grid roads leading away from the centre are not entirely straight. They curve and take account of the natural geography of the area. The boulevards of the central district, however, are perfectly straight. Milton Keynes is not supposed to be like Los Angeles, but brings together planning for commerce and planning for some kind of sacrality.

All this has been extended by the planners, artists and architects involved in the surrounding parklands. Near the Buddhist Peace Pagoda in Willen Park there is a Circle of the Hearts Medicine Wheel (based on an amalgam of popular ideas about several Native American cultures), which includes stones aligning the site to Midsummer Boulevard, a 'needle stone' by the lake and the Tree Cathedral in Newlands Park. All these sites are thus aligned to the summer solstice sunrise and winter solstice sunset. Another nearby landscape artwork is a vast maze, based on the esoteric traditions of the **Rosicrucian Order**. It includes alignments to the four cardinal directions (north, south, east and west), but also contains four bronzes, echoing others in the central shopping centre alongside Midsummer Boulevard. Although these sites and alignments are often presented as 'art' or as representing human aspirations for peace, they draw on religious themes, traditions and styles of construction. In John Michell's 'science of enchantment' (Michell and Rhone, 1992), alignments to solar or stellar events (the rising of zodiac signs or solstices) are said to aid the formation of an ideal society in harmony with itself and the cosmos. Streets become more than thoroughfares for people in pursuit of business or leisure; they become conduits for cosmic energies and influences. Midsummer Boulevard may, therefore, be perceived not only as the heart of Milton Keynes' shopping and business centre, but as the means of bringing harmony into the lives of all the city's inhabitants. Hopes for peace expressed in artwork in city parks are intimately linked and aligned with all activities in the city centre.

In addition to claims that Milton Keynes is linked to Stonehenge, Avebury and Glastonbury by ley lines, there is also at least one more empirical and deliberate link to Glastonbury. The Glastonbury Thorn School (opened in 1993) is named after the Christmas-flowering thorn tree planted in the nearby churchyard and descended from the tree allegedly planted in Glastonbury by Joseph of Arimathea two thousand years ago. More offshoots were planted in the Tree Cathedral that you can see on the DVD Video.

Activity

Note that there is one factual error in the film: it is the midwinter (not midsummer) sunset that is observable in the Midsummer Boulevard alignment in the opposite direction from the midsummer sunrise.

Now turn to the DVD Video 'Sacred Space and Landscape' and watch the film about Milton Keynes. Consider what the people in the film do and say in relation to sacred places. Do you think it is possible to construct a sacred city? We are not asking if the planners of Milton Keynes have done so – or even whether they have tried. We are interested in your thoughts about how the notion of sacred places might relate to shopping centres, entertainment, offices and other workplaces. Can they mix, or does there need to be an obvious boundary to separate sacred places from everyday life?

Discussion

For some people, clearly, it is possible to create sacred places, or perhaps they would insist that all they do is mark the sacredness that already exists in a place. But in Milton Keynes the planners of the boulevards started from scratch: no one previously had suggested that this area was in any way special. They and their successors who developed the midsummer sunrise alignment in the parks proposed that this was a way of making a thoroughly modern, rational town different, more 'meaningful'. Our discussion and the people in the film both participate in a debate about whether sacred places are entirely separate from 'ordinary' ones. All the places we have considered in this chapter contain shops and workplaces as well as constructions (standing stones, churches or alignments) that are somehow different. Just as some people seem uneasy about the ordinariness of parts of Glastonbury, so most people we have talked with, including colleagues who work and/or live in Milton Keynes, are surprised by any claim that the town contains anything sacred. Distinctive, yes, but 'sacred'?

Your views are just as valid as those of others. Questions about what makes a place sacred may be personal, but they are, without doubt, open to debate and contest. Milton Keynes' central district reveals this with absolute clarity.

Activity

Near the end of this consideration of places that are identified as sacred by some people, we invite you to reflect on the whole of this chapter. You may find it helpful to watch all three films right through now, rather than in separate sections. Perhaps a quick jotting down of notes on each of the places we have discussed will be useful. Identify similarities and differences both between the places and also between the activities that take place in them. You should also now revisit the notes you wrote earlier about Stonehenge and Avebury, Glastonbury, and Milton Keynes. These will remind you of your initial thoughts and feelings about these places. What are your impressions of them now that you have considered a range of understandings and activities? Do your responses to all this material aid you to think afresh about what makes some places sacred and others profane? Are you now able to offer a more detailed definition of 'sacred place' than you could initially?

Discussion   In addition to noting that clearly religious activities take place in all these venues, and that clearly religious understandings of them are expressed, we hope you will have noticed other activities and understandings indicative of people's valuation of the sites. In addition to tourists and shoppers, there are also people whose jobs involve managing the places so that a wide range of interests can coexist in them with a degree of harmony, or at least with minimal disturbance to others. Then there are people who provide services to the various kinds of visitors (e.g. pilgrims, tourists, archaeologists). It is also vital to remember that people may combine several reasons for living in or visiting these places. For example, people who watch the midsummer sunrise in Milton Keynes or Stonehenge may also shop for food or postcards there. Some archaeologists are also celebrants of sacred ceremonies at Avebury. Glastonbury shopkeepers may also meditate. It is not only that one person's sacred place or ceremony is another's venue for shopping, leisure or work, but that people are able to benefit from religious activities in more than one way. What they do in sacred places may result in religious, recreational and economic benefits at the same time.

Your definitions of 'sacred', 'profane' and 'sacred place' may continue to vary from those of other people. They should, however, now arise from greater reflection on a wider range of possibilities and information than was available to you before.

CONCLUSION

Sacred places are visited by a great diversity of people with differing motivations. Chapter 1 discussed the possibility that leisure can be defined as activity with no purpose but itself, yet it can also refer to *chosen* activities that enrich our lives and aid our quest for meaning or fulfilment. These definitions resonate with understandings of religion as activities with no economic or material purpose but central to the pursuit of meaning. However, activities at sacred places clearly require the expenditure of considerable effort, not only to support specifically religious activities (e.g. by those who work in hotels that cater for pilgrims), but also to achieve particular results. Rituals in sacred places are often understood to enhance the value of the whole of a person's life, not just the 'religious' bits. Some people go to Stonehenge and Avebury to realign their lives with the natural or cosmic cycles of seasonal change. Some visit Glastonbury to find physical, emotional and mental health by imbibing its sacred waters and/or mystic energies. A few people are working to convert the modernist town of Milton Keynes into a place imbued with more than mundane significance. All these activities may require leisure from the demands and locations of the everyday working world, but they often require specific kinds of labour that pursue the goal of a better life (however that is defined). Many religious people would object strongly to the suggestion that religion is a leisure activity or hobby. However, there are undoubtedly links between leisure as the quest for value and the good life and many of the activities that occur at sacred places.

In this chapter we have hardly done more than survey some of the obvious features of three locations that present themselves when we ask what places religious people consider sacred. We have paid attention to the diversity of activities that take place in sacred places. Some such activities can only, it seems, occur in sacred places. They are the essence of religion for practitioners. Other activities can take place anywhere. But the two kinds of act – religious and secular acts perhaps, or sacred and ordinary (not to say profane) acts – are hardly ever totally disconnected. For this reason, our chief focus has been on the contested nature of sacred spaces. Even spaces that some people wish were absolutely set apart from ordinary working, leisure and living places are undeniably places in which at least some people have to work to support those who perform rituals and other religious acts. Indeed, religion *is* work for some people. Places that are *only* venues for religious rituals or sacred acts are rare, or perhaps non-existent. On the other hand, although sacred places are the location for activities that may require time away from everyday pursuits, they are never entirely separated from concerns about well-being and the achievement of a better life. For all these reasons, it is helpful to think about the relationship between religious activities and those that may be identified as work or leisure. In doing so it is best to avoid making any absolute distinctions.

REFERENCES

Blake, W. (1979 [1804]) 'Jerusalem: the emanation of the Giant Albion' in Blake, *Complete Writings with Variant Readings*, ed. Keynes, G., Oxford, Oxford University Press.

Bowman, M. (1993) 'Drawn to Glastonbury' in Reader, I. and Walter, T. (eds) *Pilgrimage in Popular Culture*, Basingstoke and London, Macmillan, pp. 29–62.

Bowman, M. (2000) 'More of the same?: Christianity, vernacular religion and alternative spirituality in Glastonbury' in Sutcliffe, S. and Bowman, M., *Beyond New Age: Exploring Alternative Spirituality*, Edinburgh, Edinburgh University Press, pp. 83–104.

Bowman, M. (2004) 'Procession and possession in Glastonbury: continuity, change and the manipulation of tradition', *Folklore*, vol. 115, no. 3, pp. 273–85.

Bowman, M. (2005) 'Ancient Avalon, New Jerusalem, heart chakra of planet Earth: the local and the global in Glastonbury', *Numen*, vol. 52, pp. 157–90.

Carley, J.P. (1996) *Glastonbury Abbey: The Holy House at the Head of the Moors Adventurous*, Glastonbury, Gothic Image Publications.

Chidester, D. and Linenthal, E.T. (eds) (1995) *American Sacred Space*, Bloomington, IN, Indiana University Press.

Clapson, M., Dobbin, M. and Waterman, P. (eds) (1998) *The Best Laid Plans: Milton Keynes since 1967*, Luton, University of Luton Press.

Coleman, S. and Elsner, J. (1995) *Pilgrimage Past and Present in the World Religions*, Cambridge, MA, Harvard University Press.

Eade, J. and Sallnow, M.J. (2000) *Contesting the Sacred: The Anthropology of Christian Pilgrimage*, Urbana, IL and Chicago, University of Illinois Press.

Eliade, M. (1961) *The Sacred and the Profane*, New York, Harper & Row.

Hazeley, J., Halstead, R., Morris, J. and Morris, A. (2006) *Bollocks to Alton Towers*, Harmondsworth, Penguin.

Ivakhiv, A.J. (2001) *Claiming Sacred Ground: Pilgrims and Politics at Glastonbury and Sedona*, Bloomington and Indianapolis, IN, Indiana University Press.

Jones, K. (2000) *In the Nature of Avalon: Goddess Pilgrimages in Glastonbury's Sacred Landscape* , Glastonbury, Ariadne.

Knott, K. (2005) *The Location of Religion: A Spatial Analysis*, London, Equinox.

Maltwood, K.E. (1964) *A Guide to Glastonbury's Temple of the Stars: Their Giant Effigies Described from Air Views, Maps, and from 'The High History of the Holy Grail'*, London, James Clarke & Co.

Michell, J. (1973) *The View over Atlantis*, London, Sphere.

Michell, J. and Rhone, C. (1992) *Twelve Tribe Nations and the Science of Enchanting the Landscape*, York Beach, ME, Phanes Press.

Morrison, V. (1980) 'Summertime in England' on *Common One*, Warner Bros. CD 26399.

Roberts, A. (1992) 'Glimpses of eternity: a visionary voyage into the Glastonbury Zodiac in A. Roberts (ed.) *Glastonbury: Ancient Avalon, New Jerusalem*, London and Sydney, Rider, pp. 18–25.

UNESCO (1998–2008) 'Stonehenge, Avebury and associated sites', available at http://whc.unesco.org/en/list/373 (Accessed 3 April 2008).

3 LEISURE IN THE ROMAN VILLA

Paula James and Janet Huskinson

MATERIALS YOU WILL NEED

- Audio CD: Aetatem tibi agere (Doing your own thing)
- DVD ROM: Roman Villa
- Illustration Book

AIMS

This chapter will:

- focus on the Roman villa in order to ask key questions about leisure as an activity and as a concept in the Roman empire
- show how answers to these questions have to rely on surviving evidence pieced together from various sources
- explore leisure in relation to Roman social status
- encourage you to read the literary evidence with an appreciation of its historical and cultural context
- demonstrate how you can critically examine material evidence (archaeological remains and Roman artistic representations) of villas as places for leisure
- introduce the notion of the 'villa' as an ideal that continued into later societies.

INTRODUCTION

Janet Huskinson

In the first chapter of this book you were introduced to two important philosophers of the ancient world, Aristotle and Epicurus, who – though for different reasons – both accorded leisure a central role in human life. Simple pleasures and intellectual reflection were an important part of this. In this chapter we shall consider how these ideas became a very conscious part of the lifestyle associated with Roman villas. We shall also look at various social and economic factors which affected leisure activities in the Roman world.

A villa – in the country or by the sea – was an ideal location for well-to-do Romans to spend their leisure. So strong was the appeal of this lifestyle that it was copied by many later societies and can still be enjoyed today, for example by visiting stately homes, designed according to villa ideals, or by staying in holiday villas in the sun. One particular reason for the enduring attraction of the villa is that its lifestyle balances elements of city life – status, sophistication, competition, control – with qualities traditionally linked with the countryside, such as an idea of 'the simple life' and an enjoyment of nature. This relationship is neatly summed up by James Ackermann, a scholar who has written a history of the villa across the centuries: 'The villa cannot be understood apart from the city: it exists not to fulfil autonomous functions but to provide a counterbalance to urban values' (Ackermann, 1990, p. 9). This relationship is a key factor in understanding the place of the villa in Roman leisure.

In this chapter you will be exploring how the arts – literary and visual – work together to present a picture of this lifestyle at the Roman villa. As you read various poems and letters in which educated Romans wrote about their villas it will become apparent that they had a very visual appreciation of this environment. The literature can convey a vivid and engaging picture of the villa's relaxing ambience, and this can be considered alongside the evidence from the art and archaeology that survives from villas in Italy and in other parts of the Roman empire such as Britain.

But the survival of evidence is a crucial issue. Because so much ancient material – literary as well as archaeological – has since been lost, the picture of the Roman villa as a place of leisure has to be compiled from what are sometimes rather patchy remains. This means that piecing together evidence from various sources is a central theme in this chapter: as you will see, these individual pieces of evidence sometimes complement each other, sometimes contradict each other, and sometimes provide far more questions than answers.

You will look at some different literary views of Roman villa life (in Section 3.2) and then at various kinds of evidence from villa buildings (in Section 3.3). Finally, the conclusion aims to draw the discussion together and also offers some points to ponder.

You will also hear a discussion about Roman leisure on the Audio CD and be introduced to poetry and prose from Latin authors who were able to enjoy time off in villas. Through the DVD ROM 'Roman Villa' you will have a chance to visit some villa sites in Britain (of which the visit to Chiswick House is an optional part of your study).

3.1 ROMAN LEISURE IN PUBLIC AND PRIVATE
Paula James

Before we look at all this in detail, it is important to place leisure at the villa into its wider historical context, and in particular to relate it to other, far less genteel aspects of Roman leisure which you may have encountered.

Activity

This activity involves listening to the Audio CD 'Aetatem tibi agere'. But first read the following quotation from Jerry Toner, whose book on Roman leisure raises searching questions about the political and social aspects of 'doing your own thing'.

> Ideas about leisure were some of the sturdiest pillars on which Roman perceptions of society and selfhood stood – Leisure was not a neutral area. Strains and conflicts existed within Roman society, between the emperor, the elite, and the masses, and these found their most telling expression in anxieties over the use and misuse of free time.
>
> (Toner, 1995, p. 8)

Media notes relating to the Audio CD can be found at the end of the chapter.

I would like you to keep in mind Toner's points about strains, conflicts and the social hierarchy as you listen to the discussion on the Audio CD. This discussion covers a range of leisure activities popularly associated with Rome and asks what different kinds of evidence can tell us about Roman attitudes to duty, obligation and living life for oneself. Toner puts us on alert about an ideology of leisure which our conversation does touch upon here and there.

But in the first part of the discussion we are mainly aiming to identify preliminary questions about Roman society and culture. You should note, but not worry about, an absence of 'tightly packaged' answers here – just try to work out for yourselves whether any further questions are prompted by the discussion. After listening to tracks 1 to 7, you should start reading the chapter in earnest – its first section follows on from and fleshes out issues that the discussion has raised.

Now listen to the discussion on tracks 1–7 of the Audio CD.

The audio discussion ranges over the leisure activities of the Roman people, both the organised variety (such as the Games in the Arena, the chariot races at the Circus Maximus, religious festivals and imperial birthday celebrations) and the more informal (for instance, going to the taverns or the public baths). The public executions, gladiator combats to the death and slaughter of exotic beasts have made the Roman amphitheatres infamous in history. The Roman emperors used the profits of empire to invest in and to expand entertainments such as these for the people, 'democratising' leisure if you like, but also controlling leisure activities and making leisure the social cement that kept social tensions at bay. The emperor could portray himself as the 'father' of the people, who was above any faction and was the architect of entertainments, whether private or public, religious or triumphal, where 'the whole of Roman society could meet [...] in a spirit of public concord' (Toner, 1995, p. 127).

Perhaps this was so; but Toner also points out that the Roman elite was inclined to be judgemental and dismissive about the 'lower orders', whether they were at work or at play. On track 4 of the Audio CD Helen Lovatt suggests that high-ranking Romans felt obliged to be present at public entertainments like the Games. Whether they attended with enthusiasm or with varying degrees of disapproval, they must have felt it was even more necessary to preserve time and space for the forms of leisure that distinguished them from the common people, since the style of their leisure was a keystone of their upper-class identity. For these wealthy, educated Romans the villa provided just such a place. It was associated with *quies* (peace and quiet), and offered time for civilised intellectual exchanges and for literary pursuits.

Yet even so, it seems, the villa was not altogether a place of total escape from city life, with its social demands and its noisy mass entertainments. After all, gladiators were a popular subject in the **mosaics** and wall-paintings that decorated villas (alongside other more intellectual topics), and many villas were near enough to amphitheatres in local towns to allow for visits. Perhaps viewing the Games from a safe distance reinforced the owners' sense of calm and put the peace of the villa into sharper relief.

3.2   LITERARY PICTURES
Paula James

Even more evidence to suggest this constant tension between town and country values comes from literary pictures of different styles of villa life – from the nostalgically simple, to the hedonistically luxurious, to the well-run country estate.

The three examples you will look at now were written at different times. Notice how they differ in the image of villa life which they consciously construct, but also think about the shared ideals which underpin them.

The poet Horace and 'getting away from it all'

Horace (65–8 BCE) lived in interesting times. During his lifetime Octavian (63 BCE–4 CE), the teenage heir to Julius Caesar, became the sole ruler of the Roman empire, taking the title Augustus in 27 BCE. Horace's family property had been confiscated when he fought on the losing side in the civil wars that culminated in the battle of Actium between Antony and Octavian in 31 BCE , so he had to work for a living. He took a post as secretary in the Treasury, but his poetic skills brought him to the attention of influential figures in Rome. He was befriended by the wealthy Maecenas, confidant and cultural attaché of Octavian, and it was Maecenas who gave Horace his country estate in the Sabine hills (see Figure 3.1). Benefiting from the new regime's politically astute patronage of the arts, Horace now had more time and a congenial locality in which to realise his creative talents – and, of course, in his poetry he took the opportunity to show his gratitude towards Maecenas and to celebrate Rome's first emperor, Octavian Augustus.

Figure 3.1   View of 'Horace's farm', Licenza. Photo: Mary Evans/Deagostini Editore.

However, Horace's Sabine farm was also important to him as a haven where he and his friends did not have to be on show, or to impress influential people at the centre of power. Away from the stress of the city, they could discuss all kinds of matters, from the light and frivolous to the philosophical and aesthetic. Horace's love for his country retreat is discussed on the Audio CD. For example, on track 3 you can hear a snippet from one of his *Satires*, where the pressures of the city are presented in stark contrast to life at the Sabine farm (the passage about Horace at the Games with Maecenas is read out in both Latin and English). In this same poem Horace celebrates his time off in the country – and this is how the *Satire* begins, with a celebration of his Sabine farm.

Activity   Study the first part of Horace's *Satire* 2.6 (Reading 3.1), up to the line 'I'm the champ of Roman reticence', and consider the following questions:

- What does Horace value most about his time on the Sabine farm?
- Why do you think the god Mercury is singled out for special thanks?
- How does Horace convey the stress of the city?

Discussion   Horace's description suggests that his countryside farm provides a bracing and healthy environment, with none of the city's sicknesses – here he cites natural phenomena and also economic and political imperatives: the disease of social climbing, for instance. His country home is on the moral as well as the physical high ground, perhaps. Because it is a working farm, Horace is not necessarily totally at leisure here, although he does have slaves as bailiffs, managers, and so on. All the same, this country retreat sounds rather modest and Horace suggests it would be foolish to ask for more.

Mercury, the god Horace singles out for his expressions of gratitude (I allude to this at the end of the Audio CD discussion on track 7) is probably best known as a divine messenger, the Roman equivalent of the Greek god Hermes. He was also the god of luck and gain, and so an appropriate divinity to approach, appease and thus guarantee that Horace's delightful farm is not suddenly snatched away. Mercury was also sacred to merchants (and to thieves!) a 'wheeler and dealer' in business and commerce. To my mind Mercury makes the perfect god to straddle the poet's divided life, as Horace is suggesting that his country existence is a privilege predicated upon his service in the stressful bustle of Rome.

To Horace, the most attractive aspect of the country life is its blessed relief from the capital city. Indeed, his poem is partly about a polarisation between *otium* and *negotium* – but perhaps not entirely. The capital city is a maelstrom of machinations, and Horace gives us a vivid picture of the ducking and diving he does, both physically and verbally, while he is about his business there. He seems to spend a great deal of his time fending off requests for favours as he walks through the main **forum**. You will remember from the discussion on the Audio CD that both business and politicking went on in the 'leisure' places of the city, especially the public baths and in this case the public thoroughfares too.

Horace rather disingenuously insists that the topics of his conversations with Maecenas in the city consist of sport (the prospects of a gladiator from Thrace known as the Thracian Cock) and the weather (the health hazards of morning frosts). Horace protests that he is not a trusted confidant of Maecenas and that they keep off the subject of politics and current affairs when they talk – fancy footwork from Horace, I would say; he is clearly stressed by the fact that so many people want a piece of him when he is in Rome.

You can find Alexander Pope's reworking of this fable in The Faber Book of Beasts, *pp. 128–9. It is included on the Audio CD 'What am I? Beasts and Tradition' in Book 2.*

Away from it all at the villa

The second half of Horace's poem contains the story of the town and country mouse and is told by one of Horace's guests, Cervius.

Activity   Study the second part of Horace's *Satire* 2.6 (Reading 3.1), from 'I squander time like this' to the end. As you read, consider the following questions:

- How does Horace justify relaxing with his friends?

- Does the fable clarify or complicate the relationship that educated Romans had with the countryside?

Discussion   Horace's very first statement suggests that the hasty and hectoring exchanges he endures in the city waste his time. In contrast, the topics of conversation at the Sabine farm, far from being trivial or focused on material concerns, are often weighty and philosophical, even though the dinner party itself is portrayed as a place to be frivolous and self-indulgent. So the reader might expect the entertaining little fable that follows to have hidden depths.

The moral of the fable seems to reinforce the positive view of the countryside as a safe haven and to promote the benefits of a simple life far away from the pretensions, the pressures and the real dangers of the city. The town mouse encourages his country friend to become parasitic at the tables of the rich (remember Helen Lovatt's reference in the Audio CD to such opportunistic characters). There may also be an allusion here to the sometimes humiliating position of a client, which in the Roman system of patronage meant relying upon a wealthier acquaintance, who might hope for a slap-up meal but then have the tables turned upon him (and even the dogs set on him) if he were to fall from favour. The country mouse is soon to learn that the high life is indeed precarious at the banquets of the rich and that he is far better off in his modest woodland hole where he owes no one a living.

On the other hand, the town mouse, fussy and urbane little creature that he is, talks in the rather lofty language of an educated and literary Roman (perhaps more in tune with Horace and his guests?). He persuades the peasant mouse to sample the delights of a city banquet in a rhetorical speech. The tone of the Latin here is rather pompous: the language of high epic poetry ends in a flourish, with the exhortation '*carpe viam*', or 'come along with me' (literally translated as 'seize the road'). The Latin sounds remarkably like the phrase '*carpe diem*', or 'seize the day' (or 'live for the moment'), which Horace himself later coined in one of his *Odes*. This passage could demonstrate that the poet is having a little bit of fun at the expense of his educated guests and perhaps laughing at his own philosophy of life.

On the surface, Cervius' fable can be seen as celebrating the simple life somewhere as far away from the city as possible, and as a compliment to Horace and his country hospitality. Horace's estate, with its range of produce and array of wines, is a far cry from the rough rural fare on offer in the country mouse's woodland hole, but Horace would not have said that he lived in the lap of luxury. Even when they were sending it up in a comic vignette, Roman writers still liked to conjure with the part-legendary, part-historical image of their origins as a hardy and rustic race.

To delve a little deeper, the fable ties in neatly with the tensions Horace felt in dividing his life between his work commitments in the city of Rome and his time away on his Sabine farm. Perhaps, too, Horace is here indicating the compromises he himself has to make in order to live the good life, as he is in some ways a client of Maecenas even though he classes himself as a friend. Self-irony and the recognition of necessity underlie the fable that Horace puts into the mouth of Cervius – and, after all, the poem in which it is told is a satire and Horace himself contributed significantly to the development of the Roman satiric genre. Poetry was the usual medium for this genre, and Roman satirists ranged in their literary personae from the amused observer (like Horace in this poem) to vituperative commentators on every aspect of Roman society.

Activity

In the remaining part of the discussion on the Audio CD we elaborate a little more on the notion of leisure and its link to study and intellectual pursuits for educated Romans. When you have listened to the rest of the discussion, think back to the introduction to this book. In your opinion, do our general conclusions about leisure and our final definition confirm or challenge these earlier sections?

Listen now to the tracks 8–10 on the Audio CD.

Moving on: Statius, Pliny and taking refuge in the villa from politics?

Statius (c.50–c.95 CE) was a Latin poet, born in Naples.

On tracks 8–9 of the Audio CD, Helen Lovatt talks about Statius and his *Silvae* poems, a book of literary vignettes produced to entertain his aristocratic patrons in their sumptuous villas. The subtext to Statius' celebration of a life of conspicuous consumption is that the Roman elite who occupied these villas formed a guarded and claustrophobic circle who found it necessary to stay away from Rome in a kind of voluntary exile. The reason for removing themselves from the seat of power was that Domitian (the emperor 81–96 CE) did not disguise the autocratic nature of his rule by a deferential and tactful treatment of the wealthy elite. This elite could feel very nervous about putting a foot wrong when they were close to the court. It was wiser to exhibit their status at a safe distance.

In Statius' time, then, the villa was not just a place of leisure but also a relatively safe retreat from the ruling regime. Domitian jealously guarded his monopoly of status and power, so it was in any case unwise to keep sumptuous town houses in the imperial capital. As we discuss on track 5 of the Audio CD, Pliny the Younger had a number of villas. Yet he suggests in his letters that his town house on the Esquiline hill in Rome was far less ostentatious than those further from the capital and the emperor.

Focusing on Pliny's villas

Pliny the Younger (61–c.112 CE), nephew of Pliny the Elder, was a lawyer and career administrator who wrote nine volumes of literary letters.

Pliny the Younger served under a succession of emperors, Domitian, Trajan (98–117 CE) and Hadrian (117–138 CE), and had risen to a high position in the imperial government by 100 CE. He even managed to pursue his political career during Domitian's reign by being a good civil servant and keeping a low profile in matters of display and self-advertisement when at Rome.

Pliny the Elder (23–79 CE) wrote the multi-volumed encyclopaedia *The Natural History*, and commanded the Roman fleet at Misenum. He was killed by volcanic fumes in the vicinity of Vesuvius during its eruption in 79 CE.

Laurentum lay on the west coast of Italy, to the south-west of Rome, and was the location of various large seaside villas.

Baiae was a seaside town near Naples, famous for its hedonistic lifestyle.

Pliny was a member of the municipal aristocracy at Como, and had excellent family connections. He had inherited property from his wealthy uncle, Pliny the Elder, and was thus a very privileged man. Pliny the Younger left a fascinating record of his life and times as his correspondence covers a wide range of topics: personal, political, social and cultural. He took pains to polish his letters for publication; for this reason the historian has to keep in mind that even messages to family and friends have been (re)crafted to showcase Pliny as an intellectual and artistic force of his times.

Pliny clearly valued the time he spent at his villas in Tuscany and at Laurentum near Ostia (see Figure 3.2). In his letters he describes his country estates with great pride and affection. Like Horace nearly two centuries earlier, Pliny felt a great sense of relief when he was away from the demands of Rome and had time to concentrate on intellectual pursuits. The educated classes continued to promote the idea of *otium* as productive leisure in intellectual terms and something that distinguished them from the common herd.

Pliny even characterised his villas at Lake Como in literary terms. In one letter he writes:

> One is built on the rocks with a view over the lake, like the houses at Baiae, the other stands on the very edge of the water in an equally Baian style, and so I have named one Tragedy, because it seems to be raised on actors' boots, and the other Comedy, because it wears low shoes.
>
> (Pliny the Younger, Letter 9.7, in Radice, 1969, p. 237)

Here Pliny is making an elegant joke about the look and locality of his villas, but he is also perhaps reminding the reader that these are places he associates with enjoyment of the arts and intellectual reinvigoration.

Activity   Turn to Pliny's Letter 9.36 (Reading 3.2). Does Pliny's villa lifestyle contrast with Horace's picture of time off from the duties he associated with Rome?

Discussion   Pliny's day in the country has a clear timetable and also might involve keeping open house for quasi-dependants. These large-scale villa complexes were not purely a place of escape from the responsibilities of public life. Pliny, like Horace before him, enjoys the civilised company of educated friends at his villas but civic duties, not just estate-related responsibilities, intrude into his rural retreat. Pliny complains in later books of letters that he increasingly takes work to his countryside villas in the form of court case preparations.

Pliny's attitude to using his diminishing free time in an intellectually productive manner demonstrates that he is following in the footsteps of his famous uncle Pliny the Elder, a highly studious man who was an enormously productive author, writing the epic-length *Natural History*. The younger Pliny had been at one time rebuked by his uncle for walking when he could be carried in a sedan chair and read to on subjects of scholarly interest. Any

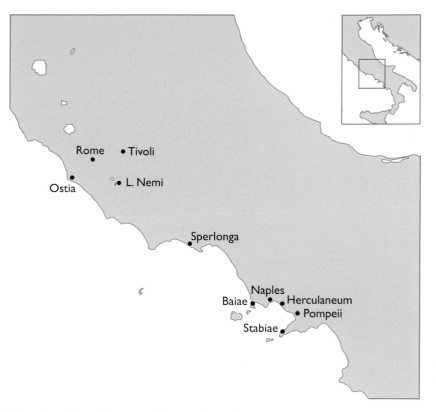

Figure 3.2 Map of Rome and the Bay of Naples.

hard-pressed student snatching a moment to study on the move might read this advice with a wry smile. And, of course, Pliny seems to be emulating his uncle when he paints the rather comical picture of himself taking his books on a boar hunt (the letter you heard on the Audio CD, track 6).

Activity Turn to Pliny's Letter 2.17 (Reading 3.3). Does the layout of the villa at Laurentum reinforce the picture you already have of the man and his life as a gentleman in the country?

Discussion As he celebrates his villa's attractions during this literary tour, in which he pauses to reflect on how he has achieved the perfect design for reading, writing and studious leisure, Pliny is proud of his choice of site, its suitability as a winter villa and the fact it is in easy travelling distance from Rome. It benefits from being in the country and near the sea, away from urban sounds and smells. The exercise area, the bath suite, the ball court and the beautifully laid-out gardens and orchards all contribute to the nurturing of his mental and spiritual health.

Pliny has designed his rooms so that he can view the world outside on his terms and with his choice of changing perspectives. He enjoys different aspects of the sea, and of the woods and mountains, all from windows in the same anteroom. The windows facing east and west in the small annexe to the left of the dining area have been carefully placed to give the occupant a daily display of the rising and setting sun.

Pliny illustrates how the Roman elite had found a way of communing with nature while having plenty of protection against its rougher features. A similar claim, taming the landscape to maximise aesthetic pleasure, was made by Statius for his patrons' villas (as you heard on the Audio CD, track 8).

Pliny's extension comprises a carefully thought-out self-contained suite of rooms where he can study and write. There he is undisturbed by the voices of his slaves and he can shut out the sound of the sea and the wind. He remarks that he is very glad of this during the festival of Saturnalia in December. Slaves and masters sometimes reversed roles in true carnival tradition during this midwinter celebration, so a certain amount of controlled anarchy could take place. Pliny's arrangement means that he can escape here to carry on with his cerebral pursuits, while his household can create a carnival atmosphere with its more raucous entertainments.

All the same, Pliny has to make allowances for duty to intrude upon leisure time. The Laurentine villa also has an atrium – a reception hall where he can receive casual visitors and deal with complaints and requests from his tenant farmers.

Literary pictures: summing up

Horace utters a poignant prayer of gratitude for the gift of land and property after the loss of his family estate. Pliny unashamedly embraces his privileges and his well-furnished villas as proper payment for his commitment to civic duty. Both men negotiated a good life in spite of the constraints of public duties and the potential pitfalls of working for autocratic rulers. When they write about leisure they also provide evidence of a stratified society with distinct political and social tensions. Statius lets us in to an intimate aristocratic circle, surviving the repressive regime of a jealous emperor, but quietly affirming its status through its leisured lifestyle. Pliny's letter about his Laurentine villa, like Horace's poems about his Sabine farm, gives an illuminating if partial portrait of the man and the impression of studiousness and gentility he wished to leave to posterity. All three writers bear out Toner's observations about the importance of leisure for the Roman self-image and how it identified one's place in the social hierarchy.

3.3   SOME PICTURES FROM ART AND ARCHAEOLOGY
Janet Huskinson

The literary passages you have just read have their own different emphases, but taken together construct a picture of the villa as a retreat from the city, a place where rich and educated Romans could enjoy intellectual pursuits and the beauties of nature.

But how does this idealised lifestyle show up in Roman villa buildings? What evidence do they provide about what leisure meant for their residents? To find some answers to these questions we shall now explore aspects of their art and architecture, looking mainly at villas in Italy. There are many archaeological remains of Roman villas to be studied, both in Italy and across the Roman empire. These show that some were more like working farms (where life might have had some of the simplicity advocated by Horace) but others reveal a much more sophisticated lifestyle dedicated to leisure, and we shall now concentrate on the latter.

A secondary theme in this section concerns some visits that you can make to villas, raising thoughts about the ways that study and leisure can still interact today, as they did in the lives of Pliny and his contemporaries. There is the chance to make two such 'visits' via the DVD ROM.

But first there are some important reminders about the sheer patchiness of the available archaeological evidence.

So much has failed to survive that we can only get a partial picture from archaeology. There may be many villa sites to be explored, but often little remains at them. Some (for example along the coast of the Bay of Naples) have been lost beneath later buildings, and we only know that they ever existed because of written accounts. Sometimes in such cases, evidence from literature and art can help to fill gaps in the archaeological record, as we shall see when it comes to considering villa buildings.

It is also the case that archaeology, like other sources, may reveal more about some subjects than others. In the context of leisure, it tends to privilege the wealthy, whose lifestyle left more enduring traces. Although objects used in menial work (from pots to wine presses) also survive in large numbers, other aspects of the lives of the countless slaves who worked in villas are scarcely visible in archaeology. In short, more archaeological evidence survives for the few for whom the villa was a place of leisure than for the many who laboured there; like literature, it tells far more about what leisure meant for the rich and educated.

Evidence from villa art

To answer questions about what leisure meant to wealthy villa owners, one useful (and attractive) source of evidence is the art chosen to decorate their rooms and gardens – wall-paintings, mosaic pavements, sculptures. Even though relatively little survives, it can give fascinating insights into how villa owners thought about leisure and what they wanted from it. Given the traditional values attached to leisure by the educated classes (think back to the ideals of Aristotle and Epicurus you met in Chapter 1) it is not surprising to find a frequent emphasis on serious cultural pursuits and on the appreciation of natural pleasures such as gardens and sea vistas. Showing all this off also seems to have been important, to judge from much of the art. This is also unsurprising, since villas were part of the social competition that their elite residents brought with them from the city, and interior decoration played a prominent part in this.

In this section we shall look first at some examples of such decoration from some Italian seaside villas. We conclude with a visit on DVD ROM to a Roman villa on the Isle of Wight, off the south coast of England, which sums up some of the opportunities and problems posed in using art as a source of evidence for leisure.

Pompeii and **Herculaneum**, towns in the southern area of the Bay of Naples, were destroyed by the eruption of Vesuvius in 79 CE.

The natural beauty of the Bay of Naples (see Figure 3.2) led many wealthy Romans to build lavish leisure homes there. Although few survive, we can get some idea of their art from houses in nearby towns (such as Pompeii and Herculaneum) that were preserved under volcanic lava after the eruption of Vesuvius in 79 CE. Rooms were richly decorated with sculptures, mosaics and wall-paintings (as in Figure 3.3), and their subject matter is a good source of evidence about what leisure meant to the owners. As we shall now see, two themes were prominent: enjoyment of nature and of the heritage of classical learning and mythology. These resonate with the ideals you have already met in the literary passages.

Figure 3.3   Wall-painting in the *tablinum* (reception room) of the house of M. Lucretius Fronto, Pompeii. © Sites & Photos, www.sitesandphotos.com.

Nature and landscape

Since Roman villas were often built in places of great natural beauty, it is not surprising to see an appreciation of nature reflected in the art that decorated them. Paintings could bring the refreshment of the garden indoors (useful when it was too hot to relax in the real garden outside). Figure 3.3 has an example in the frieze that runs along the base of the wall (although you can only see the top of it here), while a painting from Herculaneum shows a garden that is also enjoyed by large birds (Plate 4.3.9 in the Illustration Book).

But its trellises, pergolas and fountains make another important point about the natural world in relation to the ideals of the villa – the idea that its beauties could be enhanced even further by manmade features. Garden ornaments, the design of the grounds and even the situation of the villa itself are all aspects of this intervention, which has wider significance in relation to man's control over the natural world (remembering, of course, the villa owners were usually men who exercised great influence in Roman society).

Nature and buildings can be seen in another popular subject: landscape paintings of villas themselves, which often appeared as vignettes (as in Figure 3.3). As you can see from three paintings from Stabiae, a seaside town to the south of Naples (Plates 4.3.5–7), the style is often quite impressionistic, blurring distances and making natural features (such as water and trees) and architecture blend together. (We shall return to these paintings later, as evidence for villa architecture.) In this way these paintings evoke something of the seaside atmosphere, just as Pliny did by talking of the sights and smells of the sea. All is shown as calm and peaceful, and with a certain mystical quality that is also found in another type of Roman landscape painting, usually known as **sacro-idyllic** since it depicts shrines or landscapes in a pastoral setting (as in Plate 4.3.8). Yet despite this idealisation and hints of spirituality, there seems to me something rather self-regarding about these scenes, given their particular setting; they suggest rather an exclusive social group that enjoyed displaying paintings of 'desirable residences' in their houses.

Odysseus was the legendary king of Ithaca in Greece who fought with the Greeks at Troy. His adventurous journey home forms the subject of Homer's *Odyssey*.

A spectacular example of art used to enhance natural surroundings has been found at Sperlonga on the west coast of Italy, south of Rome and north of Naples, near a seaside villa associated with Emperor Tiberius (14–37 CE). Here a natural grotto in the cliffs (see Figure 3.4) was extended to form a dining room, with an island dining area, and was decorated with several large sculptures depicting episodes from Homer's *Odyssey*. The statues were found as fragments but have been reconstructed.

Figure 3.5 is a dramatic (but not unique) illustration of just how far wealthy villa owners would go in converting the natural environment to serve their leisure needs. It was not enough just to enjoy the natural

Figure 3.4   View of grotto, Sperlonga. Photo used with the permission of the Soprintendenza Archeologica di Lazio.

view. Instead they wanted to control and 'improve' it through manmade art which, particularly in this case, exemplified the other aspect of leisure for Roman elites: their heritage of classical culture and mythology. Guests at Sperlonga would have known that ancient traditions and literature set some of Odysseus' adventures on this coast, and, surrounded by these statues, they might have felt as if they were dining in the company of true local heroes.

Images from classical mythology and 'high culture'

Sperlonga involves a particularly ambitious use of mythology, but subjects from myth –many also known from famous works of classical literature – were also popular in the art that adorned villas. Often these figures must have been chosen simply to illustrate familiar tales. For instance, the panel in the centre of the wall shown in Figure 3.3 depicts two famous lovers: Bacchus (the god of wine) and Ariadne (a heroine with whom he fell in love). But mythological subjects could also offer particular intellectual, moral or spiritual themes and they were often depicted in thematic groups for viewers to ponder. All this made them subjects well suited to the contemplative aspect of leisure. You can see examples of this in the House of Menander in Pompeii, whose final phase of interior decoration included many favourite combinations of

Figure 3.5 Pellico, reconstruction of the sculptural display, Sperlonga. Reproduced with the permission of the Soprintendenza Archeologica di Lazio.

Troy in north-west Asia Minor, near the Aegean coast and the Hellespont, was the legendary site of the war between Greeks and Trojans described in Homer's *Iliad*. The sack of Troy is described in Book 2 of Virgil's *Aeneid*.

Menander (c.344–292 BCE) was an Athenian playwright.

Euripides wrote tragedies in Athens during the fifth century BCE.

The Muses were nine goddesses, each associated with a different art, who inspired writers, artists and intellectuals in creating their work.

subjects, such as the goddesses Diana (associated with hunting) and Venus (goddess of love) who were depicted like cult-statues in niches (Plate 4.3.1), and Bacchic subjects (with connotations of pleasure and abandonment to Bacchus, who represented the liberating effects of intoxication). It also included literary themes, with scenes of the sack of Troy (Plates 4.3.2 and 4.3.3) and portraits of two famous Greek playwrights, Menander and Euripides (Plate 4.3.4).

Sculpture shows a similar predominance of subjects from myth or high culture, chosen particularly to decorate rooms dedicated to the more intellectual aspects of leisure, such as reading or study. Portraits of great intellectuals of the past, images of the Muses, and copies of famous artistic masterpieces were especially popular. Examples of all of these were found in the great collection of statues at the Villa of the Papyri at Herculaneum, including a bronze bust of the philosopher Epicurus (see Figure 3.6). This was particularly appropriate because the villa housed a specialist library of texts relating to Epicurean philosophy (and it may also have had a general relevance to villa ideals, if you think back to the Epicurean views on leisure discussed in Chapter 1).

Summing up these themes: Brading Roman Villa

So far this discussion of themes – of nature and high culture – in art has focused on villas around Naples, which belong to the first centuries BCE and CE. But to conclude we shall look at the floor mosaics that were used about three to four hundred years later to decorate a **Romano-British** villa. The reason for making this move is to enable us to consider in greater depth and on site some of the questions that surround the use of surviving artwork as evidence for attitudes to leisure in a villa. After all, this material can only work effectively as such if it is carefully analysed and evaluated.

Activity
*You should allow about an hour
for this activity.*

Now turn to the DVD ROM 'Roman Villa' and work through 'Brading Villa'.

Here three people, whose work involves mosaic in different ways, address some of the issues raised above. The villa at Brading, on the Isle of Wight, combined a working life, in a beautiful setting near the sea, with a demonstrable interest in the traditional values of Roman elite leisure.

Evidence about villa buildings

Visiting a place like Brading, with its many well-preserved mosaics, can give a real immediacy to the values that Romans attached to life at the villa. We can also get a good idea of the layout of the building and some sense of the activities (relating to both work and leisure) which it supported. Future archaeological investigations may be able to tell us more.

Unfortunately many other villa sites are far less informative, usually because they have been largely destroyed or have not been fully excavated. Systematic excavation is one of the most effective means of revealing evidence for villa buildings, but even so there can be problems arising from misguided investigations in the past or limits as to what can be dug or known. It can be hard to give accurate accounts of a villa's layout or changing usage over time. So to get a fuller picture of villa buildings as places for leisure we can try to supplement the archaeological information with evidence from other sources, principally art and literature. Sometimes this process can prove useful, but sometimes it can be problematic, as can be seen from the following brief review of some examples from Roman Italy which you have already met.

Relating evidence from paintings and archaeology

The first of these examples involves the paintings of seaside villas in which, as we noted earlier, nature and buildings appear to blend. Here our question concerns the realism of the architecture: how far does this fit with the archaeological evidence for some contemporary buildings?

Look again at the three paintings of seaside villas from Stabiae (Plates 4.3.5–7), but this time consider what are the main characteristics of the villas shown here. Perhaps the most conspicuous

Figure 3.6   Bust of Epicurus from the Villa of the Papyri, Herculaneum, bronze. Museo Archeologico Nazionale, Naples 5465. Photo used with the permission of the Ministero per I Beni e le Attività Culturali.

feature of these houses is their size: they are extensive buildings, set in a wider landscape by the sea. They have enclosed gardens or face on to private jetties (sometimes you can see figures fishing or in boats) and have large **porticoes** where people can take their leisure in the fresh air, but sheltered from the sun.

These particular characteristics – size, setting and porticoes – are the kinds of tangible feature that can be checked out against the archaeological evidence.

Activity   Now compare these features with the building shown in the drawing in Figure 3.7. This was made for an archaeological report on the Villa San Marco at Stabiae (from where Plates 4.3.6 and 4.3.7 come). What similar features can you see?

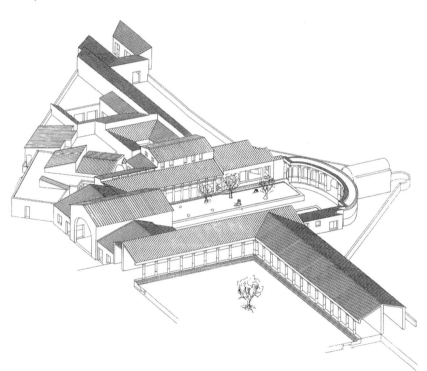

Figure 3.7   Jean-Pierre Adam, 'Axonometric drawing of the Villa San Marco, Stabiae, in its final phase', from *La Villa San Marco a Stabia*, ed. A. Barbet and P. Miniero, Napoli-Rome-Pompeii, 1999.

Discussion   The archaeological drawing in Figure 3.7 reconstructs the Villa San Marco as it would have been at the eruption of Vesuvius in 79 CE. It is **axonometric**, which means that vertical lines are rendered vertically and lines on the ground plane (e.g. wall lines) are drawn at either 45 or 135 degrees to the horizontal. It is as if you are looking directly at a corner. The value of this kind of perspectival drawing in reconstructions is that it indicates different parts of the building in relation to each other and suggests its volume. 'Suggests' is an important word to note in this case: this is all that the plan can do, since the archaeological data is incomplete. The drawing differs from the paintings in Plates 4.3.5–7 in that it represents a particular villa, and is to scale; yet like them it is not completely accurate or objective as it – inevitably – incorporates some of the archaeologists' uncertainties or imagination.

Even so, as I think you will agree, Figure 3.7 instantly confirms that the paintings do show some of the main architectural features of real-life seaside villas in the area. The Villa San Marco is large and rambling, has several porticoes, and is on the seafront (the large reception room opened on to a seaside terrace not represented here). In this case the evidence of paintings and archaeology confirm each other.

Relating evidence from literature and archaeology

But when we turn now to look at a particular example from literature, the situation is more complex. Pliny's description of his seaside villa at Laurentum (see Reading 3.3) has had a great influence on the study of Roman villas, and also on how villas were designed in other periods and places. But the process of relating it to archaeological remains raises some important questions about combining different sources of evidence in the quest to picture antiquity.

The first question concerns how far literary accounts are reliable as a basis for reconstructing ground plans and elevations of houses. In general this depends on the purpose of the written text and the accuracy and detail of its observations. But if the question is asked specifically about Pliny's villa, then the answer has to be that his description has only a limited use, for, as you have already seen, despite all its vivid detail it did not set out to give an accurate account of the villa's layout. Drawing up a definitive plan on the basis of Pliny's description is therefore out of the question.

Even so, many architects and historians – from at least the seventeenth century – have been inspired by Pliny's first-hand description to attempt reconstructions of his villa, or even to use it as an ideal template for houses of their own (as in the eighteenth-century Chiswick House explored on the DVD ROM). As a result, Pliny's villa has been re-created in many different versions; and these in turn can be used to help us to picture it. Furthermore, these variations are a reminder of just how many different interpretations there can be of the same piece of ancient evidence.

Activity
You should allow about half an hour for this activity.

Now turn to 'Pliny's villa at Laurentum' on the DVD ROM. This activity on Pliny's villa is based around some different attempts at reconstructing this building from the detailed description Pliny the Younger gave in his letter. They date from different periods, and were done in different media and from different orientations (north, south, east and west).

In this part of the DVD ROM you will need to focus on identifying:

- particular parts of the building, as described by Pliny, which are apparent in the various reconstructions

- any elements in Pliny's description that can't be reconstructed in terms of buildings (e.g. sights and smells). Think about how we might go about recapturing these effects.

Discussion   On the basis of this evidence, I would say that Pliny's description can still give a flavour of his villa and his enjoyment of it , even though it does not provide a precise account of its structures.

A second important question in relating literary accounts to surviving archaeological remains concerns the identification of specific sites. Is it possible to find Pliny's actual villa among the remains at Laurentum, on the coast south of Rome? Although some sceptical scholars have suggested his description might have been a complete fiction, others have argued that Pliny was so specific in his account that he probably was describing a real house; and since that part of the coast is dotted with the remains of Roman luxury homes, there might be a good chance of finding a site that would match his description. Even so, there has been no conclusive identification so far, since none of the different sites suggested has completely fitted the written account. What's more, this archaeological search has been beset with many of the usual problems mentioned earlier, with sites made hard to investigate because of later over-building or destruction.

Yet it is also the case that the kinds of question that are being asked of villa sites (and of many other material remains) have changed – a reminder of the constantly shifting relationship between the past and present and between different types of evidence. Past classical scholarship tended to be dominated by a study of the ancient texts, so the approach to archaeological sites was often led by a desire to identify them as the house of some 'big name' from literature, like Pliny or Horace. But nowadays text-based studies are not automatically considered pre-eminent. Archaeological material is valued as a source in its own right, used to investigate broader social, cultural and economic issues rather than the identity of a particular villa owner. Villas and their place in Roman elite leisure comprise just one such issue.

Epilogue: 'Roman' villas in later centuries

On the course website there is a gazetteer of eighteenth-century houses in Britain you can visit.

The ideals of leisure that shaped villa life for rich and educated Romans were also espoused by the leaders of later societies, and especially in eighteenth-century Britain. They made references in the design and decoration of their houses to the art and architecture of Roman villas, as they knew about this from archaeology and classical literature, and especially from the letters of Pliny. Their main purpose in doing this was usually to promote their own authority in terms that were familiar in a society heavily imbued with classical culture; but many of them were also motivated by genuine antiquarian interests.

A leading example was Lord Burlington (1694–1753), who was a great patron of the arts and a classical scholar. Between 1726 and 1729 he built an addition to his house at Chiswick, now known as Chiswick House. It was intended to be a place for cultural leisure-time pursuits, as many Roman villas had been, and its buildings and grounds had many features based on Roman models, including conscious references to Pliny and his villa.

Exploring places like these is yet another way of experiencing the Roman ideal of the villa, as well as appreciating that it has bequeathed a heritage that is still significant today.

Activity   On the DVD ROM you can visit Chiswick House and look at some of its features that are based on Roman models. This is an optional exercise in terms of your study time.

CONCLUSION
Janet Huskinson

In this discussion of the Roman villa you have seen again how perceptions of leisure relate to time and place, and how time spent in leisure can be reconstructed from evidence from various sources.

You have had a chance to see how various ancient attitudes to leisure which you met in Chapter 1 were reflected in the villa lifestyle. These were the concept of leisure as something crucial to living well, and as allowing pursuits that were valuable in themselves – such as reflective study, the enjoyment of pleasure and the provision of a safe haven 'in a dangerous and uncomfortable world'. All these attitudes are – on the face of it – thoroughly supported by the evidence we have considered here. Images of villa life created by the writers you have read and the decorative art you have looked at, along with much that we can tell from surviving buildings, seem to reinforce these ideals, and do so with such consistency that they continued to be used to promote similar values in much later times and places. So although these sources differ in type, date and emphasis, they seem to point to the same fundamental conclusions: everything looks neatly tied together.

However, looking at it all again from another angle reveals some important loose ends. After all, this discussion of the villa could only ever present a very partial view of Roman leisure. The representations of villa life presented in our examples from art and literature were not objective, factual records of the situation; rather, they were concerned to create images which would reflect a somewhat exclusive social world back to its participants to enjoy. The Romans we have discussed here were the rich and educated who had the necessary resources to make choices about their leisure pursuits (whether intellectual or self-indulgent), and – even more important – were able to take leisure time in the first place. Pliny is a classic illustration of this as he writes – self-consciously, of course – about what he does at his villa: it is easy to see how his chosen pursuits made for a very civilised lifestyle.

So what about the vast majority of other people who were not so privileged? Examples of mass entertainment have been discussed in the Audio CD, while 'leisure' occasions like the Roman games notoriously raise all kinds of ethical considerations that the *otium* of wealthy individuals does not. Yet what about all the domestic slaves and other workers whose toil created the leisure opportunities for the few? If we were able to paint the picture of Roman leisure from their point of view, its humanising qualities and positive choices would surely be obscured by the very different situation facing most of them.

But, of course, we cannot do that, because of another important factor that prevents a tidy conclusion. This is the partiality of the ancient evidence about villa life. It is not simply a matter of what has survived, but rather its inherent bias: the art and literature both shaped and were shaped by the leisure of the elite. The great workforce that supported the leisure of these images does not appear in them, unless in passing anecdotes (about favourite slaves) or romanticised images of fisherfolk and shepherds. Even the archaeology of Roman villas reveals surprisingly little about the people who made them function.

These factors will always remain loose ends and mean that the villa lifestyle can only ever be a partial illustration of Roman leisure, although that would also be largely true if we had instead discussed gladiatorial games, or bathing, for example. Yet as a topic for this course it remains particularly powerful, I would argue, simply because it does show the ideals valued by those who were actually able to take leisure time and to make choices. It shows, too, how these ideals relate to views of leisure expounded earlier by influential Greek thinkers, and how they could be worked out in terms of buildings and the natural environment. Roman reverence for nature links with some of the material you met in Chapter 2, while love of the seaside is a perennial aspect of leisure that you will turn to now.

REFERENCES

Ackermann, J. (1990) *The Villa: Form and Ideology of Country Houses*, London, Thames & Hudson.

Radice, B. (trans. and ed.) (1969) *The Letters of the Younger Pliny* (revised edn), Harmondsworth, Penguin.

Toner, J.P. (1995) *Leisure and Ancient Rome*, Cambridge, Polity Press.

FURTHER READING

D'Arms, J.H. (1970) *Romans on the Bay of Naples: A Social and Cultural Study of the Villas and their Owners from 150BC to AD400*, Cambridge, MA, Harvard University Press.

Du Prey, P. de la Ruffinière (1994) *The Villas of Pliny from Antiquity to Posterity*, Chicago, University of Chicago Press.

Kiernan, V.G. (1999) *Horace: Poetics and Politics*, London, Macmillan.

Levi, P. (1997) *Horace: A Life*, London, Duckworth.

McKay, A.G. (1998) *Houses, Villas, and Palaces in the Roman World*, Baltimore, MD, Johns Hopkins University Press.

Myers, K.S. (2000) 'Miranda fides: poets and patrons in paradoxical landscapes in Statius' *Silvae*', *Materiali e discussione per l'analisi dei texti classici*, vol. 44, pp. 100–38.

Myers, K.S. (2005) '*Docta Otia*: garden ownership and configurations of leisure in Pliny and Statius', *Arethusa*, vol. 38, pp. 103–29.

RESOURCES

Reading 3.1

Horace's Sabine farm: retreating from town

I've prayed for this: a modest piece of land,
a garden, near the house a spring, above
it all a patch of woodland. The gods have done
me well: life's good. I've nothing more to ask,
o Mercury, except to keep these blessings
all my life. If you're persuaded I've not
grown rich through shady deals, or want to waste
my wealth through either prodigality
or neglect, if I'm not so stupid as to pray
'Good lord, couldn't you just procure me that
finger of land which spoils my farm's proportions?
Or win me the jackpot, like that lucky man
enriched by Hercules who found a treasure
chest and bought the land he'd worked on?' If
I'm happy with my lot, then this will be
my prayer: fatten my flocks and funds, if not
my head; remain, as you have been, my master.

Now that I've left the city for my hilltop
retreat, what better subject for the satires
of my pedestrian muse? Up here, I'm far
removed from the throng around the greasy pole,
from palsied autumn and the ashen Auster
bringers of gain to bitter Libitina.

Father of dawn, or Janus, if you wish,
who oversees the start of the working day
as the gods dictate, I'll start my song with you.
In Rome, you waken me to advocate:
'Get your arse in gear or someone else
will take your place.' It doesn't matter if
the North wind's blowing, or that winter drags
the snowy day into a tighter loop,
I have to go. Then, having said my piece
in ringing tones – against my own best interests –
I have to navigate the crowd and bruise
the slowcoaches. 'What's the hurry, friend,
where's the fire?' Some oik gives me earache: 'You think
because you run Maecenas' errands you can
just barge through?'

                              That's as sweet as honey, I
admit. But once the dreary Esquiline's
in view, then other people's worries dance

This refers either to a story that **Hercules** persuaded Mercury to show a man a treasure, or to a belief that Hercules appeared in dreams to reveal hidden wealth.

Auster was the south wind.

Libitina was a Roman goddess associated with funerals (the suggestion here is that winter brings death).

Janus was the Roman god of doorways, but also of all thresholds, boundaries and beginnings – physical, temporal and metaphorical.

The Esquiline hill was the site of a cemetery.

around my head. 'Couldn't you meet with Roscius
tomorrow, by the Wall, before seven?'
'Horace, the guys in the office need to see
you later on today: there's something big
in the offing.' 'Get Maecenas' signature
on these papers.' If I say I'll try,
then he insists, 'Try harder and you will.'

The years fly past. It's seven or eight since
Maecenas started to treat me as a friend –
at least, to take me with him on long journeys
and let me trade in little nuggets: 'What's
the time?' 'D'you think the Thracian Cock could take
Syrus?' 'The frosts are biting – people should
take care,' – the kind of chat you might entrust
to any leaky ear. For all these years,
for every hour of every day, yours truly
has been the butt of envy. Someone sees
me sit beside him at the games, another
swears he's seen us playing ball, now all
cry out 'That lucky sod!' Imagine there's
an icy buzz abroad – all want to know
the inside track. 'Excuse me asking, but
you must be in the loop: what's going on
with the Dacians?' 'Not a clue.' 'Taking the mick
again?' 'I swear, I honestly don't know.'
'Really? But won't you tell if Caesar's chosen
Sicily or the mainland for the veterans?'
When I repeat that I don't know, they say
that I'm the champ of Roman reticence.

I squander time like this. And yet I dream
of getting back to this sweet place where I'll
be free to read the classics, or to drift
and drink away life's worries; of when I'll
be treated next to a humble stew of beans
(the brothers of Pythagoras) seasoned
with kale and bacon. O those sacred nights
and suppers, when we dine beside my hearth,
give thanks, then let the breezy slaves eat up.
We have no truck with crazy rules: each guest
can drink whatever he wants – large or small,
the harder stuff to test the strength, or else
the mild relaxing wines. And then we start
to talk. But not about the price of other
peoples' houses, nor about the style
of Lepos' dancing – our concerns are closer
to home and more essential: whether money

The **Thracian Cock** and **Syrus** were
gladiators.

The **Dacians** were a Balkan people
who regularly raided Macedonia
and sided with Mark Antony against
Octavian.

A reference to where Octavian
(**Caesar**) might settle his troops
after the battle of Actium.

The philosopher and
mathematician **Pythagoras** (6th
century BCE) forbade the eating of
beans as well as animal flesh – here
Horace is making fun of the notion
that beans might contain
reincarnated human souls.

Lepos (meaning charm or grace)
may have been a mime actor.

or morality makes men happy; if
self-interest or affection quickens friendship;
what goodness really is and where it's found.

Sometimes our neighbour Cervius will tell
a pithy fable of the kind beloved
by old women. Suppose that one of us
waxes lyrical about the riches
of Arellius while taking no account
of the anxieties, then he begins:
A country mouse once entertained a town
mouse in his meagre hole, the pair of them
old friends. He had no airs and graces, lived
within his slender means, yet he would stretch
himself for company. He had no qualms
about his hoard of grass and grains; he brought
him in his mouth old raisins, nibbled bits
of bacon, trying all he could to vary
the carte to cater for his faddy guest
who turned his nose up at every morsel.
Throughout all this, the master of the house,
stretched out on fresh straw, must content himself
with spelt and darnel, saving the best dishes
for his friend. At length, the towny says, 'My dear,
I wonder how you stand this wretched life
marooned beneath a cliff edge? Surely you'd
agree the city and society
outpoint the wild woods? Come along with me
and see the difference. Everything that lives
is born to die: the great and small alike
have mortal souls, so make the best of every
fleeting moment you have.' This speech bewitched
the bumpkin into jumping from his hole.
The pair sped off towards the city, keen
to creep within the walls before daybreak.

And now the night was half way through her journey
when they made it to a palace filled
with throws of costly scarlet over benches
of ivory. Close at hand there was a feast
of leftovers, still warm in baskets from
a banquet held that evening. Now the town
mouse makes his guest luxuriate across
the purple fabric, then he plies him with
course after course, bustling like a waiter
doing the office of a house slave, trying
each dainty first. The other one, delighted
by his change of state, lolls at ease and plays

Arellius may have been a local wealthy landowner.

Spelt and darnel are types of inferior grain.

the role of happy guest, till suddenly
a dismal clang of doors disturbs the pair,
propels them from their couches. Terrified,
the mice scurry along the hall – the howl
of huge Molossian hounds makes them panic.
'I've had enough of this,' the country mouse
then says, 'I'm going home. My woodland hole
will be my fortress, grass and grain my banquet.'

> **Molossian hounds** (from Molossia in Epirus) were large and fierce, and commonly used as watchdogs.

Horace, *Satires*, Book 2, poem 6, translated by Richard Danson Brown.

Reading 3.2

Pliny the Younger in Tuscany

You want to know how I plan the summer days I spend in Tuscany. I wake when I like, usually about sunrise, often earlier but rarely later. My shutters stay closed, for in the stillness and darkness I feel myself surprisingly detached from any distractions and left to myself in freedom; my eyes do not determine the direction of my thinking, but, being unable to see anything, they are guided to visualize my thoughts. If I have anything on hand I work it out in my head, choosing and correcting the wording, and the amount I achieve depends on the ease or difficulty with which my thoughts can be marshalled and kept in my head. Then I call my secretary, the shutters are opened, and I dictate what I have put into shape; he goes out, is recalled, and again dismissed. Three or four hours after I first wake (but I don't keep to fixed times) I betake myself according to the weather either to the terrace or the covered arcade, work out the rest of my subject, and dictate it. I go for a drive, and spend the time in the same way as when walking or lying down; my powers of concentration do not flag and are in fact refreshed by the change. After a short sleep and another walk I read a Greek or Latin speech aloud and with emphasis, not so much for the sake of my voice as my digestion, though of course both are strengthened by this. Then I have another walk, am oiled, take exercise, and have a bath. If I am dining alone with my wife or with a few friends, a book is read aloud during the meal and afterwards we listen to a comedy or some music; then I walk again with the members of my household, some of whom are well educated. Thus the evening is prolonged with varied conversation, and, even when the days are at their longest, comes to a satisfying end.

Sometimes I vary this routine, for, if I have spent a long time on my couch or taking a walk, after my siesta and reading I go out on horseback instead of in a carriage so as to be quicker and take less time. Part of the day is given up to friends who visit me from neighbouring towns and sometimes come to my aid with a welcome interruption when I am tired. Occasionally I go hunting, but not without my notebooks so that I shall have something to bring home even if I catch nothing. I also give some time to my tenants (they think it should be more) and the boorishness of their complaints gives fresh zest to our literary interests and the more civilized pursuits of town.

Source: Pliny the Younger, Book 9, letter 36: to Fuscus Salinator, in Radice (1969), pp. 256–7.

Reading 3.3   **Pliny the Younger's description of his villa**

You may wonder why my Laurentine place (or my Laurentian, if you like that better) is such a joy to me, but once you realize the attractions of the house itself, the amenities of its situation, and its extensive seafront, you will have your answer. It is seventeen miles from Rome, so that it is possible to spend the night there after necessary business is done, without having cut short or hurried the day's work, and it can be approached by more than one route; the roads to Laurentum and Ostia both lead in that direction, but you must leave the one at the fourteenth milestone and the other at the eleventh. Whichever way you go, the side road you take is sandy for some distance and rather heavy and slow-going if you drive, but soft and easily covered on horseback. The view on either side is full of variety, for sometimes the road narrows as it passes through the woods, and then it broadens and opens out through wide meadows where there are many flocks of sheep and herds of horses and cattle driven down from the mountains in winter to grow sleek on the pastures in the springlike climate.

The house is large enough for my needs but not expensive to keep up. It opens into a hall, unpretentious but not without dignity, and then there are two colonnades, rounded like the letter D, which enclose a small but pleasant courtyard. This makes a splendid retreat in bad weather, being protected by windows and still more by the overhanging roof. Opposite the middle of it is a cheerful inner hall, and then a dining-room which really is rather fine: it runs out towards the shore, and whenever the sea is driven inland by the south-west wind it is lightly washed by the spray of the spent breakers. It has folding doors or windows as large as the doors all round, so that at the front and sides it seems to look out on to three seas, and at the back has a view through the inner hall, the courtyard with the two colonnades, and the entrance-hall to the woods and mountains in the distance.

To the left of this and a little farther back from the sea is a large bedroom, and then another smaller one which lets in the morning sunshine with one window and holds the last rays of the evening sun with the other; from this window too is a view of the sea beneath, this time at a safe distance. In the angle of this room and the dining-room is a corner which retains and intensifies the concentrated warmth of the sun, and this is the winter-quarters and gymnasium of my household for no winds can be heard there except those which bring the rain clouds and the place can still be used after the weather has broken. Round the corner is a room built round in an apse to let in the sun as it moves round and shines in each window in turn, and with one wall fitted with shelves like a library to hold the books which I read and read again. Next comes a bedroom on the other side of a passage which has a floor raised and fitted with pipes to receive hot steam and circulate it at a regulated temperature. The remaining rooms on this side of the house are kept for the use of my slaves and freedmen, but most of them are quite presentable enough to receive guests.

On the other side of the dining-room is an elegantly decorated bedroom, and then one which can either be a bedroom or a moderate-sized dining-room and enjoys the bright light of the sun reflected from the sea; behind is another room with an antechamber, high enough to be cool in summer and a refuge in winter, for it is sheltered from every wind. A similar room and antechamber are divided off by a single wall. Then comes the cooling-room of the bath, which is large and spacious and has two curved baths built out of opposite walls; these are quite large enough if you consider that the sea is so near. Next come the oiling-room, the furnace-room, and the antechamber to the bath, and then two rest-rooms, beautifully decorated in a simple style, leading to the heated swimming-bath which is much admired and from which swimmers can see the sea. Close by is the ball-court which receives the full warmth of the setting sun. Here there is a second storey, with two living-rooms below and two above, as well as a dining-room which commands the whole expanse of sea and stretch of shore with all its lovely houses. Elsewhere another upper storey contains a room which receives both the rising and setting sun, and a good-sized wine-store and granary behind, while below is a dining-room where nothing is known of a high sea but the sound of the breakers, and even that as a dying murmur; it looks on to the garden and the encircling drive.

All round the drive runs a hedge of box, or rosemary to fill any gaps, for box will flourish extensively where it is sheltered by the buildings, but dries up if exposed in the open to the wind and salt spray even at a distance. Inside the inner ring of the drive is a young and shady vine pergola, where the soil is soft and yielding even to the bare foot. The garden itself is thickly planted with mulberries and figs, trees which the soil bears very well though it is less kind to others. On this side the dining-room away from the sea has a view as lovely as that of the sea itself, while from the windows of the two rooms behind can be seen the entrance to the house and another well-stocked kitchen garden.

Here begins a covered arcade nearly as large as a public building. It has windows on both sides, but more facing the sea, as there is one in each alternate bay on the garden side. These all stand open on a fine and windless day, and in stormy weather can safely be opened on the side away from the wind. In front is a terrace scented with violets. As the sun beats down, the arcade increases its heat by reflection and not only retains the sun but keeps off the north-east wind so that it is as hot in front as it is cool behind. In the same way it checks the south-west wind, thus breaking the force of winds from wholly opposite quarters by one or the other of its sides; it is pleasant in winter but still more so in summer when the terrace is kept cool in the morning and the drive and nearer part of the garden in the afternoon, as its shadow falls shorter or longer on one side or the other while the day advances or declines. Inside the arcade, of course, there is least sunshine when the sun is blazing down on its roof, and as its open windows allow the western breezes to enter and circulate, the atmosphere is never heavy with stale air.

At the far end of the terrace, the arcade and the garden is a suite of rooms which are really and truly my favourites, for I had them built myself. Here is a sun-parlour facing the terrace on one side, the sea on the other, and the sun on both. There is also a room which has folding doors opening on to the arcade and a window looking out on the sea. Opposite the intervening wall is a beautifully designed alcove which can be thrown into the room by folding back its glass doors and curtains, or cut off from it if they are closed: it is large enough to hold a couch and two arm-chairs, and has the sea at its foot, the neighbouring villas behind, and the woods beyond, views which can be seen separately from its many windows or blended into one. Next to it is a bedroom for use at night which neither the voices of my household, the sea's murmur, nor the noise of a storm can penetrate, any more than the lightning's flash and light of day unless the shutters are open. This profound peace and seclusion are due to the dividing passage which runs between the room and the garden so that any noise is lost in the intervening space. A tiny furnace-room is built on here, and by a narrow outlet retains or circulates the heat underneath as required. Then there is an ante-room and a second bedroom, built out to face the sun and catch its rays the moment it rises, and retain them until after midday, though by then at an angle. When I retire to this suite I feel as if I have left my house altogether and much enjoy the sensation: especially during the Saturnalia [the week starting on 17 December] when the rest of the roof resounds with festive cries in the holiday freedom, for I am not disturbing my household's merrymaking nor they my work.

Only one thing is needed to complete the amenities and beauty of the house – running water; but there are wells, or rather springs, for they are very near the surface. It is in fact a remarkable characteristic of this shore that wherever you dig you come upon water at once which is pure and not in the least brackish, although the sea is so near. The woods close by provide plenty of firewood, and the town of Ostia supplies us with everything else. There is also a village, just beyond the next house, which can satisfy anyone's modest needs, and here there are three baths for hire, a great convenience if a sudden arrival or too short a stay makes us reluctant to heat up the bath at home. The sea-front gains much from the pleasing variety of the houses built either in groups or far apart; from the sea or shore these look like a number of cities. The sand on the shore is sometimes too soft for walking after a long spell of fine weather, but more often it is hardened by the constant washing of the waves. The sea has admittedly few fish of any value, but it gives us excellent soles and prawns, and all inland produce is provided by the house, especially milk: for the herds collect there from the pastures whenever they seek water and shade.

And now do you think I have a good case for making this retreat my haunt and home where I love to be? You are too polite a townsman if you don't covet it! But I hope you will, for then the many attractions of my treasured house will have another strong recommendation in your company.

Source: Pliny the Younger, Book 2, letter 17: to Gallus, in Radice (1969), pp. 75–9.

Reading 3.4　　## Pliny the Younger: A boar hunt

Ridebis, et licet rideas. Ego, ille quem nosti, apros tres et quidem pulcherrimos cepi. 'Ipse?' inquis. Ipse; non tamen ut omnino ab inertia mea et quiete discederem. Ad retia sedebam; erat in proximo non venabulum aut lancea, sed stilus et pugillares; meditabar aliquid enotabamque, ut si manus vacuas, plenas tamen ceras reportarem. Non est quod contemnas hoc studendi genus; mirum est ut animus agitatione motuque corporis excitetur; iam undique silvae et solitudo ipsumque illud silentium quod venationi datur, magna cogitationis incitamenta sunt. 3 Proinde cum venabere, licebit auctore me ut panarium et lagunculam sic etiam pugillares feras: experieris non Dianam magis montibus quam Minervam inerrare.

Vale.

I know you will think it is a good joke, as indeed it is, when I tell you that your old friend has caught three boars, very fine ones too. Yes, I really did, and without even changing any of my lazy holiday habits. I was sitting by the hunting nets with writing materials by my side instead of hunting spears, thinking something out and making notes, so that even if I came home emptyhanded I should at least have my notebooks filled. Don't look down on mental activity of this kind, for it is remarkable how one's wits are sharpened by physical exercise; the mere fact of being alone in the depths of the woods in the silence necessary for hunting is a positive stimulus to thought. So next time you hunt yourself, follow my example and take your notebooks along with your lunch-basket and flask; you will find that Minerva walks the hills no less than Diana.

Farewell.

Source: Pliny the Younger, Book 1, letter 6: to Cornelius Tacitus, in Radice (1969), p. 39.

Reading 3.5   **Statius at his own villa in Alba Longa (not far from the capital), writing in celebration of Septimius Severus**

Parvi beatus ruris honoribus,
qua prisca Teucros Alba colit lares,
fortem atque facundum Severum
non solitis fidibus saluto.

iam trux ad Arctos Parrhasias hiems
concessit altis obruta solibus,
iam pontus ac tellus renident
in Zephyros Aquilone fracto.

nunc cuncta veris; frondibus annuis
crinitur arbos, nunc volucrum novi
questus inexpertumque carmen,
quod tacita statuere bruma.

nos parca tellus pervigil et focus
culmenque multo lumine sordidum
solantur exemptusque testa
qua modo ferbuerat Lyaeus.

Richly blessed with my little farms rewards
Where Alba tends old Trojan paths, I greet
      Forceful and fluent Severus
      Without my lyre's usual song.

Now savage winter has retreated North,
eclipsed by the suns up higher in the sky,
      now the sea and land are beaming,
      because zephyrs broke the North Wind.

> Zephyr was the west wind.

Now every tree is coiffed with yearly leaves
for spring, and now are heard renewed laments
      of birds, their unfamiliar song,
      which they composed in winter's hush.

My frugal land and ever-wakeful hearth,
and ceiling dark with soot from much firelight,
      give me comfort, wine too, from jugs
      where Bacchus just had been a-boil.

Statius, *Silvae*, Book 4, poem 5, 'Ode to Septimius Severus', lines 1–16, in B.R. Nagle (trans.) (2004) *The* Silvae *of Statius*, Bloomington, IN, University of Indiana Press.

Reading 3.6   **Celebrating the baths of Claudius Etruscus**

alios poscunt mea carmina coetus.
Naidas, undarum dominas, regemque corusci
ignis adhuc fessum Siculaque incude rubentem
eliicuisse satis. paulum arma nocentia, Thebae,

ponite: dilecto volo lascivire sodali.
iunge, puer, cyathos et ne numerare labora
cunctantemque incende chelyn; discede Laborque
Curaque, dum nitidis canimus gemmantia saxis
balnea dumque procax vittis hederisque, soluta
fronde verecunda, Clio mea ludit Etrusco.

A reference to **Vulcan**, the Roman blacksmith god.

                                    this song of mine
demands ensembles of another sort.
Our lady water-nymphs, the flashing lord
of fire, still tired and red from Etna's forge—
to have lured them will be enough. Put down
destructive arms awhile, my Theban epic;
I want to fool around for my dear friend.
Pour cup after cup, boy, but take no trouble
to count; fire up my dawdling lyre. Away
with Toil and Trouble, while I sing the baths
that bloom with gleaming stone, while frisky Clio,
my history's Muse, no fillets in her hair,
nor modest ivy, plays for my Etruscus.

Statius, *Silvae*, Book 1, poem 5, lines 5–14, in B.R. Nagle (transl.) (2004) *The* Silvae *of Statius*, Bloomington, IN, University of Indiana Press.

Media notes

Notes on the Audio CD 'Aetatem tibi agere'

Participants

Dr Helen Lovatt, Lecturer, Department of Classics, University of Nottingham.

Dr Deborah Brunton and Dr Paula James, Faculty of Arts, The Open University.

Purpose

The purpose of recording an informal exchange with a focus on Roman leisure was to identify preliminary questions about the society and culture under study. You should note, but not worry about, an absence of 'tightly packaged' answers here – just try to work out for yourselves whether any further questions are prompted by the discussion. After listening to tracks 1 to 7, you should start reading the chapter in earnest – its first section follows on from and fleshes out issues that the discussion has raised.

Some terms and allusions

The concept of *otium* is mentioned in the discussion. *Negotium* (from *neg* and *otium*: literally, 'not leisure') for the well-off citizen, who did not have to work in order to live, covered public and political duties. *Negotium* was 'business' for those engaged in trade and manufacture.

The Labours of Hercules comprised twelve seemingly impossible tasks, all of which the hero accomplished.

The Roman poet **Virgil** (70–19 BCE) wrote, among other things, the *Aeneid*, an epic tale of the Trojan hero Aeneas, who founded a new home in Italy that led to the origins of Rome.

Gaius **Suetonius** Tranquillus was born in 70 CE and wrote biographies of several emperors (*The Twelve Caesars*).

Martial (40–103/4 BCE) wrote short and often satirical poems on a variety of everyday subjects.

The Latin word *labor* (labour) was used to define hard graft and physical toil but also described epic missions and heroic deeds (think of the Labours of Hercules). *Labor* is the word chosen by a contemporary of Horace's, the poet Virgil, for the great but painful task of founding Rome in his epic, the *Aeneid*.

When talking about Baiae and the Romans taking 'holiday' breaks at the seaside or playing at country squires in their rural retreats, Helen refers to Propertius (born 54 or 47 BCE; date of death unknown but before 2 BCE) and Tibullus (*c*.50–19 BCE). These accomplished love poets lived in the same era as Horace.

Petronius' *Satyricon* is mentioned in the context of highly elaborate and vulgarly ostentatious banquets. The date of this long, largely comic and salacious prose narrative is uncertain (and major sections of it have not survived), but the author may have been Gaius Petronius, Emperor Nero's (54–68 CE) *arbiter elegentiae*: a style guru in literary and aesthetic terms. This would date the work to some time in the first century CE, as Nero ruled from 54 to 68 CE. (Suetonius is quoted as a source for his reign.)

The outrageous and over-drawn Trimalchio in the *Satyricon* was not simply a self-made man but a freed slave who became rich in shipping and trade, so this was a case of rapid upward mobility. Classical scholars have tentatively linked Trimalchio's embarrassing and pretentious behaviour with Emperor Nero himself, and the whole banquet scene could possibly be a satire on the imperial court at Rome. Petronius was implicated in one of several conspiracies to assassinate Nero and forced to commit suicide by the regime. The poet Martial is brought into the discussion as further evidence for the tedious round that clients performed in paying court to their patrons. In his *Epigrams* (Book 10, poem 47 and Book 4, poem 8) Martial describes a typical day in Rome, hour by hour, with its mix of duty calls, business deals and court cases in the morning but suggests that the afternoon has a more relaxed pace to it – for example going to the baths and exercise grounds, taking time off for reading or writing poetry, and perhaps rounding off the day at dinner with the 'good and the great' (the Emperor Domitian gets a special mention). Martial also regrets that there is so little opportunity to enjoy the good things in the capital city; for instance, riding, gossiping, and walking round the shaded colonnades and waterfalls.

Tracks 8–10

In the concluding tracks which you were asked to listen to at the end of the section 'The poet Horace and "getting away from it all"', Helen Lovatt puts a spotlight on Statius (she has published work on both his epic and his lighter poetry). This moves you a couple of centuries on from Horace, who was living on the cusp of an imperial autocracy (i.e. when government by a Senate of wealthy men was replaced by, effectively, a single ruler, the emperor).

Helen's little sketch of Statius, his life and times, should complement your encounter with Pliny the Younger in the chapter, as Statius was a contemporary of Pliny, producing celebratory poems on the villas and their owners' lifestyles in the second century CE.

Glossary for the DVD ROM 'Roman Villa'

Abraxas a mystical figure often shown with a chicken's head, a man's body, and snakes as legs.

Achilles a legendary Greek hero who in his youth was hidden on the island of Scyros to escape his destiny in the Trojan war, and was discovered there, disguised as a girl, by Odysseus.

Apollo a god associated with, among other things, healing and music.

Aratus a philosopher (*c*.315 – 240 BCE) famous for his poem *Phaenomena* about the constellations.

Attis a mythological devotee of the goddess Cybele, who castrated himself in her honour.

Caesar Gallus Flavius Claudius Constantius Gallus, appointed 'Caesar' (i.e. a ruler subsidiary to the emperor) in the eastern part of the Roman empire in 351 CE, known for his repressive style of government. He was executed in 354.

Ceres a Roman goddess associated with growth, especially of crops, equivalent to the Greek Demeter.

Daphne a nymph changed into a laurel tree after praying to be saved from seduction by Apollo.

Lycurgus a mythological king strangled by vines for attacking the god Bacchus.

Medusa one of three mythological sisters whose monstrous appearance turned humans to stone. Perseus beheaded her with the help of the gods.

Orpheus a mythological hero, son of Apollo and one of the Muses. His music had superhuman powers.

Sagaritis a water nymph associated with Attis.

Triptolemus a mythological hero who was given corn and knowledge of agriculture by Ceres.

Contents

MATERIALS YOU WILL NEED

- Audio CD: Seaside Music
- DVD ROM: The Seaside
- DVD Video: Interview with Gurinder Chadha
- Illustration Book
- *Bhaji on the Beach*, dir. Gurinda Chadha (set DVD)

AIMS

This chapter will:

- introduce the main features of the history of the seaside resort
- help you to appreciate some of the ways in which the seaside has been presented in a range of art forms
- show how different academic disciplines bring different approaches and insights to the study of the seaside.

HOW TO STUDY THIS CHAPTER
Deborah Brunton

So far in Book 4, the chapters have been of the same length and style as those in the earlier books and have required similar study patterns. This chapter uses a slightly different format to consider the themes of place and leisure in relation to the subject of the seaside. It includes seven short sections, plus associated audio-visual and DVD ROM materials. These are as follows:

Victorian Seaside Music (Section 4.1) explores how different styles of music became a feature of the Victorian seaside, appealing to a range of audiences.

Painting the Seaside (Section 4.2) considers how paintings by W.P. Frith and Eugène Boudin represented the seaside and how they reflected broader changes within the visual arts.

Dressing for the Beach (Section 4.3) uses photographs and films as sources of evidence for distinctive seaside fashions between the late nineteenth and early twentieth centuries.

Technology and the Seaside: Blackpool and Benidorm (Section 4.4) considers the role that technology has played in the development of resorts and of seaside holidays.

The Healthy Seaside (Section 4.5) explores the origins and changing nature of beliefs about the healthy qualities of seawater, sea air and sunshine.

Seaside Music: The Beach Boys and The Who (Section 4.6) examines the contrasting representations of the beach in the music of The Beach Boys and The Who.

Bhaji on the Beach (Section 4.7) looks at Gurinder Chadha's award-winning 1993 film: an entertaining portrayal of the experience of British Asian women on a day trip to Blackpool.

There are two aims behind this change of format. The first is to give you a further taste of interdisciplinary work, which you may choose to pursue in your future studies. You have met this approach already in studying the chapters in Book 3 on Benin, which draw on both history and art history. The sections in this chapter draw on a wide range of the disciplines you have already studied, and offer you a new topic of study – the feature film. Each section brings its own viewpoint to a different aspect of the seaside, but they complement each other, allowing you to build up a rich picture of the changing experience of the seaside. They can be split into two broad categories: sections which consider the historical reasons for the rise and development of seaside holidays; and those which consider artistic representations of the seaside from different periods and art forms. These are not absolute categories – a holiday snap is just as much a representation of the seaside as a Frith painting. But here we look at photographs more as historical sources, and at paintings more as conscious works of art which adapt and extend the techniques of the art of painting.

See the Course Companion, Section 2.5, 'Productive reading', for tips on skim reading.

The second aim is to develop further your study skills, by giving you an opportunity to study more independently. Independent study gives you more control – the chance to make choices about what to concentrate on. It involves a variety of skills, including the ability to make appropriate choices. An important skill you need to acquire in independent study is that of selecting material. In your future studies, you may well find yourself going into a library with a reading list, looking for material to help you write an essay. Some of the books on your list may have lots of information to help you write that essay; others may have a little relevant information yet others may not be helpful. It would be very time-consuming to read all the books – instead you need to quickly skim through them, selecting the ones with material relevant for your essay, and spending most of your time studying just those books. That's what you'll do – on a small scale – in this part of the course, skimming through all the materials, and then selecting some for detailed study.

Activity

Your first task in this chapter is to work through 'Resort history' on the DVD ROM 'The Seaside'. This provides a brief outline of the rise and development of seaside holidays in the nineteenth and twentieth centuries. You can then test your understanding by building your own resort in the 'Virtual resort' section. These two activities will give you a basic grasp of the history of the seaside holiday, and lots of background information on the more detailed studies of different aspects of the seaside.

Your next task is to skim through all the materials in the chapter – skim the introductions, the section headings and look at the pictures to get an idea of the sorts of topic covered. One aspect of this, which you will discover as you skim through, is that the sections vary in length and in what they ask you to do, so you need to bear that in mind as you go.

Now you are ready to make your selection of materials for detailed study.

On what basis should you make your choice? The case studies in the different sections will certainly enhance your understanding of 'place' and 'leisure' developed in the first part of this book. They also offer you a further chance to consider some of the AA100 disciplines (which may help you to decide what to pursue in your future studies) and will develop your independent study skills. You may also find some of the topics particularly intriguing or attractive.

There is another factor. Practically speaking, your study of Book 4 cannot be separated from the requirement to complete the end-of-course assessment (ECA). You will have a choice of questions for the ECA, covering different aspects of Book 4. Which question you choose to answer will influence your approach to the materials.

Remember you are not expected to read every section of this chapter. In total, the materials add up to more than three weeks' work – so you should pick which sections to study.

As you can see, then, the combination of case studies and the ECA questions allows you quite a lot of scope for choice within the course context. We certainly recommend that you at least familiarise yourself with all of the sections of this chapter before making any choices. In making your decision on what to study in more depth, we suggest you should study at least four sections.

4.1 VICTORIAN SEASIDE MUSIC

Trevor Herbert

'OH! I DO LIKE TO BE BESIDE THE SEASIDE'

Let's start by listening to a song that is synonymous with the British seaside – it's almost an anthem for the seaside resort. You'll find it as the first track on the Audio CD 'Seaside Music'. It is a marvellously evocative performance by the music-hall entertainer Mark Sheridan (see Figure 4.1). The exact date of the recording is not known, but it

"Oh! be careful!"

Figure 4.1   George Cooke, portrait of Mark Sheridan, 1905. Mary Evans Picture Library.

was probably October 1910. Sheridan was one of the great stars of the British music hall, and this became his signature tune. As the recording is so old, the sound quality is understandably somewhat flawed, but I think it conveys a lot about the way this song was performed in the opening decades of the twentieth century. 'Oh! I Do Like to be beside the Seaside' was written by the otherwise relatively obscure light-music composer John Glover-Kind in 1907, and it made an immediate popular impact, largely through Sheridan's championing of it.

Activity

Listen to 'Oh! I Do Like to be beside the Seaside' on track 1 of the Audio CD, and think about these questions:

- What qualities does the song possess that make it so popular?

- What do the words, the mood of the song and its performance on this recording tell us about the social class of the people who liked 'to be beside the seaside'?

Discussion

I've always loved this song, and I especially like Sheridan's performance of it. Its success comes from two primary features. First, the tune is catchy because it is made up of short, simple, repeated phrases that stick in the memory as soon as they are heard. Second, the words fit the tune like a glove, one note to a syllable – listen to the song again if you didn't notice this at first. This simple device really is potent, and with the foot-tapping rhythm that prevails throughout, it is hard not to be carried away by it.

The structure of the song is equally simple: a **verse/chorus structure** in which each verse leads to the chorus as if it were a magnet. Furthermore, the words are interesting even though they may seem bland; they carry a little narrative that the listener hears, subscribes to and eventually (usually quite literally) joins in with. Here is the first verse and the chorus:

Verse

Everyone delights to spend their summer's holiday
Down beside the side of the silvery sea
I'm no exception to the rule
In fact, if I'd my way
I'd reside by the side of the silvery sea.
But when you're just the common or garden Smith or Jones or Brown
At bus'ness up in town
You've got to settle down.
You save up all the money you can till summer comes around
Then away you go
To a spot you know
Where the cockle shells are found.

Chorus

Oh! I do like to be beside the seaside
I do like to be beside the sea!
I do like to stroll upon the Prom, Prom, Prom!
Where the brass bands play:

'Tiddely-om-pom-pom!'
So just let me be beside the seaside
I'll be beside myself with glee
And there's lots of girls beside,
I should like to be beside
Beside the seaside!
Beside the sea!

The point, of course, is that this is a communal song: it conforms to a format that was prevalent in music halls and other mass entertainment venues at the end of the nineteenth and in the early twentieth centuries, when Sheridan was so popular. Like most songs of its type it contains not just the musical devices I have already mentioned, but also this narrative element that the popular audience can identify with – 'the common or garden Smith or Jones or Brown'. The song is aimed unambiguously at the mass of working people, who by the opening of the twentieth century believed the seaside to represent the epitome of leisure, pleasure and fun. They toiled all year to earn those couple of weeks down by the 'silvery sea' – and the music soundscape of the seaside was as important an ingredient in the mixture that made it such an object of desire and anticipation as was the smell of the salt air.

The place of music in the *idea* of the seaside resort was always crucial, and John Glover-Kind's song – down to its references to, for example, the 'brass bands' and the 'Prom, Prom, Prom' – reflects a process that had been developing in the Victorian period. That development is fascinating, and it provides a splendid example of how musical practices can both form and reflect the socio-historical process. So, to look at this development in more detail, we need to draw on the techniques of the music historian and the social historian.

REPERTOIRE, PERFORMANCE AND RECEPTION

When they investigate the music of the past, music historians generally think of three factors: *repertoire* – the music that was played or sung; *performance* – the way that the music was played or sung, the instruments that were used and the spaces in which the performances took place; and *reception* – the nature and expectations of the audiences who listened to it, and how it was received or appreciated.

The Victorians had eclectic tastes as far as music was concerned, so Victorian musical repertoire was plentiful and varied. In an age without radios or gramophones, print was the medium through which music was disseminated for performance. A vast quantity of cheaply priced music was in circulation, and it covered many different styles. In order to understand Victorian music culture, it is particularly important to consider the ways in which the music was performed, the places where it was performed and the expectations that different audiences had of it.

Some Victorian popular music originated in live public entertainment, especially the music hall, but an even greater proportion was produced to serve the needs of domestic music-makers, particularly pianists and singers of what is sometimes referred to as 'parlour song'. There was also a wide and genuinely popular appreciation of what we would today call 'classical music', including opera. Italian opera might have been performed at London opera houses, but songs derived from operas were played in drawing rooms and popular concerts throughout the country. There was a yet wider appreciation of classical music through the performance of 'arrangements' (music re-scored so that it can be played by different instruments) by any number of instrumental groups, including brass bands, pipe bands, concertina bands and orchestras made up of miscellaneous instruments. Thus, while the popular music/classical music divide existed, both categories seem to have been enjoyed by most people.

Little Victorian musical repertoire was specific to the seaside; rather, seaside venues echoed the musical life that prevailed generally around the country throughout the year. 'Seaside music' was essentially music transplanted from urban venues to the resorts, as the easy availability of rail travel allowed increasing numbers of people to migrate to the coast in the more clement seasons. It is difficult to overstate the social and commercial consequences of this migration for the entertainment industry. Music was an essential ingredient in leisure, and it did not take long for the impresarios who ran the Victorian music business to realise that what others called a 'holiday' created for them a market with vast potential.

'SELECT' AND POPULAR VENUES, AND THE DIFFERENT MARKETS FOR MUSIC

You can read more about the development of resorts in 'Resort history' on the DVD ROM and in Section 4.4, 'Technology and the Seaside'.

From the 1870s onwards there was a tension between the two main market sectors that developed at the Victorian seaside: the middle-class holiday-makers (often quite literally the descendants of the eighteenth- and early nineteenth-century leisured classes who had frequented the fashionable seaside resorts for their health and recreation); and the new working-class day-trippers who appeared in abundance at the larger resorts and were understood to be a new mass market with an apparently insatiable appetite for leisure products. These groups can be seen as two different musical markets. Impresarios sought to capture both sectors. To retain the well-off, high-class market, there was an attempt to maintain a 'select tone', while simultaneously catering for an increasingly lucrative lower-class market.

Not all seaside resorts targeted the same social groups to the same degree, and the music that was heard in them reflected this. Different resorts, and indeed different venues at these resorts, purveyed repertoires in spaces that were designed to project a particular social tone. In the dignified environs of Brighton's Winter Gardens, for example, small bands playing string instruments and the softer **woodwinds** entertained a clientele with a repertoire that was derived from the popular classics and sedate dance music. It was not uncommon for such bands to be entirely female, and typically they would dress in white to emphasise their own purity and the respectability of their musical endeavours.

Figure 4.2   Women's orchestra, New Spa, Bridlington (Yorkshire). Unknown photographer.

On the other hand, in order to attract the mass working-class holiday-makers, a great deal of music was played outdoors by bands of an altogether different sort. Some resorts were able to engage the services of bands of the regular military, but many featured performances by brass bands. The distinction between a military band and a brass band is important. Military bands are made up of **brass** and woodwind instruments with **percussion**. While there were amateur military bands, there were also many bands of the regular army, and they were seen as an important element of military ceremonials and equally important in conveying patriotic sentiments among the populace in general. This they did to great effect. They were highly trained (the training for military musicians was much more sophisticated than the training available at the conservatoires, or music schools, at this time), and they made a striking visual impression with their colourful uniforms. Brass bands, on the other hand, were entirely amateur and made up of only brass instruments with percussion. In fact, the brass instruments they played were almost all members of a newly invented species of instrument which produced a characteristically homogenous and mellow tone. The repertoire of both types of band, but particularly brass bands, overlapped with the salon-type music heard in the palm-lined rooms of hotels – light pieces, almost all derivative of some other area of music (drawn from the opera house, the dance hall, parlour song, and so on); but, as you would expect, military band programmes were punctuated by rousing marches which summoned up images of British patriotism.

Blackpool

In Blackpool, trainloads of Lancashire mill-workers became increasingly central to the town's economy as the nineteenth century wore on, throwing the tension between the lower- and higher-class markets into particularly sharp relief:

> A theatrical company is quartered here, playing, I believe, every night, and concerts and dances are frequent. I hear, however, complaints from pleasure's votaries [...] that still more ought to be done in the way of providing amusement, and that, as Blackpool can make no pretensions to the charms of a quiet watering-place, and is yearly getting far too crowded and noisy for sober folk who come to the sea-side only for rest and good air, it ought to go in utterly and uncompromisingly for the opposite system. [...] The principal hotel, the Imperial, has adopted these tactics to a certain extent, and every Saturday night during the season gave 'scratch' dances, which were considered a great success.

(*The Times*, 26 October 1869, p. 7)

You can read more about this in Section 4.5, 'The Healthy Seaside'.

From this tension came the need to effectively segregate music through the establishment of discrete venues aimed at specific types of audiences. The first Victorian resorts – those established in the first half of the nineteenth century – tended to set themselves up as spas, with an emphasis on the health-giving properties of relaxation and sea-bathing, and the upper- and middle-class entertainment they offered was similarly modelled on spa towns such as Bath. Thus, as in spa towns, many seaside resorts had assembly rooms (their names are still commonly found today) where the musical fare consisted of sedate concerts and balls. The importance of assembly rooms to the social life of seaside resorts waned over the course of the century, though they continued to serve a significant function well into the 1870s.

New types of venue were also designed with respectable holiday-makers in mind – Blackpool's North Pier, for example, was a 'select' venue where orchestral concerts were held (with a charge for admission to discourage 'undesirables'), while the town's South Jetty (now the Central Pier) offered more varied entertainment including all-day open-air dancing, aimed at the working classes. In 1874 the North Pier gained a 35-piece orchestra to serve the elevated tastes of high-class visitors and provide a conspicuously more genteel alternative to the fare that was available for the working classes. In contrast, like the South Jetty, Raikes Hall also offered dancing, as well as 'spectaculars' featuring acrobats, fireworks and novelty acts, as opposed to the more educational attractions that were advocated by social reformers.

The Blackpool Winter Gardens, with its multiple venues, could offer a mixed bag of entertainment, and aimed ambitiously at all sectors of the market. The Winter Gardens Opera House opened on 10 June 1889 with the aim of expanding the opportunities for 'select' entertainment in the town, presenting for its inaugural performance Gilbert and Sullivan's most recent work, *Yeoman of the Guard*, premiered in London only eight months earlier. Music festivals aimed at 'serious' music-lovers featured prominently in the entertainment programmes of the Winter Gardens, and in 1901 the Blackpool Musical Festival was formally established there.

Municipal orchestras and itinerant bands

Seaside municipalities with single-minded pretensions to respectability were especially strategic in their approach to entertainment. New Brighton appointed the respected and ambitious composer Granville Bantock (1868–1946) as its director of music, while in Bournemouth a full-time municipal orchestra was established (the first municipal orchestra in the country, now the Bournemouth Symphony Orchestra). This orchestra was set up under the directorship of Dan Godfrey (1868–1939), the greatest military band conductor of the day and one of the most prolific arrangers of orchestral music for amateur brass bands.

At the other end of the performance spectrum were umpteen itinerant musical groups of varying degrees of musical proficiency, who moved speculatively from resort to resort in the hope of engagement or at least modest sponsorship from passers-by. 'German bands' were frequently encountered. These literally were groups of German musicians who busked in the open air, much to the irritation of many. 'A Correspondent' to *The Times*, writing in 1885 about 'Sandiford', a fictional place that was supposed to represent a typical small seaside resort, probably described the experience of many seaside visitors:

> [Music], alas, abounds, and, with the exception of the town band, is of the very worst quality. I do not know whether the performers or their instruments are most at fault, but the latter are in the last stages of decrepitude. There is a wheezy, wasted trombone, which is evidently in a consumption, though,

You encountered Tara, the legendary meeting place of the Irish Kings, in Book 2, Chapter 5.

unhappily, a lingering one; and a harp so old that it suggests the idea that it is the very one which once hung in Tara's halls, and has been brought hither to utter its dying strains. This superabundance of music is the one crumpled rose-leaf which interferes with the repose and quiet joy of Sandiford.

(23 September 1885, p. 8)

Black-face minstrels (known at the time as 'nigger minstrels' – see the quotation from *The Times* below) and later another species of musical entertainers known as **pierrot troupes**, were also in circulation, and typically they performed outdoors, often on the beach itself. The minstrels and pierrots were variety acts (performing songs, dances and comic sketches), and were regarded as acceptable family entertainment for the respectable lower-middle and working classes. However, another fictionalised account, this time of a large seaside resort, 'Spaville-on-Sea', published in 1885, suggests that the higher social classes often regarded these acts as vulgar intrusions – precisely because of their ubiquity and popularity. But here it is obvious that the writer is actually satirising higher-brow attitudes, rather than simply deriding popular entertainment itself:

It is needless to say that there are also the nigger minstrels, for are they not always with us on our sea-side holiday, proving, by the crowds they attract by their odious vulgarities, how superior we who hate them are to our fellow-creatures?

(*The Times*, 26 September 1885, p. 6)

Some town committees tried to guard against noisy and intrusive competition between itinerant bands and minstrel troupes by raising subscriptions to employ a regular band or troupe. By the 1890s, municipal bands were being established by seaside councils across the country. The respectability that these bands were intended to embody was often emphasised by giving them the title 'spa band' (as in, for example, 'The Scarborough Spa Band').

SEASIDE MUSIC AND RATIONAL RECREATION

'Rational recreation' was a relatively new concept that became a sustained theme of Victorian life. It had a special meaning in respect of music, and it should be seen against a background of genuine concern on the part of the dominant classes that an increasingly large, urban, working-class population held the potential to undermine key social values. The term 'rational recreation' was invented by (mainly higher-class) social reformers to describe working-class pastimes that were by definition self-improving and wholesome, as opposed to boisterous and morally corrupting. Thus the reading room of a workmen's institute was a place of rational recreation, but the smoking room of a pub – or any other room in a pub, for that matter – was decidedly not.

Participating in or listening to 'good' music was invariably seen as a rational recreation because performing music could only come about through studious endeavour, and listening to good music was considered at best educative and at the very least to encourage docility.

The views of the rational recreationalists were influential until the late nineteenth century. At that time, the significance of the working classes in the economy of the seaside became the dominating factor in determining the nature of the entertainment that was offered, but before that development was fully in place the values of the rational recreationalists provided a focus against which most seaside music could be measured. As late as 1885 a journalist writing in *The Times* complained about the 'very doubtful second-rate watering-places' of the east coast which offered dubious pleasures to the London working classes in particular, describing these resorts as:

> A Seven-Dials-on-Sea, of squalor indescribable, a perpetual Derby Day, too painful to look at, a saturnalia of lounging and drunken and card-playing humanity, freely intermixed with vulgar music-halls and stands for the sale of cheap imported oysters.

(The Times, 16 September 1885, p. 4)

Seven Dials was a notorious slum area of London.

You can see an image of Derby Day in Figure 4.4 in the next section.

Leaving aside the oysters, this extract illustrates the extent to which certain resorts and the activities that went on within them were emblematic of the social stratification of Victorian society.

A seaside entertainment that offered a resolution of these tensions was the amateur brass band contest. The man who laid the greatest claim to having invented this was a self-made impresario from Hull called Enderby Jackson (1827–1903). Jackson said he was inspired with the idea of such contests while observing the attitude of spectators at agricultural shows. If they were fascinated by the prospect of which pig would be judged the fattest in a show, how much more happily would they try to second-guess adjudicators at a brass band contest? Furthermore, audiences would readily travel to support their local band, and the railway companies keenly collaborated: brass band contests were often sponsored by railway companies, and there is persuasive evidence to show that the phenomenon of the cheap day excursion, and indeed the actual term itself, was invented specifically to attract audiences to these contests.

During a contest, bands competed with each other by playing a piece of their choice, and most chose to play an arrangement of an Italian opera overture. The quality of their playing was extremely high, and because their repertoire was mainly made up of arrangements of classical music it was viewed as morally 'improving' for performers and audiences alike. Its basis in classical music also meant that the repertoire formed a common cultural ground that could be occupied by

Figure 4.3   View of bandstand, Marine Gardens, Morecambe (Lancashire), *c*.1910. Unknown photographer. Mary Evans Picture Library. Bandstands such as this proliferated throughout England in the nineteenth century as open-air band concerts became more commonplace.

people of different backgrounds. Most of the players were working-class, but engravings and photographs of the period show that the audiences appear to have been made up of people from most sectors of society. Furthermore, because the audiences – or, should we say, spectators – at these open-air events were engaging in a process of appraisal in judging the bands against the views of the official adjudicators, it could be argued that they were not just listening but listening analytically. It should be said that the virtue of these events was sometimes marred by the fist fights that broke out among rival supporters when a controversial result was announced, but this regrettable if recurrent detail did not entirely undermine one of the most sustained popular music events of the period. Brass band contests became one of the great attractions of the seaside.

Repertoires and venues

Having read this section and looked at the illustrations that accompany it, I now want you to listen to some music. The purpose here is partly to provide aural illustrations for some of the features I have described, but I also want you to return to the themes I mentioned at the start of this section: repertoire, performance and reception.

There are three pieces of music (three pieces of repertoire) on tracks 2 to 4 of the Audio CD. Obviously, none of the performances was recorded in the Victorian period, but each originates in that period, and I have chosen the recordings because, in different ways, they provide really vivid resonances of the sounds that would have been heard in the late Victorian era. I think they provide a really good insight into aspects of Victorian seaside performance. The pieces are:

Track 2 'My Daughter's Schottische' by W.H. Montgomery (1810–1886), played on original instruments of the Victorian period by the Wallace Collection, conducted by Simon Wright. Montgomery was one of the Victorian period's most prolific writers of dance music, the schottische being a type of dance that was favoured in Victorian times. This piece appears in seaside programmes in the second half of the nineteenth century. It was arranged for a particular band, the Cyfarthfa Band from Merthyr Tydfil in south Wales, by its bandmaster George Livesey, and it is played here directly from the original Victorian band manuscripts.

Track 3 'Overture, Poet and Peasant' by Franz von Suppé (1819–1895), arranged for brass band by Riviera (the first name is not known). It is played here on a 78 rpm recording made in 1936 by the Fodens Motor Works Band under its conductor Fred Mortimer. The band was based in Sandbach in south Cheshire. This is one of the great British brass bands, playing at a time when it was at its zenith. Though the recording was made more than 30 years after the Victorian period ended, the piece and the mode of its performance are very close to what would have been heard in the 1890s.

Track 4 A modern recording of 'Winter Stories' by Alphonse Czibulka (1842–1890). The piece opens with a prolonged reference to another popular Victorian piece, 'Hearts and Flowers', and then moves into a multi-sectioned waltz. I have chosen this because its performance by the London Salon Ensemble is not just attractive, but also makes use of the type of unorthodox, pragmatic (i.e. using whatever was available) instrumentation that must have been common in Victorian times – three violins, a cello, bass, piano and harmonium (a small portable organ of the type that was used in Victorian chapels).

Activity

Now listen to the three pieces. As you listen, think about the two questions posed below. Both questions are based on rather crude hypotheses about the reception of these performances and the places in which they might have been given, but I think they are broadly illustrative of the themes I have been discussing. As you listen to the music, think about the different types of resort that I have discussed, the different sectors of society that frequented them and the role that music had in different seaside locations.

1   I think that one of these pieces is especially suitable for performance indoors before a fairly genteel audience; one is especially suitable for performance out of doors on a promenade; and one could be

performed indoors or out of doors and to just about any sort of audience. What do you think? Which piece fits which type of venue, and why?

2   In the light of the first question and of the themes I have explored in this section, think about the type of listening that each piece demands. Does each of the pieces serve simply as background music, or do any of them require something more?

Even though the full/complete version of each piece is given, you may find that you can answer these questions without listening to every piece all the way through.

Discussion   I think that Track 2 could be performed anywhere to great effect. It is a jaunty piece of dance music and has plenty of contrasting sections, but they are all relatively light and entertaining. It could, quite literally, be danced to, but I could also imagine it as the soundscape for a healthy and relaxing day out at the seaside, indoors or out. The instruments are all brass instruments (with some percussion), so the sound would carry well out of doors, but it is neither imposing nor overwhelming.

Track 3 could be performed indoors in a large hall, but it is also well suited for performance in the open air. Apart from the fact that the sound of the brass instruments would carry well, the instruments would not suffer any damage if it happened to rain (not a trivial issue).

Track 4 is best suited to a genteel indoor setting. It is a charming, engaging piece, and could be danced to, but it also provides a suitable backdrop for polite conversation over tea. It simply would not be heard in the open air, and the string instruments, piano and harmonium would be extremely vulnerable to temperature changes and variations in moisture and humidity out of doors.

As to my second question, I think that the second piece – the 'Poet and Peasant' overture – is of a quite different order to the other two. The main reason is that while the other two pieces might provide perfect background music for restrained (if not refined) leisure activities and might well capture an enthusiastic audience if the presentation was right, the Suppé overture demands to be listened to. It is not a collection of tunes but *a work* which is more descriptive and complex and which poses considerable demands on performers. Musical contrasts in this piece are much greater than they are in the other two tracks and you may have sensed that it is explicitly dramatic. Now the significance here is that 'Poet and Peasant' was a brass band test piece, the type of piece that a band would have played in a contest. Those who listened to a performance of this piece would have done so with intense scrutiny. Despite the obvious partisanship with which people listened to their 'own' band, there was always a sense of drama about these occasions. Everyone in the audience considered themselves a music critic, and it was precisely that level of concentrated discernment that marked brass band contests out as a form of rational recreation.

FURTHER READING

Books about music and the Victorian seaside are few and far between, but the following list (and the bibliographies they contain) will be a helpful starting point if you want to look further:

Ehrlich, C. (1985) *The Music Profession since the Eighteenth Century: A Social History*, Oxford, Clarendon.

Herbert, T. (2000) *The British Brass Band: A Musical and Social History*, Oxford, Oxford University Press. The relevant chapter of this text (Chapter 1: 'Nineteenth-century bands: making a movement') is freely available online through the Oxford University Press online 'Bookshelf' facility.

Hern, A. (1967) *The Seaside Holiday: The History of the English Seaside Resort*, London, Cresset.

Howell, S. (1974) *The Seaside*, London, Studio Vista.

Pimlott, J.A.R. (1976 [1947]) *The Englishman's Holiday: A Social History*, New York, Harvester.

Russell, D. (1997) *Popular Music in England, 1840–1914: A Social History* (2nd edn), Manchester, Manchester University Press.

Walton, J.K. (1983) *The English Seaside Resort: A Social History 1750–1914*, Leicester, Leicester University Press.

Walton, J.K. (2000) *The British Seaside: Holidays and Resorts in the Twentieth Century*, Manchester, Manchester University Press.

Walvin, J. (1978) *Beside the Seaside: A Social History of the Popular Seaside Holiday*, London, Allen Lane.

The following two books are mainly devoted to pictures of holiday venues in the period (many more are published locally):

Craven, A.B. (1971) *Victorian and Edwardian Yorkshire from Old Photographs*, London, Batsford.

Green, I. (1978) *The Book of Dover*, Chesham, Bucks., Barracuda Books.

4.2 PAINTING THE SEASIDE

Charles Harrison

INTRODUCTION

For this section, it may help to refer back to the description and analysis of pictures that you undertook in the chapter on Cézanne in Book 1.

The principal purpose of this section is to compare two different pictures of life at the seaside in the mid-nineteenth century, one from England and one from France, and in the process to consider different purposes, techniques and achievements in the art of painting. Though the comparison is specific to the type of subject and to the period in question, it is intended to encourage you to think about the more general priorities and techniques of pictorial composition and to introduce you to certain kinds of contrast relevant to study of the art of the modern period: in particular between description and expression, between narration and representation, and between works that appear to invite interpretation and others that seem more resistant.

'ON MODERN LIFE'

The first painting to be considered is *Life at the Seaside: Ramsgate Sands* (Plate 4.4.1 in the Illustration Book) by the English painter William Powell Frith (1819–1909). It was first shown at the Royal Academy in 1854, when the artist was 35 years old. The painting was a great popular success, and its purchase by Queen Victoria made Frith's reputation. The picture remains in the Royal Collection and at the time of writing is on display in the Queen's Gallery at Buckingham Palace. In his *Autobiography and Reminiscences* (Frith, 1887–8, p. 171), the artist claimed that he had been weary of the kind of **costume painting** that was prevalent among academic painters (see, for instance, Plate 4.4.2); instead, 'I had determined to try my hand on modern life'. This was the first of a series of pictures in which Frith constructed densely populated scenes from contemporary Victorian life, each full of character and incident. The best known of those that followed are *Derby Day* (Figure 4.4 and Plate 4.4.3) and *The Railway Station* (Plate 4.4.4)*,* both of which earned the artist considerable sums from the sale of reproduction rights.

To understand the importance of these pictures in the development of art in England, it may help to consider the alternative – costume painting – that Frith claimed he had grown weary of. Costume painting refers to pictures of people and episodes from the past – a past that was often romanticised or used to introduce moralising content into art. In the teaching and criticism of painting, it had been understood for the previous two centuries that history painting was the highest of the genres of art. This categorisation of painting by type of subject owed much to the influence of the French Academy of Painting and Sculpture, founded in 1648, and to the respect accorded within the Academy to the neoclassical painter Nicholas Poussin (1594–1665). Plate 4.4.5 shows Poussin's *Exposition of Moses.* Representing a moment from the biblical story of Moses being hidden in the margins of the river Nile (Exod. 2:3–4), this would have been thought of as

Figure 4.4   William Powell Frith, *Derby Day*, 1856–8, oil on canvas, 102 x 224 cm. Tate Britain, London. Photo: © Tate, London 2007.

a history painting. The implication was that such works as this were possessed of an elevated intellectual and moral content that was demanded by the nature of their subject matter. As a consequence they tended to be favoured by those – whether hereditary monarchs or elected representatives – who saw themselves as responsible for the conduct of public life, and by those who were in a position to purchase works for public collections. By contrast, a far lower status was accorded to the painting of still lifes, landscapes or ordinary scenes from everyday life, genres in which the Protestant Dutch painters of the time tended to specialise. Figure 4.5 (also reproduced as Plate 4.4.6) illustrates an early seaside scene, painted by the young Adriaen van de Velde (1636–1672) four years later than Poussin's picture. It shows the beach at Scheveningen near The Hague in the Netherlands.

While many of the most interesting and popular developments in painting did indeed take place in the 'lower' genres, and notably in landscape, a belief in the primacy of history painting persisted in academic practice down to Frith's day, and particularly at the Royal Academy Schools in London where he was trained. But many of the costume pieces that featured during the mid-nineteenth century, either in the annual academy exhibitions in London or in the French **Salon**, were actually sentimental illustrations to literary texts, or mawkish evocations of an idealised classical world, with little of the vitality and gravitas that had characterised work such as Poussin's (see, for instance, Plate 4.4.7, which illustrates a work by Jean-Léon Gerôme shown in the French Salon in 1847). In his review of the French Salon of 1846, the French poet and critic Charles Baudelaire noted the decline of the classical tradition and suggested that 'since all centuries and all peoples have had their own form of beauty, so inevitably we

Figure 4.5   Adriaen van de Velde, *The Beach at Scheveningen*, 1658, oil on canvas, 50 x 74 cm. Gemaeldegalerie Alte Meister, Kassel. Photo: © Museumslandschaft Hessen Kassel/The Bridgeman Art Library.

have ours' (Baudelaire, 1846, p. 302). Proposing, with only a modicum of irony, that artists should seek out 'The heroism of modern life' (a subheading in his review), he continued:

> The pageant of fashionable life and the thousands of floating existences – criminals and kept women – which drift about in the underworld of a great city [...] all prove that we have only to open our eyes to recognise our heroism. [...] We are enveloped and steeped as though in an atmosphere of the marvellous; but we do not notice it.
>
> (Baudelaire, 1998 [1846], pp. 303–4)

Ciaran Carson's poem 'The Albatross', in The Faber Book of Beasts, *is a version of Baudelaire's 'L'Albatros', from* Les Fleurs du Mal.

In his series of poems collected as *Les Fleurs du Mal* (*Flowers of Evil*), Baudelaire gave his own form of expression to what he saw as the character of modern life.

Though we tend nowadays to take it for granted, this idea that art's proper business is to engage with modern life was still relatively controversial at the time. The acceptance of the principle by some artists rather than others led to the division between modernists and traditionalists that we saw at work in France in Book 1, Chapter 3, and that can be observed in the musical and literary spheres in the early twentieth century. While it is unlikely that Frith read Baudelaire's writings, he certainly seems to have been motivated by a similar view that appropriate material for an ambitious modern art was to be found in the life of the modern city – and of its populations at leisure.

LIFE AT THE SEASIDE: RAMSGATE SANDS

You can read about the nineteenth-century seaside in 'Resort history' on the DVD ROM.

Frith's painting of *Life at the Seaside: Ramsgate Sands* was the fruit of three years of work. It contains some 70 separate figures. Its composition was largely based on drawings that the artist made on visits to the town in the south-east of England in 1852–4. There is a limit, though, to the extent to which the artist could have based his work on observations of actual holiday-makers and on transcriptions of their likenesses. The dramatis personae of his picture are clearly designed both to play out a number of scenarios within its composition and, in many cases, to conform to stereotypes that would be recognisable to its audience. They need to appear not just as believable people but also as animated characters. *Ramsgate Sands* is really still a kind of costume painting, though one that is staged in modern dress.

One source, however, is easily enough discovered. Frith was an acquaintance of the novelist Charles Dickens, who in 1842 had commissioned the artist to illustrate two characters from his novels – Dolly Varden (from *Barnaby Rudge*) and Kate Nickleby (from *Nicholas Nickleby*). Earlier, in 1836 Dickens had published his anecdotal text 'The Tuggses at Ramsgate' in *Sketches by Boz*, with illustrations by Robert Seymour (Plate 4.4.8). This is a laboriously comic account of how the recently prosperous but naive and pretentious Tuggs family – London grocers out of their element at Ramsgate – are easily fleeced by a trio of con artists. In Dickens's sketch the Tuggses arrive at Ramsgate pier by the 'City of London Ramsgate steamer':

> If the pier had presented a scene of life and bustle to the Tuggses on their first landing at Ramsgate, it was far surpassed by the appearance of the sands on the morning after their arrival. It was a fine, bright, clear day, with a light breeze from the sea. There were the same ladies and gentlemen, the same children, the same nursemaids, the same telescopes, the same portable chairs. The ladies were employed in needlework, or watch-guard making, or knitting, or reading novels; the gentlemen were reading newspapers and magazines; the children were digging holes in the sand with wooden spades, and collecting water therein; the nursemaids, with their youngest charges in their arms, were running in after the waves, and then running back with the waves after them; and, now and then, a little

sailing-boat either departed with a gay and talkative cargo of passengers, or returned with a very silent and particularly uncomfortable-looking one.

(Dickens, 1836, p. 50)

Frith's painting does not literally illustrate Dickens's story in the way that Seymour's engraving does, but its conception and composition are grounded in an understanding of 'modern life' that is clearly compatible with that of the novelist, and perhaps influenced by the cast of characters that he picks out. *Ramsgate Sands* is in this sense entirely of a piece with the type of account that Dickens gives of a specific kind of social circumstance – the urban middle class disporting itself on holiday at the seaside – and, as contemporary commentators on the picture were quick to demonstrate, the careful characterisations Frith gives to his various figures encourage the viewer to engage in comparable kinds of ironic narrative reading. A reviewer in *The Art Journal* in June 1854, for instance, observed of the family group to the right centre of the foreground:

> That family in the centre are remarkable for their exclusiveness; at Peckham, their garden wall is higher than that of anybody else; and here they turn their backs upon everybody, living as it were within a ring-fence. The papa wears his slippers and reads *The Times*. The mama, who is yet pretty, shades her complexion [...] The young ladies read Bulwer and Disraeli, and keep worrying their matter of fact father for the newspaper to look over the list of marriages.

(Quoted in Arscott, 1995, pp. 162–3)

Baron Edward Bulwer Lytton (1803–73) was the author of the historical novel *The Last Days of Pompeii* (1834); **Benjamin Disraeli** (1804–81), later to be prime minister, was the author of the political novels *Coningsby* (1844) and *Sybil* (1846).

In England as in France during the mid-nineteenth century, the same point is made over and over again by artists, writers and critics anxious to establish their own positions as sophisticated observers of the social world: that one of the clearest signs of modernity is the rise to prominence of the urban bourgeoisie. For those whose business is the *representation* of modern life, it is through observation of the distinctive occupations, manners and appearances of the class in question that the particular qualities of that life are to be caught. In the 1850s, Ramsgate was the kind of place one would go to watch the urban bourgeoisie at leisure.

Activity

The purpose of this activity is to encourage you to practise careful observation, and also to provide material for a comparison of Frith's painting with the beach scene by the French artist Eugène Boudin (reproduced in Plate 4.4.9), which is discussed below.

Looking at Frith's painting of *Life at the Seaside: Ramsgate Sands*:

1   Try to pick out the imagined viewpoint from which Frith organises the scene as it appears to the spectator.

2   Write brief notes on the basic organisation of the composition. What I have in mind here are the framing of the subject matter; the division of elements into foreground, middle-ground and background; the distribution of the main contrasts of light and dark; and the principal accents of colour.

3   Pick out some of the principal groupings and say what you see as occurring within them.

Discussion   1   Frith wants to present a panoramic view of the assembled holiday-makers crammed on to the sands. As is the habit of people on the beach, they face out to sea. In order to picture them from the front, the artist therefore establishes a viewpoint within the sea as the tide advances up the beach. The effect of the high horizon line is to suggest a high viewpoint, and to emphasise the sense of proximity to the scene while allowing the variety within it to be displayed. (Dropping the horizon line would have the effect of lowering the view into the composition, with the consequence that the foreground figures would obscure the rest.)

2   The harbour wall at left and bathing machines at right frame the edges of the composition, while the municipal buildings, hotel and raised terraces form a kind of backcloth to the scene. (For other views of bathing machines, see Plates 4.4.10 and 4.4.11; the first of these shows horses harnessed ready to tow a machine out into the shallows.) The advancing tide is in the very front of the picture space, while a main cast of characters occupies a broad band across the foreground. Further groups of figures occupy the middle distance, receding from foreground to background and interrupted by passages of unpopulated sand at right and left. A large hut appears in the centre. To the left of this it is possible to make out an empty Punch and Judy booth. The composition is lit from above, as we might expect, with the sun overhead and slightly to left of centre. Between the mid-tone browns and greys of the sand and the buildings, the assembled figures form a darker mass, punctuated by the highlights of white newspapers and women's clothes, and by occasional patches of bright colour, the most notable being provided by the pink and yellow dresses in the foreground group to right of centre.

3   The principal groupings I note in the foreground, reading from left to right, are these: at the far left a woman reading a paper with a man looking over her shoulder and another looking out to sea with a telescope; next a woman under an umbrella surrounded by small children, to whom a kneeling man in a green coat is trying to sell what looks like a Chinese doll, with his hand on the handle of a basket presumably containing other wares; next there are two women accompanying a small child who is being encouraged – if not forced – to paddle (it is notable that this figure and the small girl with a telescope at the far left both appear to look directly out of the picture at the imaginary spectator); then there are a man and a woman sitting together under the same large umbrella; to the right a man reads a newspaper, while what we may assume to be his wife and daughters

attend to a kneeling man with a pair of white mice; next there is a group around a foppish young man lounging on a chair; and finally, at the far right, there is a shy or alarmed young girl hiding her face in her mother's skirts. In the very centre of the middle-ground there is a magician with a hare, while at the far left there is a group of black musicians. The middle distance to the far right is taken up with donkeys and the figures around them and with the bathing machines. This is not an exhaustive list, but if you have noticed most of these you have done very well.

BEACH SCENE, TROUVILLE

The second painting considered in this section (Figure 4.6 and Plate 4.4.9) is by the French artist Eugène Boudin (1824–1898), one of a generation of artists, immediately preceding the Impressionists, who concentrated on landscape themes studied from life in the open air. Probably painted around 1870, *Beach Scene, Trouville* shows fashionably dressed holiday-makers spread out across the sand, with a flagpole to the left of centre of the composition. Boudin is particularly known for his small beach and harbour scenes, many of them painted on the French Channel coast (see also Plate 4.4.10). He provided support and encouragement to the young Claude Monet, whom he met at Le Havre in northern France in 1858. Monet was to be one of the principal members of the Impressionist group, who first exhibited together in 1874. Boudin was also represented in that first exhibition, though he was not to exhibit again with the group. Plate 4.4.12 illustrates a small sketch made in 1870 by Monet on the beach at Trouville in northern France, where Boudin's picture was also painted.

Figure 4.6   Eugène Boudin, *Beach Scene, Trouville. c.*1860–70, oil on wood, 22 x 46 cm. National Gallery, London, NG 6309. Bequeathed by Miss Judith E. Wilson, 1960. Photo: © National Gallery, London.

The figure at the left is Monet's wife and the other figure may well be Madame Boudin. *Beach Scene, Trouville* is one of two pictures by Boudin that may have belonged to Monet. (A further painting of Trouville by Monet is shown in Plate 4.4.13.)

Activity   Make brief notes comparing Boudin's painting (Figure 4.6 and Plate 4.4.9) with Frith's (Plate 4.4.1). I suggest you make your points in the following order:

1   Consider any evident similarities between the two paintings.

2   Note the relative sizes and media (study the captions to these paintings to pick up this information), and consider what these might tell us about the works' intended audience and possible market.

3   Note any obvious differences in technique. By this I mean the way the respective compositions, and particularly the figures, are delineated and the manner in which the paint is applied.

4   Compare the placing of the horizon, the imagined viewpoint (where you, as the spectator of the scene, appear to be placed), and the **angle of vision** into the composition (do you feel as though you are looking in any particular direction, or with any specific focus?).

5   In some pictures the imagined viewpoint of the spectator may carry with it a sense of specific imaginary identity and even emotional attitude. In others, while some impression of mood or atmosphere may still be conveyed, this is something we tend to associate more with the nature of the scene as it is pictured than with any imaginary state of mind. Can you distinguish in this sense between different kinds of viewing that Frith's and Boudin's paintings, respectively, might invite? Such questions are rarely easy to answer, but they can lead to an understanding of the particular means by which paintings convey a sense of mood or emotional effect. For those used to the study of literature, it may help to think of the way in which the narrative voice of a short story or novel can function to convey the sense of a particular observing mind and sensibility at work.

Discussion   Though I offer here much fuller responses than I would expect you to have given, you should not assume that what follows is complete. Nor, of course, is my interpretation of either painting immune to challenge or argument. While certain factual points about works of art can be established beyond dispute, there is always a possibility of disagreement over matters of judgement and interpretation. What matters is that whatever one says should be open to being tested against a careful view of the works in question.

1   Points of similarity include the wide 'landscape' formats and the multi-figure subjects, with groups of figures spread laterally across the picture space; also the use of a marked vertical motif to break the horizon line. It is clear that for both painters the idea of a 'modern' painting depends upon the representation of 'modern life', and this in

turn depends upon the faithful depiction of the urban middle class at leisure in all its assumed finery, with the clothing of fashionably dressed women providing colour and highlights.

2   Boudin's painting is far smaller than Frith's. It is the size and type of painting that could – just plausibly – have been completed in a single session out of doors in front of the scene. That it is painted on a wood panel rather than canvas is consistent with the relative informality of its composition. Where painting on canvas generally requires an easel, a wooden panel can more easily be worked on the painter's lap. While the size of Frith's painting suggests that it is designed for public exhibition, and its detail and variety indicate that it invites prolonged study, Boudin's picture is of a size appropriate to hanging in a private domestic context, where it might add a scenic but undistracting element to the decoration. Though his subject may have much in common with Frith's, Boudin's work seems to have no sense of ambition with respect to art's higher-status genres. In other words, if Frith's painting is intended to build on an academic tradition of history painting, Boudin's relates back to the more modest observations of the Dutch painters such as van de Velde (Figure 4.5 and Plate 4.4.6). Where Frith's work was purchased by royalty, Boudin's would have been quite appropriate as a casual gift to a fellow artist.

3   Despite the smaller size of Boudin's painting, it was executed with a much larger brush than Frith used. The paint was applied in more liquid form, and the technique is much sketchier and looks more spontaneous. While the figures are much less carefully described than Frith's, Boudin appears more concerned to capture a particular quality of light and atmosphere and to convey a sense of the overall appearance of the fashionable costumes, using a much lighter palette overall, with less use of black and with frequent accents of bright colour. It was this technique for providing an atmospheric *impression* of a given scene, rather than a detailed description, that led the French critics in 1874 to label the independent group 'Impressionists' – a title the artists subsequently adopted.

4   The horizon level of Frith's picture is set high and the foreground figures are set close to the front of the composition. The effect is to establish a viewpoint that is close to the picture-plane, looking *into* the scene represented. Boudin's horizon is set very low and the figures are set some distance into the picture space. And – a very important point – where Frith's spectator looks from the sea at the assembled figures facing him or her, Boudin's looks from the beach out to sea, so that the majority of the figures are observed from the back. The effect is to establish a more detached and undiscriminating viewpoint and a more far-reaching gaze.

5   I see Frith's painting as having a kind of narrative voice not unlike that of Dickens, or of other engaged observers of the Victorian social scene. He virtually invites us to weave entertaining stories around the various groupings and incidents that his picture portrays. Boudin's work, on the other hand, is concerned with visual effects and impressions – even

with the bourgeoisie at leisure as a type of sight, and their representation as a kind of decoration – rather than with the possibility of narrative. It is in this sense much further from literature than Frith's, and therefore, perhaps, harder to associate with a particular imagined viewer of the scene depicted. Boudin's spectator is more clearly the spectator of a *painting* and not just of an imaginary scene. Where Frith's picture-plane is transparent, Boudin's never quite separates itself from the literal painted surface.

Despite the industry, ambition and great popularity of his work during his lifetime, Frith did not fare well under the subsequent regime of modernism in criticism and art history. The theories of modernism in art that prevailed for most of the twentieth century were those that tended to look for a significant distinction between art and literature, to disparage the narrative and descriptive as *literary*, and to promote the decorative and expressive as specifically *artistic* virtues. From a modernist perspective, Frith's painting was disqualified by the relative

Figure 4.7   Philip Wilson Steer, *Walberswick, Children Paddling, c.*1889–94, oil on canvas, 64 x 92 cm. Fitzwilliam Museum, Cambridge. Photo: © Fitzwilliam Museum, University of Cambridge/The Bridgeman Art Library. © Tate, London 2007.

conservatism of its technique. For the critic Clive Bell, writing in 1914, 'pictures in the Frith tradition are grown superfluous'. *The Railway Station* (Plate 4.4.4), Bell wrote,

> is not a work of art; it is an interesting and amusing document. In it line and colour are used to recount anecdotes, suggest ideas, and indicate the manners and customs of an age; they are not used to provoke aesthetic emotion. [...] With the perfection of photographic processes and of the cinematograph, [...] pictures of this sort are becoming otiose.
>
> (Bell, 1914, pp. 18–19)

In contrast, and for all the apparent modesty of his representative works, Boudin was hailed as an important precursor of Impressionism – and as a significant contributor to the emancipation of painting from literature, and from sentimental viewpoints on human life, whether of the past or of the present. Where *Life at the Seaside* and *Beach Scene, Trouville* share an interest in the symptomatic appearances of modern life, they treat those appearances in very different ways, and they thus occupy very different positions in the history of modern art.

By way of conclusion, Plates 4.4.14 and 4.4.15 (the latter is reproduced as Figure 4.7) illustrate pictures by two English painters working around the turn of the century, each of whom was then looking principally to recent French art for ideas about how life at the seaside might be represented in paint. What seems to matter here is not the kinds of characters that might be attributed to the pictured figures, but rather what the scenery of the seaside has to offer in the way of painterly effects.

REFERENCES

Arscott, C. (1995) '*Ramsgate Sands*, modern life, and the shoring-up of narrative' in Allen, B. (ed.) *Towards a Modern Art World*, Studies in British Art, vol. 1, New Haven, CN and London, Yale University Press.

Baudelaire, C. (1998 [1846]) *Salon of 1846* in Harrison, C., Wood, P. and Gaiger, J. *Art in Theory 1815–1900*, Oxford, Blackwell.

Bell, C. (1914) *Art*, London, Chatto & Windus.

Dickens, C. (1836) 'The Tuggses at Ramsgate' in *Sketches by Boz*, London, Chapman & Hall.

Frith, W.P. (1887–8) *Autobiography and Reminiscences,* 2 volumes, London, Bentley & Son.

4.3 DRESSING FOR THE BEACH

Lucy Faire

INTRODUCTION

In this section you will examine what people in the late nineteenth and first half of the twentieth centuries wore when they went to the seaside, using photographs and films to help you understand what these clothes actually looked like. You will begin by looking at clothes that people considered to be appropriate for the beach and how what they wore changed between the 1860s and the 1950s. You will then go on to look at changes in bathing costumes. Throughout this section you will consider how clothing differed between men and women, between adults and children, and between the different classes and different generations. You will also need to think about how the seaside acted as a place where people could throw off their inhibitions and evade the normal codes of conduct expected of their class and gender. By the end of this section you will understand more about how people perceived the seaside and how experiences of being on the beach changed between the latter half of the nineteenth century and the 1950s. You will be able to explore the topic further by studying a series of early twentieth-century films on the DVD ROM 'The Seaside'.

PHOTOGRAPHS OF THE BEACH

Photographs are a wonderful source to study something as visual as costume. Photos and films can provide us with images of what people were actually wearing at the seaside and how they wore these clothes. Fashion drawings, on the other hand, show only what people were being *advised* to wear. However, as dress historian Lou Taylor has explained, 'in trying to "read" clothes from photographs some fundamental questions have to be considered. Why was the image taken, by whom, under what conditions, for what audience and for what use?' (Taylor, 2002, p. 163). The professional, and in some cases the amateur, photographer was often trying to produce an image that was aesthetically pleasing or startling. This could result in posed photos of individuals or groups which did not represent actual circumstances. Many of the photographs in the Hulton Archive (a major picture library) are of this kind, taken by professional photographers in the 1940s and 1950s for magazines such as *Picture Post*.

But even if the events recorded did take place, we need to be aware that these tended to be special rather than mundane occasions, and that the people in the photographs may have consented to be photographed only if they felt they looked their best. Of course, for historians, the motivation behind the posed image can be as interesting as whether the picture shows a typical scene. Panoramic views are more reliable at representing what people were actually doing, but with this kind of photograph it is still possible to pick and choose what will be in the frame.

The photograph also exposes the interests of the photographer. For example, many photos of beaches are of groups of young people, particularly young women. Although this might reflect the fact that young adult earners could afford to make their own trips to the coast with friends or as part of a work outing (Fowler, 1995) it might also be that photographers found young women more photogenic. You can get round the problem of representativeness by referring to a variety of different kinds of photograph, just as you would refer to a variety of written sources (Becker, 1979, p. 106).

However, there are aspects of photography that are beyond the photographer's control. The photographer can be confined by accepted ideas of what can be photographed – as you will find later on in this section, photographing ordinary women in swimming costumes around 1900 was surrounded by taboos. Then there are the limitations of film and photography as a medium. The majority of the films and photographs you will look at here are black and white, and it's important to remember that monochrome film makes some very bright colours look dark and dingy (Yearsley, 2004, p. 188).

DRESS AT THE SEASIDE

The late nineteenth century

More information about seaside pasttimes can be found in 'Resort history' on the DVD ROM.

When you look at the photos and films, you will see that dress was evidently important to many people at the seaside. There were two main reasons for this: first, when people went on holiday they liked to feel special; second, the seaside provided ample opportunities to dress up and impress friends and strangers (Walton, 2004, pp. 159–60). Although the promenade was the best place to show off, the beach also had this function, as William Porter explained in his 1865 guide to Blackpool in Lancashire: '[e]very day during the season [the sands] are crowded – at least in the vicinity of Blackpool – with the beauty and fashion of the neighbourhood'. He added that it was possible to see people from all walks of life walking, sitting, reclining and riding 'in every variety of costume along the sands or on the parade above' (Porter, 1865, p. 42). Similarly, the *Keble Gazette* noted in 1886 that at Margate in Kent the jetty was for 'those who desired to exhibit their wardrobes and indulge in a little innocent "mashing"' (Walton, 1983, p. 209). In the 1860s, middle-class and working-class dress would have been quite different, but by the time Sagar Mitchell and James Kenyon filmed Blackpool in the early 1900s there was a 'new democracy of dress', at the seaside at least, because the working class could now afford Sunday and holiday clothes (Walton, 2004, p. 160). So it is apparent that dress codes at the seaside were different from those followed in everyday working life.

'Masher' was slang for a young man dressed in the height of fashion.

Activity   Look at Plates 4.4.22–24 in the Illustration Book, examine the kinds of clothes that people were wearing on the beach in the 1890s and early 1900s and consider the ways that they are different from, and similar to, beachwear today. You should think about the following questions as you do this:

- What is the design of the clothes, and do you get any sense of texture or colour from these pictures?

- Is there any sense of generational difference in what was considered suitable for the beach?

- Is there any evidence that might tell you about the class background of the people in the photos?

- What are people wearing on their heads?

- How much skin is exposed by the clothes?

- Are these posed or panoramic pictures, and what impact do you think this had on how representative each image is?

- Can you tell at what time of year the photos were taken, and what the weather was like?

Discussion   The clothing in the photos is very formal. The men are dressed in suits and ties and are wearing shoes. The women are wearing long dresses or skirts and their arms and heads are covered. The casual dress currently worn at the seaside seems a far cry from the clothes worn here. The lack of flesh seen on the beach can be explained partly by notions of propriety, but it is also because white skin was a status indicator: at this time tanned skin was associated with those who worked outside. The pictures also suggest that there were generational differences in what was acceptable beach dress. Although the child in Plate 4.4.24 is dressed as formally as the grown-ups in the picture, Plate 4.4.22 suggests that this wasn't necessarily representative of all children. Moreover, the women on the panoramic (and thus perhaps more representative) Margate photo (Plate 4.4.23) look more casual than those in the posed Blackpool one, who are dressed in heavy and seemingly dark clothes with ornate hats and fur stoles rather than white blouses and straw hats. The straw hats, on the other hand, still seem formal to us.

Class differences are harder to identify. You could make a good guess that the children in Plate 4.4.22 and the child in Plate 4.4.24 are middle or upper class, because at this time working-class families with young children generally could not afford to go to the seaside. The class of people in Plate 4.4.23 is much harder to guess at. It's also difficult to know the time of year when the Blackpool photo was taken. Are the clothes so thick and heavy because it was cold, or are they a sign of affluence? If the former was the case, then some of the differences between the Margate photo and the Blackpool one might be to do with weather conditions as much as differences between the ages and class of the people depicted.

Propriety partly explains the formal look of the clothes, but this formality was also because people wanted to feel and look good while on holiday – although working-class people, at least, were constrained by income. They often had to choose between wearing their Sunday best and their work clothes, and few wanted to wear the latter during their hours of leisure. However, because the suit was worn in leisure time, it didn't have the negative work-related connotations it has today. The children in Plate 4.4.22 were probably middle class. If so, their normal dress code had been suspended because bare feet (among the working class at least) were a sign of poverty.

Figure 4.8   Family holiday, 1930. Unknown photographer. Photo: Fox Photos/Getty Images.

The inter-war period

During the inter-war period clothing became more casual, but people still dressed to impress. In his autobiography, describing his life in Brighton on the Sussex coast, Leonard Goldman's memories of women's seaside dress from the 1920s illustrate this well: 'The young women ... wore short, knee-length dresses and skirts, with flowered designs of silky material. And those high heels.' The young men were equally frivolous, with 'enormously wide Oxford bags [trousers], some with bow ties and often wearing blue blazers, [and] shod in

Figure 4.10   Girl in two-piece swimming costume, Blackpool beach, *c*.1946–55. Photographed by John Gray. Photo: Reproduced by permission of English Heritage/ NMR.

BATHING AT THE SEASIDE

In the early years of the nineteenth century most people bathed naked. The exceptions were women of the middle and upper class. Middle-and upper-class men swam naked because it was believed you only got the full benefit of the sea if you were naked and that to wear 'drawers' was effeminate. Working-class men (and women) swam naked because they had no choice – they could not afford costumes. Given that when people were on the beach they were reluctant to show any flesh, even their feet, it seems strange that they were so insistent on swimming naked. Throughout the nineteenth century commentators on sea-bathing noted this inconsistency, pointing out that participants were happy to show parts of the body they would not have dreamed of revealing when away from the water. This attitude lingered until after 1918.

Traditionally, historians have assumed that the practice of men bathing naked disappeared during the nineteenth century, and especially after the 1860s when resorts introduced by-laws banning naked bathing. However, male nude bathing continued right up to the 1890s but was often confined either to the edges of a resort or to times of the day when the least number of people would be offended, such as before 7 o'clock in the morning (Travis, 1997, p. 23). Sometimes this meant that those who wanted to swim naked between the hours of 7 a.m. and 9 p.m. had to join the working class on their beach, as was the case at Scarborough in North Yorkshire (Travis, 1997, p. 19).

As the nineteenth century progressed, men swimming naked were increasingly a cause for concern. One way to solve this problem was by segregating men's and women's bathing areas. In early nineteenth-century Blackpool, the solution was for them to bathe in the sea at different times. The men had to leave the beach when a bell was rung so that women could come and bathe, and vice versa (Porter, 1865, p. 42). More common, especially in the second half of the nineteenth century 'because of bathing machines and bathing dresses' (Porter, 1865, pp. 41–2), was to designate a section of the beach to each sex, with a specified distance between the two. For example, at Southport in Lancashire a fine of 5 shillings was imposed on any pleasure boat which came within 30 yards (27 metres) of the ladies' swimming area, and the men's and ladies' swimming machines had to have at least 100 yards (90 metres) between them (Pimlott, 1947, p. 130). Bathing machines were considered another way of preserving modesty, although ironically the attendants were often men.

Bathing machines were mobile changing rooms which could be wheeled down to the sea.

The segregation of bathing beaches on gender lines continued in many places up to the 1900s, though once in the water it was hard to stop the different sexes mingling. By this time the bathing machines were going out of fashion in places like Minehead in Somerset where 'mixed bathing' was allowed. The town's 1905 guidebook noted that 'many prefer their own tents' (*Minehead*, 1905, p. 26). The reintroduction of mixed swimming put paid to most naked bathing, since most men found the former a greater lure.

However, young working-class men continued to swim naked because, as we noted above, the working class could afford only a limited number of clothes. Because many working-class people simply could not afford costumes, local legislation against naked swimming was often viewed as an attack on working-class sea-bathing. These laws should not, however, be taken as a reflection of what actually happened. They were often not enforced and there continued to be complaints until the end of the century about young working-class men ignoring the rules and swimming naked as they had done for centuries (Travis, 1997, p. 30).

Victorian middle-class women wore a bathing costume which was a long flannel gown tied around the neck but loose at the bottom. These costumes were almost impossible to swim in and meant segregation was necessary because of their tendency to billow up when in the water (Travis, 1997, p. 16). Since nothing was worn under the gown, it could be very revealing. In France, women's bathing clothes were

Figure 4.11   Mixed bathing, youngsters in the Thames at Weybridge (Surrey), 1914. Unknown photographer. Photo: Topical Press Agency/Getty Images.

more practical. In the 1860s John Hulley, the vice-president of the Athletic Society of Great Britain, wrote to *The Times* from Biarritz urging Britain to adopt similar costumes for men and women, thereby ensuring that families could bathe together on the beach (Hulley, 1864). He described French men as wearing loose, baggy trousers with a matching 'garibaldi' (a shirt of some kind), while the women wore a 'bloomer costume' consisting of trousers down to the ankle and a jacket. The latter certainly had the advantage of not ending up around the neck and, because men and women swam together, husbands were able to teach their wives and children to swim.

Swimming costumes did start to appear in Britain during the later decades of the nineteenth century: a Scotsman visiting the Dorset resort of Bournemouth in 1885 noted that there was unofficial mixed bathing in costumes (Walton, 1983, p. 193). At this time, and into the twentieth century, women's costumes were made of heavy serge covering most of the arms and legs, with an additional skirt for

Figure 4.12   Bathers pose on the beach, Shanklin, Isle of Wight, 1926. Unknown photographer. Photo: Central Press/Getty Images.

modesty. It is very difficult to find images of these early costumes because it wasn't acceptable to photograph 'decent' women in swimsuits: such images were 'confined to "pin-up" postcards' (Horwood, 2000, p. 657).

However, by 1913 'figure hugging female costumes' had arrived, selling as well as 'elaborate skirted costumes' (Horwood, 2000, p. 658). Figure 4.11 illustrates Horwood's findings that by 1914 women, or in this case girls, were now wearing both old and new kinds of swimming costumes, the older ones including superfluous collars and braiding. By the 1920s, as Figure 4.12 demonstrates, the figure-hugging costume was definitely 'in': it covered up quite a bit of flesh yet could be very revealing. This change was noted in a 1920 article in the *Daily Mail* which commented that 'skirted costumes are scarcely to be seen', demonstrating, the paper thought, a lack of 'modesty' among the crowds at Southsea in Hampshire (Horwood, 2000, p. 660).

Figure 4.13 'Waves by the sea', a group of tourists on the breakwater in Eastbourne (Sussex), 1930. Photographed by W.G.Phillips. Photo ©: W.G. Phillips/Getty Images.

Activity

At the end of this section, you will be asked to do a similar activity using films on the DVD ROM.

Look at Figures 4.13 and 4.14 and assess the main changes in swimwear between 1930 and 1955. You might like to make a note of the following as you do this:

- any pattern or adornment on the costume
- how much of the torso is exposed.

Discussion

The men and women in Figure 4.13 are wearing costumes of a similar design – with rounded necks and covering the tops of their thighs. The photographs show a substantial shift in costume style between 1930 and 1955. In the later photo one of the women is wearing a bikini-style costume, while the other wears a swimsuit which exposes all of her legs. Both costumes have a distinct pattern and one is made of a very light-coloured fabric.

In the 1920s men's and women's costumes were very similar – especially now that the skirt had been abandoned. Figure 4.13 suggests that these similarities remained into the 1930s. As Horwood has

Figure 4.14   Beach models, 1955. Photographed by Judy Lambert. Photo: Lambert/Getty Images.

explained, 'This was one of the rare occasions where male and female dress combined to create one of the first truly "unisex" garments' (Horwood, 2000, p. 662). However, the unisex nature of swimming costumes did not last long.

Leonard Goldman remembers the new-style cut-away costumes appearing in Brighton in the 1920s and explains that these 'new styles were expensive and had to be saved for over a long period', but they 'gave one greater freedom of movement, and, of course, greater exposure to the sun' (Goldman, 1997, p. 67). He adds that nobody, not even men, was allowed to go topless on the beach. Horwood argues that in 1934 there was a new trend for men to roll down their swimming costumes to their waists (Horwood, 2000, p. 664). Figure 4.8 suggests a slightly earlier date for this change for some men and boys. For women the biggest change was the two-piece swimsuit, officially named the bikini in 1946, which had a strong influence on swimwear.

SUMMARY

As you have seen, in the period we have looked at, and especially during the twentieth century, there was a shift from wearing formal 'best' or smart clothes on the beach, to wearing more informal clothes which exposed more of the body. While formal clothes may seem restrictive to people today, wearing the Sunday best was previously seen as liberating for the working class because it meant that you weren't at work. Swimwear has followed a slightly different pattern, in that during the early decades of the twentieth century swimming costumes covered up far more than the swimwear of the Victorian period, at least for men. Middle-class women have gradually felt able to expose more of their bodies, but it is interesting that for the first thirty years of the twentieth century there was equality in what men and women were expected to cover up. This shows that changes in clothing have not moved in a consistent direction, but reflect a whole host of shifts in attitudes and experiences.

Activity
You should allow about an hour to complete this activity.

Now turn to the DVD ROM 'The Seaside' and work through the section 'The seaside on film'.

REFERENCES

Becker, H.S. (1979) 'Do photographs tell the truth?' in Cook, T.D. and Reichardt, C.S. (eds) *Qualitative and Quantitative Methods in Evaluation Research*, Beverly Hills, CA and London, Sage.

Fowler, D. (1995) *The First Teenagers: The Lifestyle of Young Wage-Earners in Interwar Britain*, Ilford, Woburn Press.

Goldman, L. (1997) *Oh What a Lovely Shore: Brighton in the Twenties through the Eyes of a Schoolboy*, Brighton, The Author.

Harrisson, T. (1961) *Britain Revisited*, London, Victor Gollancz.

Horwood, C. (2000) '"Girls who arouse dangerous passions": women and bathing, 1900–1939', *Women's History Review*, vol. 9, no. 4, pp. 653–73.

Hulley, J. (1864) letter to *The Times*, 6 August.

Minehead (1905) Minehead, Cox and Sons.

Pimlott, J.A.R. (1947) *The Englishman's Holiday: A Social History*, London, Faber and Faber.

Porter, W. (1865) *Porter's Guide and Visitors' Companion to Blackpool, Fleetwood, Lytham, Etc., Together with a Map of the Fylde District*, Blackpool and Fleetwood, William Porter.

Taylor, L. (2002) *The Study of Dress History*, Manchester, Manchester University Press.

Travis, J. (1997) 'Continuity and change in English sea-bathing, 1730–1900: a case of swimming with the tide' in Fisher, S. (ed.) *Recreation and the Sea*, Exeter, Exeter University Press.

Walton, J.K. (1983) *The English Seaside Resort: A Social History 1750–1914*, Leicester, Leicester University Press.

Walton, J.K. (2004) 'The seaside and the holiday crowd' in Toulmin, V., Russell, P. and Topple, S. (eds) *The Lost World of Mitchell and Kenyon: Edwardian Britain on Film*, London, British Film Institute.

Yearsley, I. (2004) 'On the move in the streets: transport films and the Mitchell and Kenyon collection' in Toulmin, V., Russell, P. and Topple, S. (eds) *The Lost World of Mitchell and Kenyon: Edwardian Britain on Film*, London, British Film Institute.

FURTHER READING

Harrison, B. (1994) 'Photographs' in Catterall, P. and Jones, H. (eds) *Understanding Documents and Sources*, Oxford, Heinemann.

Probert, C. (1981) *Swimwear in Vogue*, London, Thames and Hudson.

Walton, J.K. (1998) *Blackpool*, Edinburgh, Edinburgh University Press.

Walton, J.K. (2000) *The British Seaside Holiday: Holidays and Resorts in the Twentieth Century*, Manchester, Manchester University Press.

Walvin, J. (1978) *Leisure and Society 1830–1950*, London, Longman.

4.4 TECHNOLOGY AND THE SEASIDE: BLACKPOOL AND BENIDORM

Colin Chant

BLACKPOOL

Introduction

The year 1840 was a pivotal one in the history of the British seaside. It was a time of railway fever, ten years after the opening of the world's first passenger railway between Liverpool and Manchester in north-west England. Part of the rush of construction was a new branch in north Lancashire, running from the mainline station of Preston to Fleetwood at the mouth of the River Wyre. Fleetwood was the first Victorian **new town**– a commercial port and resort, which the line's promoters also envisioned as a railhead for crossings to Ireland, Scotland and the Isle of Man. However, the line's consequences would be far from its sponsors' intentions. One of the intermediate stations at the market town of Poulton-le-Fylde happened to be some four miles east of the resort of Blackpool, at that time a backwater of some 1,000 residents. A distance of four miles was nothing to the Lancashire working folk of the time, some of whom – the so-called **Padjamers** – would make an annual trek to Blackpool, on foot or by cart, over the 20 miles or so from Preston, and the textile towns beyond (Thornber, 1985, pp. 223–5). Their goal was to bathe and drink seawater on 'Bathing Sunday', in celebration of the mid-August high tides. The railway helped turn this very particular working-class beach festival into an entire season of seaside trips for working people from the north of England, the Midlands and north Wales.

Over the half-century and more before the dawn of the railway age, Blackpool emerged as a minor sea-bathing resort equipped with a grassy promenade, several hotels – some with assembly rooms and warm and vapour baths – a library, billiard rooms and a makeshift theatre (Walton, 1998, p. 19). The resort's customary clientele of a few hundred Lancashire and Yorkshire professionals, merchants, manufacturers and retailers were taken aback by the rising tide of working-class excursionists, with their boisterous beach culture, rooted in popular traditions of drinking, dancing and the fairground. They were especially appalled by the trippers' Sabbath-breaking and nude bathing, or bathing without recourse to machines – but money talked, and a rail extension from Poulton to Blackpool itself followed in 1846. The *Preston Pilot* in 1851 glumly predicted that Blackpool property would be 'depreciated past recovery' (quoted in Walton, 1983, p. 38). As it turned out, catering for the working masses would make Blackpool a lucrative boom town: 'the world's first working-class seaside resort' (Walton, 1998, p. 11).

This was the beginning of the reconstruction of the seaside experience as pure fun and entertainment. As you already know, the British leisured classes originally embraced the seaside as a place of work and self-improvement. For working people seeking relief from the rigours of industrial labour, the pursuit of pleasure would outweigh the quest

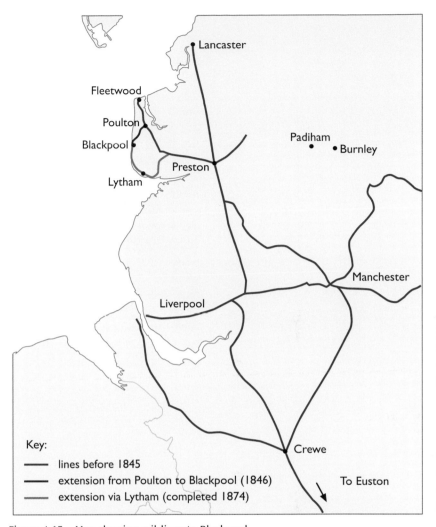

Figure 4.15   Map showing rail lines to Blackpool.

for physical and moral edification. As a social historian of technology, I am interested first and foremost in the contribution of technological innovation to this cultural transformation of the seaside. In this section I shall discuss the changing cultures of the seaside, with particular reference to Blackpool as the world's first working-class resort, and consider the contribution of technological innovation to these changes. Through this study, together with the section on Benidorm, I shall explore the relationship between technologies and a range of historical contexts.

In the case of Blackpool, technological change was clearly instrumental in focusing opposing cultural forces onto the seaside. It was through the railway that the beach became a 'crucible of conflict between classes and lifestyles' (Walton, 1983, p. 3). Before the railway, the select nature of the resort had been guaranteed by the limitations of the roads, among which, as Blackpool's first historian complained, was a lack of milestones (Hutton, 1789, p. 9); and then by the cost of the stagecoach service from Preston that started in 1781.

The advent of the railway helped break down these social, economic and physical barriers to the beach.

Railways were only the most immediate of the technological influences on seaside resorts. They were the product of another original British process, the economic and technological changes commonly dramatised as the **Industrial Revolution**. Although the pace of these 'revolutionary' changes notably quickened from the 1770s onwards, they actually took more than a century to unfold. They hinged upon the mechanisation of manufacturing processes, a complex set of developments unlocking the potential of Britain's natural endowment of coal and iron. The literal driving force of the new technological and economic order was the steam engine. This device began by draining the mines; it was then applied to textile mills, engineering plant and ironworks before setting steamships and then railway locomotives in motion. Iron and then steel became available in unprecedented quantities during the nineteenth century: as structural materials they altered the face of urban Britain, including its resorts. During the second half of the nineteenth century, the power of steam generators was translated into commercial applications of electric energy, including electric lighting and electric tramways, both of which were seized upon by ambitious seaside resorts.

Figure 4.16   Blackpool's North Pier, Tower and Gigantic Wheel, c.1925. Unknown photographer. Photo courtesy of Leisure Parcs.

Activity   Consider Figure 4.16. What evidence is there of the technological innovations listed above in this photo of Blackpool's early twentieth-century urban face?

Discussion   Many of you will have recognised the metal Tower, Blackpool's iconic imitation of the Eiffel Tower. Less familiar will be another great metal structure anticipating the London Eye: Blackpool's Gigantic Wheel. You may have spotted the electric lights on the North Pier, although the metalwork supporting the structure is mostly hidden in this view – more on this later.

My emphasis thus far has been on the influence of technological innovations on the development of British seaside resorts. But, like all social historians of technology, I would stress that the relationships between technological and social change are complex and interactive. To put it another way, a given technology can only be influential within favourable *contexts* of various kinds: cultural, economic, political, environmental, and so on. The Industrial Revolution itself demonstrates the complexity of the relationship between technological and social change. It brought with it wholesale changes in the balance and boundaries between work and leisure. Among the causes of these social and economic changes was the adoption of innovative industrial technologies; but these changes in their turn prepared the ground for the adoption of subsequent innovations, not least the technologies of the new industrialised seaside resort of Blackpool.

Let's consider some of the contexts of these innovations – you might try to categorise them as you read on. From the late eighteenth century onwards, millions of Britons moved from agricultural villages into fast-growing industrial towns and cities. Throughout the nineteenth century and well into the twentieth, life in the rapidly growing industrial cities could be punishing, even more so than the agricultural toil and squalid country cottages the migrants left behind. The drudgery and disciplines of labour in workshop, factory, mine and dock, in combination with the cramped squalor of jerry-built housing, surely fostered a craving for escape and relief (see Figure 4.17). In Lancashire this release was afforded not only in the Padjamers' annual forays to the beach, but more widely in the Wakes Week celebrations. Originally a pagan festival, this came to acquire Christian trappings, though for working people it signified a sanctioned break from work, and the fun of the fairground and alehouse. Mill owners accepted the tradition, if sometimes grudgingly. From the 1840s, the Wakes Week came to incorporate one or possibly two rail excursions to the seaside. By the late nineteenth century, urban working people – particularly those employed in the thriving textile towns of Lancashire and Yorkshire – had enough by way of surplus earnings and time off work (albeit unpaid) to take an entire week away at the seaside. As the timing of Wakes Weeks differed from town to town, the transfer of this popular tradition by rail to the seaside provided the backbone of Blackpool's entire summer season (Poole, 1984). Thus we see that the rise of Blackpool as a popular commercialised resort was enabled by the technology of the railways, but also that this technology could only be effective within a range of demographic, industrial, urban and cultural contexts.

Figure 4.17   Unknown artist, Blackpool postcard, *c.*1918. From the collection of Fred Gray. Taken from his book *Designing the Seaside: Architecture, Society and Nature*, London, 2006.

Mass movement

Having stressed that the history of any given technology must be understood within its various contexts, I shall now explore further the influence of technological innovation on the British seaside. Although the arrival of the railway was a turning point in Blackpool's history, it was not the first industrial mode of transport to affect British resorts. The pioneers were the paddle-steamer companies. Starting in 1812 with a service from Glasgow to the resort of Helensburgh on the Firth of Clyde in south-west Scotland, paddle-steamers rapidly proliferated throughout Britain, bearing excursionists and holiday-makers from London to resorts on the Thames and Kent shores, from south Wales across the Bristol Channel; and from the English mainland to the Isle of Wight and Isle of Man. However, once a national railway network had been established in the 1840s, faster locomotives largely displaced the steamers.

Throughout the land, resort growth followed hard on the establishment of a railway connection. Services to coastal resorts were one of the growth areas of railway enterprise in the late nineteenth and early twentieth centuries, and were often marketed with a gusto reflecting the development of a commercial, consumer-orientated economy at this time (see Plate 4.4.25 in the Illustration Book). But in the middle decades of the nineteenth century, resorts were seen as seasonal and prey to changing fashion. Railway companies were generally unenthusiastic carriers of working-class passengers, preferring the more lucrative return on their middle-class clientele. As we have seen, the remarkable growth of traffic to Blackpool was an unintended consequence of the construction of the Preston and Wyre Railway in 1840. The subsequent proprietors of the line, the Yorkshire and Lancashire Railway, had a reputation for inferior rolling stock and unpunctuality in their service to Blackpool; it was as though they were dragged along by an unexpected demand for travel to the resort, rather than leading it.

In keeping with the competitive temper of Victorian railway enterprise, which commonly resulted in the duplication of services, another line was subsequently laid to the resort from Preston by way of the upmarket resort of Lytham to Blackpool's south. However, the target of the promoters was not the holiday excursion business, but the carriage of agricultural produce. The town now had two separate termini, the original station in Talbot Road and a new one at Hounds Hill, the pair later known as Blackpool North and Blackpool Central. Around the turn of the century, the railway companies woke up to the potential of their market, and invested heavily in station facilities and excursion sidings (see Figure 4.18). This was just as well: on an August Saturday in 1910, 200 trains delivered 92,000 holiday-makers to the town (Richards and MacKenzie, 1986, p. 311). The railway termini also acted as nodes of development within the resort. Stalls and amusements clustered in the stretch between the Central station and the Central Pier – what would become known from the 1920s onwards as Blackpool's 'Golden Mile'. The streets around the stations also became filled with three- and four-storey guest-houses, much extended to their rear in order to accommodate the vast increase in holiday-makers. The railways were certainly busy: in the period 1865–1913, when Blackpool became a popular, industrialised resort, annual visitor numbers increased from 285,000 to 3,850,000 (Walton, 1998, pp. 2, 47).

Figure 4.18   Crowds arrive at Blackpool Central railway station, 1937. Photographed by Reuben Saidman. Photo: © NMeM Daily Herald Archive/Science and Society Picture Library.

Within industrial Britain's rapidly growing towns and cities, increased demand for mobility was initially met by descendants of the traditional horse-drawn carriage or cart – the very means by which the wealthy had made their way to the exclusive seaside resorts of the eighteenth century. It was only near the end of the nineteenth century that electric power facilitated the near-wholesale mechanisation of urban transport. In Britain, seaside resorts led the way. In 1885 Blackpool became the first town in Britain to operate an electric tramway as regular public transport. The local authority soon took it over and added suburban lines to the original route along the promenade. The technology and economics of the electric tramways were well suited to the compactness of industrial cities, an urban feature that had only intensified through development around the new railheads. Most of the original tramways were scrapped in the middle decades of the twentieth century, as planners and local authorities deemed them obsolete in a less dense, motorised world; Blackpool's pioneering vehicles, however, have continued as a sort of working tramway museum, part of the resort's tourist apparatus.

<table>
<tr><td>Activity</td><td>It should be clear by now that mechanised transport was essential to the rise of the popular seaside resort. Technology, however, can only be influential within favourable contexts. Which contexts might be relevant here?</td></tr>
<tr><td>Discussion</td><td>Social and economic considerations – such as increased spending power and leisure time – are evidently necessary in explaining the rapid growth of paddle-steamer and railway services to resorts, and in the subsequent investment in mechanised public transport within resorts. There seems to have been a great deal of potential demand for travel that was unlocked by transport innovations, even though the transport companies themselves were sometimes slow or reluctant to exploit it. When they did, they made full use of the marketing instruments of the new commercial world of late Victorian Britain. Finally, the survival of Blackpool's trams only makes sense in the context of a tourist economy.</td></tr>
</table>

There is no denying the huge influence on Blackpool – not least its developing urban form – of the adoption of mechanised transport, including its electric tramway system. But there is clearly nothing in the technology of the railways that directs passengers to the coast, or determines the kind of holiday that follows; the point is reinforced by the indifference to Blackpool's holiday trade displayed by the original promoters of the resort's railway lines. Mechanised transport was a necessary ingredient in the causal mix that explains the rise of the popular seaside resort; but an equally important ingredient was existing traditions of popular culture. The railway did no more than facilitate the transfer of these traditions to the seaside.

Industrialising the seaside: Blackpool

Mechanised transport brought many hitherto exclusive seaside resorts within the spatial and financial reach of the middle and working classes in turn. In an age of entrepreneurs, the greater spending power of the new holiday-makers created a business opportunity. It was exploited increasingly by transferring into the leisure domain some of the technologies that had proved their value in the world of industrial production. It is difficult to say which contributed most to the industrialisation of Blackpool: the extension of a vigorous working-class culture originating in the annual forays of the 'Padjamers', or the subsequent commercial drive of holiday entrepreneurs and the local authority to exploit it. It was during the 1860s that the resort's business and civic leaders changed from a policy of containing the perceived excesses of working-class excursionists to one of actively investing in the town's popular appeal. This was achieved by a partnership between entrepreneurs, who constructed Blackpool's increasing array of artificial attractions, and the local authority (among whose councillors the holiday industry was well represented) which took increasing responsibility for infrastructure: the promenade and sea defences, lighting and urban transport.

You can read more about piers in 'Resort history' and 'Virtual resort' on the DVD ROM.

Apart from the railway stations, another kind of transport terminus made its mark on the town's built environment. These were its piers, structures that proliferated on the coastline of England and Wales during the nineteenth century. The first piers were usually made of wood, and were functional transport termini, relieving steamboat passengers of the trouble of transferring to a rowing boat, or even onto the shoulders of a porter, in order to reach the shore. The advent of the railways reduced the steamboat operators to purveyors of pleasure trips. Piers served this more limited purpose, though the excursion business alone could hardly have sustained their upkeep. What saved seaside piers was their unplanned commercial value as a safely exciting promenade out over the sea. An entrance fee could be charged, and various entertainments provided to lighten the strollers' purses further. Ironically, by the time the railways were killing piers off as functional transport interchanges, designers of the new pleasure piers were adapting the technology of railway installations, manufacturing their supporting piles, girders and bracing from cast and wrought iron (Adamson, 1977; Bainbridge, 1986; Fischer, 1987). Blackpool's North Pier was opened ceremoniously in 1863 as a bespoke pleasure pier: a two-penny charge was levied, in the vain hope that this would discourage the day-trippers. These unwelcome day-trippers would be lured away by a second pier: 'the first major commitment of resources to pleasing this more plebeian public' (Walton, 1998, p. 39). The South Jetty, now known as the Central Pier, opened in 1868 and was soon offering cheap steamer trips and all-day dancing. The North Pier reaffirmed its upmarket status through the acquisition of an Indian Pavilion and an orchestra. The current South Pier was opened in 1893 as the Victoria Pier – like the North Pier, an upmarket enterprise on which dancing was banned – giving the front an unprecedented triple hand of these iconic British seaside structures.

As well as in the piers, railway engineering and architecture were evident in the iron-and-glass vaults of the Winter Gardens, opened in 1878. This structure, with its conservatories and promenades (see Figure 4.19), was initially aimed at the more middle-class holiday-maker, but from the late 1880s it went with the resort's popular trend, providing music-hall entertainment and dancing in the Empress Ballroom. The industrialisation of Blackpool was at its most intense around the turn of the century. In 1894, the iconic Tower was opened, and the great Tower Ballroom appeared beneath it five years later. The Tower was built to emulate Eiffel's Parisian showpiece of 1889, and whatever its merits it managed to outlast a clutch of other such

Figure 4.19   Unknown artist, 'The Pavilion at the Winter Gardens', taken from the *New Album of Blackpool and St Annes Views, c.*1900. From the collection of John Walton.

imitations in English resorts (Walton, 1994). The year 1896 saw the opening of the Alhambra palace of varieties next to the Tower, and the Gigantic Wheel, a 1000-ton steel structure that foreshadowed the London Eye. The Anglo-American South Beach funfair opened in the early twentieth century, and soon boasted the Sir Hiram Maxim Captive Flying Machine, which still operates (see Figure 4.20). The South Beach was an enterprise that drew investors from London and the United States, as Blackpool looked across the Atlantic to high-tech resorts such as Coney Island in New York state. Moreover, the local authority had not been slow to recognise the attraction to visitors of electric lighting: one of the first places in Britain to light up in this way was the North Pier, in 1879. Some years of technological and entrepreneurial development later, electricity was shrewdly deployed to extend the holiday season further: the famous Illuminations were first switched on in 1912 (Plates 4.4.26 and 4.4.27). Technological innovation was now to be celebrated, and used to promote resorts as well as to develop them. The industrialised seaside town became almost the antithesis of the traditional resort offering an escape from an industrialising world. Instead, the civic leaders and commercial entrepreneurs of the new resorts developed a built environment bearing witness to another kind of industry.

We have seen that as new modes of transport, power and construction entered into the holiday, and partly reconstituted it, the holiday itself became to some extent industrialised. Is there something paradoxical in this? To start with, steam-based technology as a mode of transport

Figure 4.20   General view of Blackpool, 1913. Unknown photographer. The Captive Flying Machine is clearly visible in the top left quadrant. The cars were suspended from the structure's arms, and spun round.

allowed industrial workers temporary relief from steam-based technology as manufacture. However, resorts such as Blackpool became less of a refuge from the industrial town and city, as they themselves were changed for good by the very processes of industrialisation and urbanisation that had propelled working-class holiday-makers to their beaches.

Activity   Was the industrialisation of the seaside resort therefore a self-defeating process? Do you see any problems with this line of reasoning?

Discussion   You might find the premises of the conclusion questionable. Perhaps the conception of the seaside resort as a refuge from urban-industrial living is a middle-class rather than a working-class view of leisure. It might in any case be more applicable to the earlier stages of industrialisation. Later on, conditions in industrial cities improved somewhat and there is no denying that the popular appeal of Blackpool increased massively. Seaside technology was giving people what they wanted.

Activity   You have seen how Blackpool rode a wave of technological innovations to become the most popular British resort of the twentieth century. Did the Industrial Revolution *create* Blackpool? If not, how would you put the relationship into words?

Discussion   I hope that you felt that 'creation' was an overstatement of the causal power of technology and its sponsors. I said at the beginning of this section that the railway was instrumental in Blackpool's reconstruction. You might well agree by now that it can hardly be seen as the prime cause. The resort's transformation into a popular playground says as much about changing culture as changing technologies.

In a short section like this, more questions are raised than answered. Was the pioneering industrial seaside resort of Blackpool representative? Did it give a lead that other resorts followed, or was it an exception to the British seaside norm? I shall leave those questions for your own consideration. It is clear, however, that even if technological innovations were turned to Blackpool's peculiar advantage during its heyday, they were insufficient to guarantee its long-term prosperity or that of British resorts in general. I shall next discuss the innovations that underlay Blackpool's latter-day decline.

FLIGHT TO SPAIN

Introduction: the globalisation of the seaside holiday

During the second half of the twentieth century, the seaside holiday habit spread across the world, a trend led by affluent Caucasians seeking the new status symbol of a sun-tanned skin. The horizons of the pioneering British beachcomber duly expanded beyond their own coastline, across the Channel to the Atlantic coast, to the Mediterranean, and on to North Africa, the Caribbean and South Asia. As in the earlier section on Blackpool, my focus here will be the contribution of technological innovations to this phenomenon. Again, I shall argue that technological innovations are essential to our understanding of the historical development of the seaside holiday, but that they are only part of a complex causal mix and need to be understood in relation to a variety of historical contexts. I hope that as you read, you will compare and contrast Blackpool and Benidorm as popular seaside resorts developing within distinctive technological and cultural contexts.

Let's pause and consider the various influences other than technological changes – economic, social or cultural – that might help explain the migration of the seaside holiday-maker to foreign shores. Among the possibilities that occurred to me are rising living standards after the Second World War and further increases in leisure time. Under changing cultural attitudes – apart from the new fashion for sunbathing mentioned at the outset – you might have included a lessening of traditional British insularity. Those of you who know something about the Second World War might point out that it increased Britons' exposure to foreign influences, both at home and abroad. Improved educational opportunities after the war may also have diminished fear of foreign languages; on the other hand, and perhaps more important, doggedly monoglot Britons have benefited from the establishment of English as the lingua franca of the contemporary era of global communications. And what of all the space in the print and visual media devoted to foreign holidays – is that cause or effect?

The motorisation of the British seaside

The transition from the Blackpool guest-house to the Mediterranean high-rise hotel was gradual. In between, the British seaside holiday itself was transformed. The most influential technological innovation in this process was the internal combustion engine, an invention of the 1860s. The efficiency and versatility of the new engine facilitated a variety of transport modes, both public and private, which were much less restricted in space than the track-bound locomotive or tram. These injected much greater flexibility and personal choice into everyday life in general and the field of holiday play in particular.

The majority of Britons first experienced motorisation in the communal forms of the motorbus and coach. Buses entered the seaside transport network as feeders from railway stations to outlying resorts, but coaches and **charabancs** soon entered into direct competition with the railways, helping to bring fares down and further democratising access to the seaside. The 'chara' trip was often organised on a works basis, and thereby carried on in miniature the Wakes Week tradition of communal enjoyment within the context of a stable group identity (Walvin, 1978, pp. 111–12). It also entered into the seaside holiday itself: at Blackpool, the novelty of charabanc trips to the Lake District reinforced the decline of the steamboat pleasure trip (Walton, 1998, p. 113).

The private motor car was much more radical in its effects on the seaside. It was clearly a more individualistic or family-based mode of transport. Its rise during the inter-war years gave middle-class holiday-makers more options, such as touring, camping, caravanning and picnicking. In these ways, the costs of motoring could be offset against the reduced outlay on accommodation and eating out. From the 1950s private motoring came within the reach of the working classes, who were thereby better able to resist the restrictive regime that the Blackpool guest-house landlady was reputed to impose upon the train-borne holiday-maker (Walton, 1978; O'Connell, 1998).

You read about the planning of Milton Keynes in Chapter 2, Section 2.4.

Motorisation reworked the physical form of resorts, as happened in all urban settlements throughout the twentieth century. Where geography allowed, resorts tended to sprawl outwards in a ribbon of development along the seashore or approach roads. A constant challenge in the planning of established towns and resorts was the need to adapt compact nineteenth-century development around railway termini to the land hunger of the motor car – not for them the tidy system of grid roads devised by the car-friendly planners of Milton Keynes. Blackpool already had a multi-storey car park in 1939, with 1000 spaces (Walton, 1998, p. 132). After the drastic reduction of the national railway network that began in the 1960s, disused railway sidings and engine sheds were often used to accommodate cars. Blackpool Central station was closed in 1964, and the land behind converted to car parks and roads. These roads linked up in 1975 with the resort's 'new lifeline' of the motor age: the M55 motorway (Walton, 2000, pp. 81, 89).

Benidorm: Blackpool by the Med?

The effects of motor transport in Britain's resorts were enormous, but the impact of another hugely influential twentieth-century transport innovation – the aeroplane – was potentially terminal. British resorts now had to compete with cheap holiday packages based on air travel, translating the essentials of the British seaside holiday into 'sun, sea and Sangria' on the shores of the Mediterranean. Again, it was the relative lightness of the internal combustion engine that first made powered flight possible. As early as 1928 during the era of propeller-driven aircraft, Imperial Airways launched a *de luxe* winter package tour of the Mediterranean. But it took a further development in aviation technology, the jet engine, to bring the cost of air travel within the compass of working people, starting in the late 1950s (Lyth and Dierikx, 1994; Lyth, 2002).

Just as Blackpool was the emblematic holiday resort of the railway age, Benidorm on Spain's Costa Blanca stands in the British imagination for the later twentieth-century package of air travel, coach transfer and half-board hotel accommodation. The resort is sometimes portrayed as the creation of British tour operators (Williams, 1996); indeed, the very notion of the 'Costa Blanca' has been portrayed as the brainchild of British European Airways (Bray and Raitz, 2001, p. 49). In response to these perceptions, the Spanish have justifiably insisted on the priority of indigenous officials and entrepreneurs in the resort's development (Wilson, 1999).

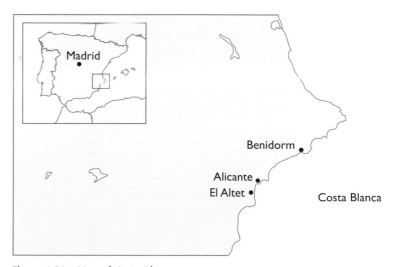

Figure 4.21 Map of Costa Blanca.

Located on Spain's east coast, Benidorm before the 1950s was a small village, dependent on deep-sea fishing and the cultivation of olives and citrus fruits. Although a small number of wealthy Spaniards had beaten a path to the village since the early twentieth century, the east coast was undeveloped in comparison with Spain's north Atlantic seaboard, where the resorts of San Sebastián and Santander had flourished since the middle decades of the nineteenth century. Again the seaside holiday was shaped by a mix of technology, topography and culture. The domestic seaside holiday industry was constrained by poverty of communications and geographical obstacles, not least the sheer size of the country compared with Britain. The north's domination of early Spanish tourism was also based on the appeal of its spas, and on the desire of the Madrid elite to escape the sweltering summer heat of the capital (Walton and Smith, 1994).

Activity   How does the early history of the Spanish resort compare with that of the British resort?

Discussion   The geographical context is clearly more extreme, but there are similarities in the attitudes of the Spanish and British upper classes to the seaside: the taste for health-giving spas and the urge to escape the city and avoid the sun.

The development of Benidorm as a popular tourist resort began in the mid-twentieth century with the decline of deep-sea fishing. This change of direction was facilitated by a rail connection from Madrid to Alicante, and then by a new road from Alicante to Benidorm. It was therefore by established modes of transport that Spanish holiday-makers prepared Benidorm for the mass tourism that would later be exploited by foreign air tour operators. In fact, Spanish holiday-makers still outnumber other European visitors to Benidorm, whether in July and August when *Madrileños* (residents of Madrid) continue their flight from the oppressive heat of the interior, or in the winter months when older people from northern Spain seek relief from the cold and wet.

A motoring guide to Spain published in 1962 could still describe Benidorm as 'one of the most attractive resorts' on the Costa Blanca. The charms of Old Benidorm were prominent in the early promotion of the package tour (Plate 4.4.28). Even at this time, the author of the motoring guide detected 'enormous' growth: her explanation was that the resort was the 'first to break the bikini ban' (Lascelles, 1962, p. 129) – a notable coup for Benidorm's enterprising mayor, who claimed to have travelled to Madrid on a Vespa motor scooter to persuade the dictator General Franco to permit this revealing beachwear (Wilson, 1999, pp. 251–2, 273; Botsford, 2002). Surely more fundamental to Benidorm's rise was its natural environment: its climate, its clear Mediterranean waters and its three miles of wide sandy beach – not quite as much sand as Blackpool, but a lot more sun (see Figure 4.22). There are two main expanses of beach: the Playa de Poniente and the Playa de Levante to its east. These are separated by

Figure 4.22   Tourist admiring the beach at Benidorm, 1963. Photographed by Phillip. Photo © Philip/Fox Photos/Getty Images.

the Plaza de Castillo (Castle Square), set upon a rocky outcrop at the end of which are steep steps leading down to a sea-level viewing platform. Along with the wall of the adjacent port, this is the nearest equivalent to one of Blackpool's piers. The Benidorm authorities have been prudent in their stewardship of their natural assets: since 1961 the beaches have at night been machine-scrubbed of their daily load of cigarette butts and other refuse, and latterly boats have gone out to clean up the seawater too (Wilson, 1999, pp. 265, 394, 397).

Benidorm's natural advantages underpin its extraordinary rise to a peak of 12 million visitors in 1977. But this peak would also be unthinkable without the adoption of modern technologies. The jet airliner was crucial: developments in engine technology brought down both costs and journey times; moreover, shorter times in the air enabled the operators to dispense with some of the comforts of the old propeller-driven aircraft. On the Spanish side, the opening of an international airport at El Altet to the south of Alicante in 1967 was a crucial multiplying factor in Benidorm's soaring growth. Aviation innovation and infrastructure were not the only causes of the rise of the popular package holiday, however. Tour operators reduced costs by other means: chartering flights rather than using scheduled services; block-booking hotels; operating from cheaper provincial airports like Luton; and involving themselves in hotel development at resort destinations.

Figure 4.23   View of Benidorm, 2007. Photographed by Jose Jordan. © JOSE JORDAN/AFP/Getty Images.

Within the resort, technologies of high-rise construction have enabled the visiting millions to be stacked up along Benidorm's beaches, at the same time maximising the number of rooms and apartments with fine sea views (see Figure 4.23). Today Benidorm claims to have more skyscrapers per kilometre than New York. It boasts the tallest hotel in Europe (at the time of writing in 2008): the 52-storey Gran Hotel Bali.

Benidorm adds to its daytime capacity for sunbathing with what a printed guide from the 1980s calls its 'extraordinary night life' (Potok et al., 1987, p. 8; the phrase 'love it or loathe it' crops up a few times in other publications' commentaries). The resort has adapted to cater for the Britons who are the largest nationality among the north Europeans pouring into the resort each summer. The main tourist quarter around the Playa de Levante has bars and restaurants with English names dispensing English fare. This raises a controversial issue, beyond the main concerns of this section: suffice to say that some modern commentators object to the typecasting of the package holiday as a dose of 'sun, sea, sex and sand', whose consumers have to be protected from their fear of the host culture by the tour operators (Wright, 2002). The issue again arises whether Benidorm and Blackpool before it 'are the subject of similar criticism because they provided what their working-class visitors wanted, which was not necessarily what middle-class commentators thought they should want' (Barton, 2005, p. 213).

Apart from the bars and clubs aimed at the young and unattached, there are several modern high-tech facilities for families, such as Aqualandia, Europe's largest water park, its chutes and slides set into the hillside on the eastern fringe of the resort. To the north-west of the town is Terra Mítica, the Costa Blanca's version of Disneyland. This is a mythologically themed park that trumpets among its thrill rides 'Magnus Colossus', the biggest wooden roller-coaster in Europe. Showing that Benidorm is a creature of the motor as well as the jet age, its main water parks and theme parks are a bus ride from the town centre. Terra Mítica's location – beyond the AP-7 motorway some 3.5 miles from the beach – surely strains the facility's seaside identity to breaking point.

Activity   You are now in a position to compare and contrast Blackpool and Benidorm. You should note down the similarities and differences between the two seafronts in Figure 4.16 and Figure 4.23. You should then consider whether any differences you see can be linked to the changing technological contexts of the two resorts.

Discussion   Both seafronts have their own distinctive characteristics, which partly reflect the technologies that made the resorts' growth possible. Blackpool's heavy investment in technologies of entertainment and construction – the piers, the Tower, the Gigantic Wheel, and later the Pleasure Beach and the Illuminations – are much more prominent in its generally low-rise seafront, along with the transport technologies that brought millions to the resort and carried them along the promenade: almost all have been used to construct a marketable identity for the resort. Benidorm's identity is partly shaped by the high-rise backdrop to its beach, but – despite its boast of Europe's tallest hotel – this aspect of the resort ('Manhattan of the Med') is nothing like as positive as its natural assets of sun and sand, and even its contrived, hedonistic night culture. There are, to be sure, high-tech leisure facilities, but these are located on the urban fringe, and hardly central to the resort's identity.

What do these differences tell us? Do they point to changed attitudes to technological innovation, or to changed expectations about holidays abroad? Does Blackpool's greater promotional emphasis on its artificial environment simply come down to the difference in climate?

Epilogue: technology and the end of the seaside?

Developments in the aviation industry, economic as well as technological, helped broaden the palate of the British sun-seeker. The archetypal package holiday to Spain, the Balearics and the Canary Islands began to decline in the 1990s, as the beaches of South Asia, North Africa, the United States and the Caribbean became attainable for the increasing numbers of the affluent. The package holiday itself is now threatened by the emergence of the internet, and the consumer autonomy and alternative modes of buying accommodation and travel that it has fostered.

Consumer horizons have expanded not only to faraway beaches, but to alternative experiences. Since the 1990s no-frills, low-cost airlines have helped popularise the weekend break at more and more continental European cities. Much of this business serves a middle-class clientele seeking culture, heritage and cuisine, although a number of cities – notably Dublin, Amsterdam, Prague, Riga and Tallinn – have become hosts for the uproarious British stag and hen weekend. Blackpool too has been involved in this trend, which has provided some relief from its decline as a traditional family resort, but the link between this and the 'seaside' is tenuous. All in all, the budget airlines show that transport developments can help to diminish as well as to broaden the appeal of the beach holiday.

The implications of technological innovations for the seaside have proved ambiguous. For more than a hundred years from the mid-nineteenth century, they helped extend the seaside holiday throughout society, and to some extent entered the fabric of the holiday experience itself. Thereafter they facilitated the transfer of north Europeans to hotter places. Further on, technological innovation has offered consumers a sanitised version of the beach, without the sand in your food or sewage in the water. A compromise with quite long historical roots is the swimming pool by the sea, a notable early example being Blackpool's South Shore, an enormous pool which opened in 1923 (see Plate 4.4.29).

Figure 4.24   Blackpool's Sandcastle, 2002. Photographed by Fred Gray. Photo: © Fred Gray. Taken from his book *Designing the Seaside: Architecture, Society and Nature*, London 2006.

Now consumer taste has left even South Shore behind. The pool has given way to the Sandcastle complex, 'whose only distinctive seaside attribute was its name' (Walton, 2000, p. 116) (see Figure 4.24). But high-tech leisure facilities with water chutes and ultimate thrill rides have no necessary connection with the coast. There are signs that the beach and the sea are becoming less than integral to the seaside holiday. By a process of technological reproduction, they might be dispensed with altogether. Is this the implication of such projects as the 'Aquacity of Tomorrow' on the Columbia River in Portland, Oregon; or the Japanese Phoenix Seagaia resort, part of which is a dome protecting an artificial beach from weather and insects (Plate 4.4.30)? Artificiality is reaching new extremes in Dubai, as its rulers look to up-market tourism to keep them going after the oil runs out. Here, artificial palm-tree shaped islands offer affluent tourists a technological paradise on earth: they may shuttle between artificial beaches and an enclosed ski slope with artificial snow. Perhaps even more paradoxically, some of the world's biggest cities are now constructing temporary 'urban beaches' for the summer season, so that their tourists can have their cake and eat it – so far have we journeyed from the seaside holiday as the perfect antidote to the stresses of urban life. Will the natural links between sun, sea and sand be severed for future generations – or is the lure of the seaside a cultural constant?

REFERENCES

Adamson, S.H. (1977) *Seaside Piers*, London, B.T. Batsford.

Bainbridge, C. (1986) *Pavilions on the Sea: A History of the Seaside Pleasure Pier*, London, Hale.

Barton, S. (2005) *Working-Class Organisations and Popular Tourism, 1840–1970*, Manchester, Manchester University Press.

Botsford, F. (2002) 'Benidorm climbs ever upward', *BBC News, World: From Our Own Correspondent*, 8 June, available at http://news.bbc.co.uk/1/hi/programmes/from_our_own_correspondent/2031726.stm (Accessed 1 December 2007).

Bray, R. and Raitz, V. (2001) *Flight to the Sun: The Story of the Holiday Revolution*, London and New York, Continuum.

Fischer, R. (1987) *British Piers*, London, Thames & Hudson.

Gray, F. (2006) *Designing the Seaside: Architecture, Society and Nature*, London, Reaktion.

Hutton, W. (1789) *A Description of Blackpool in Lancashire, Frequented for Sea Bathing*, Birmingham, Pearson and Rollason.

Lascelles, A. (1962) *Motoring Holidays in Spain*, London, Arthur Baker.

Lyth, P. (2002) '"Gimme a ticket on an aeroplane ...": the jet engine and the revolution in leisure air travel, 1960–1975', paper presented to XIII Economic History Congress, Buenos Aires, Argentina, 22–6 July, available at http://eh.net/XIIICongress/cd/papers/4Lyth8.pdf (Accessed 16 June 2008).

Lyth, P.J. and Dierikx, M.L.J. (1994) 'From privilege to popularity: the growth of leisure air travel since 1945', *Journal of Transport History*, vol. 15, no. 2, pp. 97–116.

O'Connell, S. (1998) *The Car in British Society: Class, Gender and Motoring, 1896–1939*, Manchester, Manchester University Press.

Poole, R. (1984) 'Lancashire wakes week', *History Today*, vol. 34, no. 8, pp. 22–9.

Potok, M., Harsh, P. and Satué, F.J. (1987) *Benidorm*, London, Harrap Columbus.

Richards, J. and MacKenzie, J.M. (1986) *The Railway Station: A Social History*, Oxford, Oxford University Press.

Thornber, W. (1985 [1837]) *The History of Blackpool and its Neighbourhood*, Blackpool, Blackpool and Fylde Historical Society, facsimile of 1837 first edition.

Walton, J.K. (1978) *The Blackpool Landlady: A Social History*, Manchester, Manchester University Press.

Walton, J.K. (1983) *The English Seaside Resort: A Social History, 1750–1914*, Leicester, Leicester University Press.

Walton, J.K. (1994) 'The re-making of a popular resort: Blackpool Tower and the boom of the 1890s', *Local Historian*, vol. 24, no. 4, pp. 194–205.

Walton, J.K. (1998) *Blackpool*, Edinburgh, Edinburgh University Press.

Walton, J.K. (2000) *The British Seaside: Holidays and Resorts in the Twentieth Century*, Manchester, Manchester University Press.

Walton, J. and Smith, J. (1994) 'The first Spanish seaside resorts', *History Today*, vol. 44, no. 8, pp. 23–9.

Walvin, J. (1978) *Beside the Seaside: A Social History of the Popular Seaside Holiday*, London, Allen Lane.

Williams, A.M. (1996) 'Mass tourism and the international tour companies' in Barke, M., Towner, J. and Newton, M.T. (eds) *Tourism in Spain: Critical Issues*, Wallingford, CAB International.

Wilson, C. (1999) *Benidorm: The Truth*, Valencia, Ayuntamiento de Benidorm: Agencia Valenciana de Turisme.

Wright, S. (2002) 'Sun, sea, sand and self-expression: mass tourism as an individual experience' in Berghoff, H., Korte, B. and Harvie, C. (eds), *The Making of Modern Tourism: The Cultural History of the British Experience, 1600–2000*, Basingstoke and New York, Palgrave.

4.5 THE HEALTHY SEASIDE

Deborah Brunton

INTRODUCTION

The seaside holiday is now associated simply with leisure, and a chance to relax. But in the past people went to the seaside for other, quite different reasons – to recover from illness or to improve their health. The idea of the seaside as a particularly healthy place has a long history. But where did the association between health and the seaside come from? How were the natural resources of the shore supposed to promote health? And how did they help to shape the activities now associated with the seaside holiday and the development of seaside resorts?

EIGHTEENTH CENTURY: SEASIDE CURES

The fashion for bathing in the sea as a means of curing disease grew out of a much older practice of drinking and bathing in the waters of mineral springs to treat skin complaints. During the 1730s, doctors began to recommend drinking and bathing in seawater for health reasons, and the practice quickly became popular among the upper classes. Bathing was not the same as swimming – it was a form of therapy, with the number of baths and the time spent in the water prescribed and carefully regulated by doctors. Patients were carried out from the beach in wheeled bathing machines. They emerged from these machines – either naked or wearing a loose gown – and were briefly dipped under the water by guides known as 'dippers', then taken back to shore and rubbed dry. Bathing was not supposed to be pleasant: doctors claimed that the beneficial effects came from the shock of immersion in cold water, and bathing went on all the year round. The cold water was said to stimulate the skin and nerves and thus to promote the action of all the internal organs, removing any obstructions in the bodily 'humours'. Bathing was considered to be good for the treatment of a wide range of diseases, and to alleviate the bad effects of a sedentary lifestyle. However, it was also believed to be potentially dangerous: patients going into the sea without medical advice were thought to risk inflammations or burst blood vessels which could have fatal results. Very frail patients were advised to make use of indoor seawater baths, filled with hot or tepid water.

You encountered humoural medicine in Book 3, Chapter 5.

The air at the seaside was also considered useful to the restoration of health. Taking the air was easy – and much more pleasant than bathing. Simply by sitting or strolling by the beach and sea front, visitors breathed in the health-giving air.

By the end of the eighteenth century, bathing and visiting the seaside were very fashionable activities, and these concerns drove the development of the first seaside resorts. To cater for invalids, new facilities were built in coastal towns and villages. Hotels and houses were constructed to accommodate patients, their families and servants, who would stay for several weeks or months at a time. Doctors flocked to these resorts to establish practices and dispense expert advice. Local entrepreneurs set up fleets of bathing machines, or built seawater baths for those unable or unwilling to face the waves. Invalids and families needed to be entertained during their stay too, so resort towns also had shops, libraries, assembly rooms for concerts or dancing and theatres, where visitors could while away the afternoons and evenings.

NINETEENTH CENTURY: THE SEASIDE FOR HEALTH

In the nineteenth century, seaside resorts boomed. Most of the visitors who came to the sea now were not ill, but wanted to boost their health and enjoy a holiday. Bathing increased in popularity. While invalids continued to go into the sea on medical advice, healthy visitors also took to the waves, eager to share the beneficial effects and simply to enjoy the new sensation of bathing. Although doctors were the first to advocate bathing, and had elaborate theories about the reasons for its health-giving character, these ideas soon spread to the general public.

Books and articles in newspapers and magazines, some written by doctors for a general audience, explained the benefits of sea-bathing. Bathing thus became a part of **popular medicine** – a form of treatment understood by the general public which was widely used without the supervision of doctors. Books such as Charles Parson's *Sea Air and Sea Bathing: Their Influence on Health* (1877) explained the benefits of bathing. Parsons claimed that the initial shock of the cold water stimulated the nerves of the body and caused vessels in the skin to contract, forcing blood through all the internal organs. Thus the water revitalised the nervous system and all the organs. He suggested that bathers should dive into the sea head first to achieve maximum benefit, then swim or splash about for a few minutes. ('Dippers' were no longer employed except by the very frail – although the bathing machine continued in use in order to ensure privacy while changing and to get the bather into sufficiently deep water – see Figure 4.25.) Bathing was advocated for all sorts of chronic diseases and the exhaustion brought on by the hectic pace of life, work and travel in the Victorian world. However, Parsons warned of the bad effects of reckless bathing: going into the sea too often or for too long – even paddling – could bring on headaches and stomach complaints.

Victorian visitors also wanted to take in the sea air. Beliefs about its curative properties were reinforced in the nineteenth century by medical science. Sea air was pure and clean at a time when the air in towns was increasingly filled with dust, smoke and other industrial pollutants. New chemical analyses showed that air samples taken at the shore contained iodine, 'saline particles' and ozone, a form of oxygen. Although doctors were rather hazy as to how these components acted on the body, all were convinced that the air found

Figure 4.25   Bathing machines at St. Leonards-on-Sea (East Sussex), *c*.1895. Unknown photographer. Photograph: Hulton Archive/Getty Images.

by the sea was especially invigorating, helping to restore health to invalids. From the 1870s onwards, doctors treated patients suffering from tuberculosis – a debilitating and ultimately fatal lung disease – by exposure to fresh air in the mountains or at the seaside.

This reinforced a popular belief in the health-giving properties of sea air and gave Victorian travellers a further reason to go to the seaside to improve their health. Many middle-class Victorian families enjoyed long seaside holidays in the summer, encouraging their children to go bathing and to take in the sea air in order to build up their health and help them resist the coughs and colds of the unhealthy winter months. Popular ideas about the benefits of sea air survived even after medical science showed, at the end of the nineteenth century, that sea air did not contain high levels of ozone: similar levels of the gas were found everywhere. Nevertheless, visitors continued to enjoy the air, and local councils in resort towns provided promenades with covered seats, as well as parks and gardens where people could stroll or sit. In 1858, for example, Bournemouth council built an 'Invalids' Walk' lined with pine trees, as part of a park. Elsewhere, 'Winter gardens' provided shelter for visitors in bad weather. Piers were particularly popular – as well as exposing visitors to the sea air, they gave people who walked

Figure 4.26   Redcar (Cleveland), pier and promenade, *c.*1890. Unknown photographer. Photograph: Hulton Archive/Getty Images.

along them an exciting impression of being out at sea. By the end of the nineteenth century, every seaside resort town of any size had a pier (see Figure 4.26).

TWENTIETH CENTURY: SUNSHINE, EXERCISE AND THE PURSUIT OF FUN

In the early twentieth century the seaside was still strongly associated with health, but for slightly different reasons. Bathing in seawater was no longer seen as therapeutic – rather, it was an opportunity for health-giving exercise. A popular craze for outdoor exercise began in the late nineteenth century. Hiking and camping – as advocated by the Boy Scout movement – were seen as ways of building muscles and character. Athletics, cycling, golf and tennis were also popular. Gymnastic exercise was an iconic activity. The Women's League of Health and Beauty (founded in 1930) provided cheap, accessible exercise classes in towns to bring the 'joy of movement' to women everywhere (see Figure 4.27). Its ethos was: 'Movement is Life. Stillness is the attribute of death. The stagnant pond collects the weeds which will finally choke it, but the moving river clears itself' (quoted in Matless, 1998, p. 88). Taking exercise was portrayed as both fun and good for health: it was an antidote to cancer, constipation, nerves and tuberculosis – all complaints thought to be increasingly common in the early twentieth century.

Figure 4.27   Women's League of Health and Beauty rehearsing the demonstration they will give in Hyde Park, London, of methods designed to improve the physical health of business women, 16 May 1933. Unknown photographer. Photo: Central Press/Getty Images.

Swimming fitted perfectly with the enthusiasm for outdoor exercise, and was increasingly accessible to the general population. In the late nineteenth century only the upper and middle classes could afford swimming lessons and special swimming costumes. By the early twentieth century, however, working-class adults and children were learning to swim in the new swimming baths built in many towns. By the 1930s, swimming was a popular activity. An article in the journal *Modern Woman* in 1929 enthused about the

> value of swimming to health and beauty [...] the skin, which is so vitally concerned with health, is actually cleansed [...] swimming builds pliant and well balanced muscles. It imposes little or no strain on the heart; it affords splendid spinal and pelvic exercise; it necessitates unusually deep breathing; and it is remarkably restful for the nerves.

(Quoted in Braggs and Harris, 2000, p. 71)

There is more about lidos and other sporting facilities in 'Resort history' and 'Virtual resort' on the DVD ROM.

During the 1920s and 1930s, seaside resorts built increasingly elaborate facilities for swimming. For those who wished to bathe in the sea, there were changing huts, lifeguards and refreshment kiosks on the beach. Resorts which did not have good beaches built outdoor pools which were filled by the tide. These were followed by elaborate **lidos**: complexes of pools, diving boards and lounging areas (see Plate 4.4.31). These facilities had the advantage of allowing swimming even when the sea was rough, and they guaranteed clean water at a time when resort towns discharged their sewage straight into the sea. Many were capable of accommodating hundreds of swimmers. Blackpool's lido, built in 1923, was roughly four times the size of a modern Olympic-size pool. Such large facilities were expensive: Blackpool's cost £75,000. For visitors who wished to take their exercise on dry land, resorts also boasted tennis courts, bowling greens, putting greens, golf courses (see Figure 4.28 and Plate 4.4.32).

In the 1920s, resorts also began to advertise a new means of boosting health – sunshine. The new enthusiasm for sunbathing was inspired by medical science. In the early twentieth century doctors were exploring the curative effects of sunshine. For instance, patients suffering from tuberculosis were treated by very carefully controlled sunbathing, their bodies very gradually exposed to sunlight for longer and longer times each day. Moreover, rickets – a disease which causes malformed bones – was increasingly common among city children at this time. In 1922, it was proved that the disease was caused by a lack of exposure to sunlight and could be treated by sunbathing or by exposure to ultraviolet light from special lamps. Infected wounds were also found to heal better when exposed to sunlight. Sunlight therapy was seen as a breakthrough in the war on disease. Hospitals eager to show that they possessed the most up-to-date equipment boasted of their facilities for ultraviolet light therapy – or 'bottled sunshine', as it was described.

While doctors saw sunlight as a treatment for specific diseases, 'sunbathing' – literally, bathing the skin in sunlight – was taken up by the public as a means of improving overall health. In the popular press, lack of sunlight was linked to generally poor health and an inability to fight off disease. Exposing the skin to sunlight was thought to boost the body's ability to fight off infections, to give a better 'tone' to the nerves and organs, and to bring about vigour, high spirits and even increased intelligence. Charities sent weakly children to the seaside in order to boost their health. Schools were advised to have children dance around ultraviolet lamps, accompanied by gramophone music, in order to get their dose of sunlight. Even the animals in London Zoo received ultraviolet light therapy.

Sunbathing was often combined with exercise. Books and magazine articles explained the benefits of allowing sunlight to reach the skin

Figure 4.28   Railway poster for Troon (south-west Scotland), produced by the Midland Railway (MR), and Glasgow and South Western Railway (GSWR), *c.*1910, mixed media. Artwork by J.Y. Wright. © Science and Society Picture Library/NRM – Pictorial Collection.

Ever-briefer swimsuits were ideal for sunbathing. You can read about this in Section 4.3 'Dressing for the Beach'.

while exercising. Hikers were recommended to wear shorts and light clothing in order to expose the maximum amount of skin to the sun and air. However, British authors were cautious about advocating nude sunbathing, which, it was felt, should be restricted to the privacy of home and garden.

Sunbathing was not just a means of promoting health – the resulting tan was seen as fashionable and glamorous. Many contemporary writers date the rise of the suntan to 1923 or 1925 (accounts differ) when Coco Chanel, the fashion designer, returned from a holiday on the south coast of France sporting a deep tan. A suntan carried associations of glamour, wealth and leisure, yet could be acquired by anyone.

Seaside resorts were quick to pick up on the popularity of sunbathing in their marketing literature. Resorts boasted of the number of hours of sunshine they enjoyed in the summer months, and posters inevitably showed sunny weather – so hot that visitors had to relax in the shade of verandas and beach umbrellas. Even posters for Scottish resort towns, not known for their reliably good weather, showed visitors basking in the sun (see Figure 4.29).

Figure 4.29   Tom Gilfillan, *Cheap holiday tickets to Saltcoats, the finest tidal lake on the Firth of Clyde*, railway poster produced by the London, Midland and Scottish Railway (LMS), 1935. National Railway Museum, York, 1989–7115. Photo: © Science and Society Picture Library/NRM – Pictorial Collection.

The new enthusiasm for sunshine was mixed with older beliefs about the health-giving quality of sea air. The air by the sea was still clean and unpolluted. Long after science had shown that there was no more ozone by the sea than in the city, resorts continued to advertise their 'ozone-laden breezes' (Hassan, 2003, p. 102). Great Yarmouth in Norfolk promised visitors 'an incomparable sense of well-being', while the air of Brighton in Sussex was reported to lift the spirits and to make the holiday-maker feel 'glad to be alive' (Hassan, 2003, p. 102).

OR NOT SO HEALTHY?

So far, you've seen evidence that many visitors to the seaside in the 1920s and 1930s wanted to enjoy the sun, and to swim in the sea or in a lido. We know that these activities featured heavily in advertising for seaside resorts, but were they popular with all visitors? Did everyone see these seaside facilities as a means of improving their health?

Activity   Turn to Reading 4.1, which consists of extracts from the Mass Observation records. The Mass Observation project is an ongoing attempt to compile 'an anthropology of ourselves': recording life in Britain exactly as it happens. In the extracts that make up this reading, middle-class observers record the activities and attitudes of working-class visitors from Bolton (which they call 'Worktown') on holiday at Blackpool.

Do the visitors take part in any 'healthy' activities? Do they think of a trip to the seaside as a healthy activity?

Discussion   The accounts from Mass Observation give a contradictory message. The detailed account of the time spent by the two working-class couples suggests that workers wanted to relax when on holiday, rather than taking vigorous exercise. They sleep, read, and watch films and **pierrots**. Other reports of activity on the beach suggest that this is typical: adults sleep or sit and talk. Children are the only active group. Nevertheless, visitors do still associate the seaside – and especially sea air – with health, and feel that their health is improved by a trip to the sea.

The Mass Observation data reminds us that we need to be critical when using advertising as a historical resource. The contemporary railway posters with their images of healthy, glamorous young people swimming and golfing were designed to present an appealing image, not necessarily to give an accurate representation of what all visitors did at the seaside. While some visitors – those who were able to afford sports equipment and lessons – went to the seaside with the aim of swimming, sunbathing and improving their health, others went for a chance to rest and relax, to catch up on sleep, and to feel that the holiday was in some ways 'doing them good'.

CONCLUSION

The desire for health was crucial to the rise and development of the seaside. The first resorts were created to fulfil the demand for sea-bathing, and from the eighteenth to the twentieth centuries visitors hoped to find health as well as pleasure by the sea. The idea that the seaside is a healthy place – somewhere to recover from illness or just recharge the batteries – is a persistent one. It came into being in the eighteenth century, when doctors first established the connection between sea-bathing and health. But it survived as a popular belief well into the twentieth century, long after medical practitioners had abandoned theories about the beneficial effects of bathing or breathing in ozone. The idea of the healthy seaside persisted for such a long time because it changed and adapted: at various times, the different natural resources of the seaside were fitted into medical ideas about curing disease. It also survived because a desire for health overlapped with the pursuit of leisure – of having fun on the beach, in the sea and by the shore – and because seaside resorts were happy to provide facilities for seekers after both health and pleasure.

REFERENCES

Braggs, S. and Harris, D. (2000) *Sun, Fun and Crowds: Seaside Holidays between the Wars*, Stroud, Tempus.

Hassan, J. (2003) *The Seaside, Health and Environment in England and Wales since 1800*, Aldershot, Ashgate.

Matless, D. (1998) *Landscape and Englishness*, London, Reaktion.

Parsons, C. (1877) *Sea Air and Sea Bathing: Their Influence on Health*, London, J. & A. Churchill.

FURTHER READING

Carter, S. (2007) *Rise and Shine. Sunlight, Technology and Health*, Oxford, Berg.

Walvin, J. (1978) *Beside the Seaside: A Social History of the Popular Seaside Holiday*, London, Allen Lane.

RESOURCES

Reading 4.1 **Worktowners at Blackpool**

The four people left the boarding-house at 9:48 and walked slowly up the street towards the promenade. [...] They went down a passage beside the Imperial Hydro and so out on to the promenade. [...] Having reached the Gynn Square, they went up on the cliff walk. [...] When they reached the boating pool near the lift, they went without hesitation down the slope to it. ... They selected deckchairs in the front row overlooking the water. Their walk from their lodging house had taken them 29 minutes. ...

Mr F opened a *Daily Express* across his legs and began to read. All four looked up at three yellow RAF planes as they passed over towards the North. Then they leaned forward and began to discuss them. Mrs A leaned back with her head resting against the back of the deckchairs. She had very restless feet which were always twitching and tapping. [Mr] F passed the remainder of the newspaper to his wife and took out a packet of cigarettes. Slowly he selected one and lit it. [...]

Mr A passed his part of the newspaper to his wife. Mrs A spread the newspaper on her knees and looked at the front page idly. [...] Mr F was now reading his part of the paper again. [...] The only conversation was a few remarks between Mr and Mrs F and Mrs F and Mrs A. Mr A hardly spoke at all. [...]

At 11:55 ... all moved away.... The four straggled up the slope to the cliff walk ...

They stopped near the Gynn to stare at some donkeys coming up from the sands. Later Mrs F lagged behind to watch a beach patrol calling in the bathers. The party returned by the same route that they had gone in the morning. [...]

At 1:30 they went to the south end:

[...] All four get off tram at Victoria Pier, and all go on the pier, keeping to the right side, all four walking together, the two women kept looking in the shops. As soon as they get to the end of the pier, they all lean over the side and look at the water. Three of them sit in deckchairs and Mrs A walks to the kiosk and looks at postcards and magazines.... Then all ... wait for **pierrots** to start. Both women go to sleep. The two men look around and watch people coming to the show. Mrs F sits up and says 'Oh I am tired', and goes to sleep again. Meanwhile both men fall asleep. Show starts and all sit up and observe. [...]

They leave before the pierrots have finished though near the end. Mr F seems reluctant to go, and lingers behind and looks at them. Then he runs up and catches them and all four walk off the pier. Eventually all get on a tram and sit on the top. [pp. 146–8]

[...]

Just before tea on a typical afternoon [...] 50 per cent were sleeping or snoozing, 25 per cent were looking, 10 per cent were playing, 10 per cent supervising children, and 5 per cent talking. [p. 94]

[...]

The *Blackpool Gazette* was upset (19 March 1938) when a leading London physician told the Royal Institute of Public Health that 'the idea that fresh air, as such, has any kind of miraculous effect in sustaining the health or as a recuperative factor in illness outside of movement, temperature and humidity, is a pure fallacy'. It is, however, Blackpool's air that Worktowners count as the primary health asset. The more the wind blows, the more they like it. Of some thirty people asked on the promenade what sort of weather they liked best, two-thirds said the breeze or the wind. As one man said: 'This is bracing. I can get the sun at home. This is what I like, the breeze.' But many people say that they find Blackpool air, like old beer, 'too strong' for them. It gave one woman 'headaches and made her sick'. [p. 82]

Source: G. Cross (ed.) (1990) *Worktowners at Blackpool: Mass-Observation and Popular Leisure in the 1930s*, London and New York, Routledge, pp. 82, 94, 146–8.

4.6 SEASIDE MUSIC: THE BEACH BOYS AND THE WHO

Nick Jones and Richard Danson Brown

INTRODUCTION

In this section we shall be addressing the theme of the beach in two highly contrasting ways: the first – viewing the seaside as a place of fun and enjoyment – will be concerned with early 1960s' surf music and The Beach Boys; the second – viewing the seaside as a place of danger and violence – will focus on the music of The Who.

FUN, FUN, FUN: SURF MUSIC AND THE BEACH BOYS
Nick Jones

Figure 4.30   The Beach Boys, 1962. Photographed by Charlie Gillett. Photo: © Charlie Gillett Archive/Redferns.

Activity   Turn to Reading 4.2. This is an extract from a short biography of The Beach Boys (see Figure 4.30) by John Bush. The first paragraph provides an overview of the band's history; the second and third go into more detail for the years 1961 (the year the band was formed) to 1963 (the year of the group's first Top 10 hit, 'Surfin' U.S.A.'). Make brief notes on the main points that the writer makes.

'Surfin' U.S.A.'

The Beach Boys' 'Surfin' U.S.A.', which reached no. 3 in the Billboard's Singles chart in March 1963, is one of the most celebrated examples of 1960s' surf music. You may be wondering what this style of popular music consists of. We'll be exploring this in a moment, but for now I want you to concentrate on the following question: what is it about the song that makes the listener immediately identify it with 'the beach'?

Activity Listen to the song – track 5 on the Audio CD 'Seaside Music' – and compile a short list of bullet-point responses to this question, considering both the music and the lyrics. For the music, I suggest that you focus on instrumentation, vocal style and the overall character. As the song is quite short, you might want to listen to it a few times.

Lyrics

The song's title and the opening lines – 'If everybody had an ocean/ Across the U.S.A./Then everybody'd be surfin'/Like Californ-i-a' – clearly inform the listener that the theme of the song is based around surfing, an American national craze in the early 1960s. By deliberately linking the theme of the lyrics to surf culture the song not only conjures up images of glorious sunshine with surfers racing down to the beach to catch the next wave, but also speaks directly to a teenage audience. Since the end of the 1950s, teenagers have been a key audience for, and consumers of, popular music and many commentators have been keen to point out that music which directly appeals to a youth culture – in this case a surfing **subculture** – is deliberately cashing in on the vast market that exists. Whatever your views on the matter, what it does demonstrate is that a specific section of society can identify with, and have a strong allegiance to, a particular style of popular music. This important point has already been demonstrated by Trevor Herbert in his material on Victorian seaside music (Section 4.1); the notion will be revisited and further developed later on in this section.

Music

I would argue that the music for 'Surfin' U.S.A.' is so familiar to us today – so utterly representative of surf music – that it immediately conjures up images of the easy-going, carefree and sultry beach environment. But what does this 'surf sound' consist of, musically speaking? I shall start by discussing the song's structure, something that I didn't ask you to listen out for specifically, but something that is, of course, absolutely crucial to any musical composition.

- The song's structure is simple and clear, and follows the standard verse–refrain format:

CD time reference	
0'00"	Intro (guitar)
0'02"	Verse 1
0'26"	Chorus
0'50"	Verse 2
1'14"	Chorus
1'39"	**Middle eight** (organ and lead guitar solos)
1'57"	**Outro**

- Instrumentation: guitar, bass guitar, drum kit, organ. The guitar has a thin, 'twangy' **timbre**. The organ has a sumptuous, 'jazzy' sound.

- Vocal style: the lead vocalist (Mike Love) has a rather soft, warm yet detached vocal delivery coloured by the Californian accent; the other vocalist (Brian Wilson) can be heard singing **falsetto** (listen out for 'Everybody's gone surfin'' at 0' 45"). The supporting close vocal harmonies (a Beach Boys' hallmark) – to wordless 'oohs' in the verses and to 'Inside outside U.S.A.' in the chorus – are, by contrast, much richer and thicker in **texture**.

- Musical character: the music is immediate and accessible; it has a sunny disposition – a real sense of fun – and is optimistic in every respect.

You may want to listen to the whole song one more time to make sure that the things I have discussed above have been fully absorbed. If you need to do this, then do so now before moving on.

Following the release of 'Surfin' U.S.A.', The Beach Boys continued to produce easy-going, bright and accessible surf music – a musical style that complemented perfectly the essentially white, middle-class youth lifestyle and leisure time of early 1960s' California. But this was to change with the release in May 1966 of their tenth studio album, the ground-breaking and seminal *Pet Sounds*. Making no reference to surfing in the lyrics and employing unusual and striking instrumental combinations, the album offered a sense of distance from their early work. Nevertheless, the popular image of the group as producers of catchy, perfectly formed surf pop songs has been an enduring one, and unquestionably forms the larger part of the group's musical legacy.

Track 6 on the Audio CD is the influential single 'Good Vibrations', which was recorded at around the same time as Pet Sounds.

ANTHEM FOR DELINQUENT YOUTH: THE WHO'S 'MY GENERATION'

At the same time as The Beach Boys were producing surf pop songs, on the other side of the Atlantic the British **rock** band The Who were creating songs in a very different style – here was a music that was hard-edged and shot through with nervous energy and anxiety, typified by their 1965 single 'My Generation'.

In 1964, the line-up of the group consisted of guitarist and main songwriter Pete Townshend, lead singer Roger Daltrey, bass guitarist John Entwistle and drummer Keith Moon. From the beginning, the band drew attention because of their wild stage antics: Moon would routinely smash up his drum kit and Townshend his guitar and amplifiers. The frantic and nervous energy that the band generated onstage was transferred to the recording studio to great effect for 'My Generation' (see Plate 4.4.33 in the Illustration Book).

Activity   I now want you to listen to 'My Generation' – track 7 on the Audio CD. As you listen, jot down a few words or a single sentence to describe how each instrument – guitar, bass guitar and drum kit – sounds, including the manner in which each is played. Also describe the main characteristics of the voice.

Discussion • Guitar: the song opens with 'power chords' (vigorous and forceful strums, articulated by fast downward hand strokes); it's unusual in that the guitar hardly has any melodic lines at all, mostly rhythmic chords; it also uses **feedback** towards the end of the song (from 2' 24", but especially at 2' 45"–48"), which contributes to a controlled cacophony that is suggestive of the band's auto-destructive stage act.

• Bass guitar: this stands out from the overall texture – it has a heavy, 'rumbling' and 'raspy' sound; and, most strikingly, has its own solo (0' 55"–1' 12").

• Drum kit: the drumming is energetic and inventive, powerful and aggressive.

• Voice: there's an angry, snarling vocal delivery, rough and 'bluesy' in places; the unusual vocal stuttering adds to the overall sense of rage and frustration.

You may well be wondering why Daltrey is stuttering on the record in the first place. A number of possibilities have been put forward, the most popular being that the song 'presents a picture of a confused and inarticulate adolescent, with lead singer Roger Daltrey singing the vocal in a stuttering fashion that mimics the speed-induced verbal stoppages associated with mod methedrine use' (Shuker, 1995, p. 156). The reference to 'mod' here may not have come as that much of a surprise to you, as The Who – and 'My Generation' in particular – are closely associated with the Mod subculture which developed in London in the early 1960s and reached a peak at a national level in the mid-1960s. Indeed, 'My Generation' became something of a 'beach anthem' – the essential soundtrack to accompany those hedonistic weekends when Mods would descend ritualistically on British seaside resorts to clash violently with their subcultural rivals, the Rockers (see Figures 4.31 and 4.32).

TEENAGE WASTELAND: MODS AND ROCKERS

Here we'll be undertaking two short reading activities to set the scene for Richard Danson Brown's discussion that follows. While we'll be looking mainly at the Mod lifestyle, we'll also be considering the following proposition: that we can only fully appreciate popular music by understanding the social and cultural contexts in which such music is produced.

Activity   First of all, I want to explore the lifestyle and leisure activities of the Mod subculture. So turn now to Readings 4.3 and 4.4. As you read these, make a note of the main preoccupations of this social movement.

Discussion   Both extracts highlight the Mods' obsession with fashion, dancing, drugs and music. In Reading 4.4 Peter Wicke talks of the ritualistic nature of their leisure activities: going to clubs, taking amphetamines, dancing to certain types of popular music – all carried out with monotonous frequency. Both Wicke and Simon Frith (in Reading 4.3) point out that Mods listened to American **soul music** and **rhythm & blues**, but Mods also enjoyed **Motown** and **Ska** music. Wicke states that the movement 'provided the social basis for an important branch of British rock music'; and the Mods' identification with British rock music, and the close relationship that can exist between music and society, is something that I want to explore in the next activity.

Activity   Peter Wicke, the author of Reading 4.4, has also asserted that 'It is impossible to consider rock music without placing it in its social and cultural contexts' (1990, p. 73). Pause and consider this statement for a moment. Do you agree? When you are ready to move on, turn to Reading 4.5. Do you find Wicke's argument here convincing?

Discussion   Wicke argues that there existed an intimate link between the Mod movement and the music of The Who. I find his argument convincing in this particular instance; although it doesn't apply to classical music so easily, it would be difficult to argue against the notion that individuals and social groups show a preference for particular styles of popular music. Clearly, then, there is an essential link between popular music and identity – indeed many subcultures are defined by the music that they listen to and the way that they look, and the Mod movement was no exception. But it's important and interesting to note that The Who didn't really think of themselves as a Mod band. In fact, before 'My Generation' was released, Townshend was trying to distance the band from their Mod following by aligning them instead with **Pop Art** (hence the band's use of British 'pop motifs' like the Union Jack and the Royal Air Force roundel). But with the success of 'My Generation' the band continued to exploit the Mod connection, most notably by playing at Mod music clubs like the Marquee in London's Soho.

By now, you should have a reasonably good idea of what activities preoccupied the Mod movement. But what about their subcultural rivals, the Rockers? They too had their own dress code and listening preferences:

> The rockers wore black leather jackets, jeans and boots, had greased hair and rode motorbikes. [...] The rockers' key value

Figure 4.31   Mods on scooters, 16 May 1964. Unknown photographer. Photo: Express Newspapers/Getty Images.

was freedom, and their preferred music was 1950s rock'n'roll: Elvis, Gene Vincent, and Eddie Cochrane.

(Shuker, 2002, pp. 262–3)

The many differences between the two groups bred bitter rivalry and mutual hatred and resulted in violent clashes, the most notorious of which took place in various English south coast seaside resorts. These clashes received maximum press coverage at the time (see Cohen, 1973), no doubt because they were staged in an environment usually associated with enjoyment and leisure, not danger and violence. The most infamous seaside scuffle took place on May Bank Holiday, 1964:

There was Dad asleep in a deckchair and Mum making sandcastles with the children, when the 1964 boys took over the beaches at Margate and Brighton yesterday and smeared the traditional postcard scene with blood and violence.

(*Daily Express*, 19 May 1964)

Figure 4.32   Rockers and their motorbikes, 1 July 1964. Photographed by Terrence Spencer. Photo: Time & Life Pictures/Getty Images.

QUADROPHENIA
Richard Danson Brown

We're now going to look at an LP by The Who, *Quadrophenia* (1973). While this follows on from Nick Jones's discussion of The Beach Boys and 'My Generation', it is slightly different in that I consider *Quadrophenia* as a record which also uses narrative, lyrics and photography alongside music to conjure a time and place through the filter of an individual mentality. *Quadrophenia* is a multimedia experience, and my discussion will take an interdisciplinary approach to this rock opera's representation of the seaside.

The term 'rock opera' was coined to describe records like The Who's 1969 LP *Tommy*, which tells the story of a deaf, dumb and blind child who becomes a pinball champion and the leader of an eccentric religious cult. Like most of The Who's original material, *Tommy* and *Quadrophenia* were chiefly written by Pete Townshend. They embody an almost literary ambition to put the forms and possibilities of rock music to the service of story-telling. Unsurprisingly, both LPs became the basis for successful films.

The rock critic Matt Kent points out that The Who were not alone in this endeavour:

> In the '60s rock composers began linking their songs to form a story, a cycle of songs based around a central theme. Many commentators point to the period around 1967–8 as the evolutionary period for what was to become known as the concept album, or *rock opera*.

(Kent, 2005, p. 2)

The Who routinely used the term rock opera, with varying degrees of self-parody, to describe *Tommy* when they performed it during 1969 and 1970: see *Live at the Isle of Wight Festival 1970* and *Live at Leeds* (The Who, 1996a; 2002). Rock operas have been the focus of much derision: from high-brow critics, who contend that a popular form like rock cannot aspire to the musical sophistication of classical opera; and from rock critics and musicians, who came to see in records like *Tommy* and *Quadrophenia* a disastrous triumph of pretension over passion, and a diminution of the fundamental energy of rock (see Rockwell, 1992). Yet as the music critic Jessica Duchen (2006) points out, '*Tommy* and *Quadrophenia* are as characteristic of their era as any opera by Mozart or Wagner'. To get a sense of this, we need a more detailed sense of *Quadrophenia* as an object.

When it was first released, *Quadrophenia* was a double album – two vinyl records, accompanied by a gatefold cover and a booklet which included the lyrics to the songs as well as a short story and a sequence of black and white photographs which visually represent the story conveyed in words and music elsewhere in the package. The 1996 CD reproduces this packaging (see The Who, 1996b). As a product and as a concept, *Quadrophenia* is far removed from the 'My Generation' single: it's an elaborate artefact which aims to stimulate the listener on a range of levels. Yet *Quadrophenia* is closely related to The Who's earlier work. A fragment of 'The Kids are Alright', a song from the *My Generation* LP, echoes in the fade-out of *Quadrophenia*'s 'Helpless Dancer', while the storyline centres on The Who's earliest days as a house band to the Mods in the expanding London conurbation. The record is dedicated 'to the kids of Goldhawk Road, Carpenters Park, Forest Hill, Stevenage New Town and to all the people we played to at the Marquee and the Brighton Aquarium in the summer of '65'. The record memorialises a particular moment in time when, as you have seen, The Who embodied the style and aspirations of their youthful following. *Quadrophenia* elegises both the Mod movement and The Who's early career.

Consider Plates 4.4.34 and 4.4.35, which reproduce the record's original front and back cover. These are photographs by Graham Hughes and Ethan A. Russell. Russell co-directed the design of the package with Townshend and took the booklet photographs. The front shows a Mod in a parka sitting on a Lambretta scooter with his back slightly turned towards the camera. In the scooter's mirrors, we see the reflected faces of The Who: from the bottom, Daltrey, Entwistle, Moon and Townshend. The name of the band is spray-painted onto the back of the parka, simultaneously showing the kid's allegiances and identifying them as the makers of *Quadrophenia*, the title of which frames both front and back covers. On the back, the scooter is shown abandoned in a lengthening seascape. This photo invites the viewer to ask what has happened to the Mod from the front cover, and indeed what has happened to his favourite group.

So what is the *Quadrophenia* story? The easiest way to find out is by reading the short story.

Activity   Turn to Reading 4.6, the *Quadrophenia* short story. As you read it, I'd like you to think about what sort of narrative this is, and then to consider how Townshend represents music and the seaside in this text. How are these things important to the story's protagonist?

Discussion   1   The *Quadrophenia* story is a first-person narrative of the same kind as Nadine Gordimer's 'The Ultimate Safari' (which you studied in Book 3, Chapter 4). Like Gordimer, Townshend gives voice to a young and vulnerable sensibility. Here the voice is that of a young Mod (named Jimmy Cooper for the *Quadrophenia* feature film (1979), though only referred to as 'Mod kid' on the LP credits) who suffers from mental illness. Unlike Gordimer's story, this is not a sequential narrative. Contrasting scenes, images and linguistic registers flash rapidly through the prose, so that the reader is given an overall sense of the kid's 'quadrophonic' state of mind, as he is pulled in the four mutually incompatible directions of 'tough guy', 'romantic', 'bloody lunatic' and 'hypocrite'. In essence, the story narrates how the kid's personality disintegrates after his return from a weekend of sex, violence and drugs in Brighton. In the present moment, as he ends up on 'this bastard Rock' off the coast of Brighton, he feels let down by his parents, his girlfriend, work, and even by being a Mod.

2   Music forms one of the key concerns of the story. The Who's music underpins the kid's identity as a Mod: 'They were a mod group. Well, mods liked them. [...] The guitar player [...] wrote some good songs about mods, but he didn't quite look like one.' Disconcertingly, Townshend both mythologises his group and backs away from a thoroughgoing endorsement of Mod culture; in the group's failure to acknowledge the kid, there is an ironic sense of the gathering sense of the distance between the band and their audience: 'After the show I hung around outside waiting for them to come out. When they did they never bloody well recognised me.' Plate 4.4.36 shows Russell's photographic representation of this scene: as the band leave the Hammersmith Odeon surrounded by groupies and move towards a chauffeured limousine, the kid looks on from behind his scooter. While The Who shape the kid's identity, he is excluded from their glamorous lives.

3   The seaside is equally significant as an indication of the divisions in the kid's mind. Brighton is the ideal place for a fist fight and sex on the beach; the sea is also heightened, beautiful, and removed from everyday

reality: 'The sea is so gorgeous you want to jump into it and sink.' The kid's boat trip gives him an image of an almost mystical transcendence of the limitations of his life, as the noise of the boat becomes 'Like heavenly choirs or orchestras tuning up [...] Like the sort of noise you'd expect to hear in heaven, if there is such a place.' In this respect, the seaside is a 'fantastic' place, in that it represents the meeting point between the sociological reality of the beach fights between Mods and Rockers, and a symbolic testing ground where the kid comes to understand 'the bare bones of what I am'.

In *Quadrophenia* and *Tommy*, Townshend makes inarticulate characters speak for themselves. Music and the sea endow the kid with a poetic register which evokes his inner conflicts; the seaside is the place he turns to as he attempts to resolve that turmoil. As 'Bell Boy', a song which ironically celebrates the fighting on the beaches, puts it: 'A beach is a place where a man can feel/He's the only soul in the world that's real'. *Quadrophenia*'s paradox is that in seeking to represent the experiences of the crowd, it turns ever more sharply on the emotions of the isolated, individual 'soul'. Townshend has commented on the long-standing relationship between his work and the concerns of his audience:

> all those West Londoners and Carnaby Street immigrants from Ireland or the Caribbean who sometimes turned to me and said that I had a knack of putting into words what they could party-dance away, but found otherwise hard to express. It turned out that what I was best at putting into words for them was the frustration that they could not put anything into words.
>
> (Townshend, 2004, pp. 7–8)

You may have felt some of this difficulty in reading the story: there is a disparity between the kid's isolation from the society he inhabits and the flashes of a deeper insight into the dynamics of his situation. Similarly, the stuttering vocal of 'My Generation' aptly figures the tongue-tied aggression of the young towards the older generation they wished would 'f-f-f-f-f-fade away'.

These tensions are present in the photos and the music of *Quadrophenia*. We're going to explore the music through two songs, 'Cut My Hair' and 'Love Reign O'er Me'. You should remember that the LP is a sequence of seventeen linked tracks. Our two tracks telescope *Quadrophenia* by focusing on the kid's alienation ('Cut My Hair') and his epiphany ('Love Reign O'er Me'). You also have a number of Russell's booklet photographs in the Illustration Book: Plate 4.4.37 (the breakfast scene), Plate 4.4.38 (Brighton Pier), Plate 4.4.39 (the boat), Plate 4.4.40 (the kid underwater) and Plates 4.4.41 and 4.4.42 (the Rock).

Activity Now listen closely to the two songs (tracks 8 and 9 on the Audio CD). Think about how the different elements of *Quadrophenia* contribute to the kid's story. How do you think the music compares with 'My Generation'?

Discussion   I would say that the music is different from 'My Generation'. Though all three are performed in the standard idioms of rock music (guitar, vocal, bass, drums), *Quadrophenia* uses a more elaborate musical palette. 'Cut My Hair' has a prominent piano part in the verses; this is supplemented by horns towards the end of the chorus as the lyric reaches the lines 'Why that uncertain feeling/Is still here in my brain'. The closing verse is shaped by sound effects: a radio report about the fight between the Mods and Rockers is overlaid by a whistling kettle, evoking a suburban breakfast. You might have noticed that the lead vocal is shared between Townshend in the introspective verses and Daltrey in the cockier, rocking choruses. 'Love Reign O'er Me' shows a similarly varied musical texture: after a lengthy piano intro with sound effects of rain, the song juxtaposes synthesisers and acoustic guitars with more traditional rock instrumentation. Keith Moon's rapid shifts from atmospheric cymbals in the verses to the full range of the drum kit in the choruses are particularly striking; Moon dramatically punctuates the gathering excitement of Daltrey's almost operatic vocal. By the end, the kid has reached a moment of musical and spiritual epiphany (or revelation) as the swooping chords show his exhilaration in musical form.

The lyrics are also more ambitious than those of 'My Generation'. 'Cut My Hair' gives a tangible sense of the kid's domestic and mental environment. This is done partly by musical means; as we've noted, there's a contrast between the introspection of the verses ('I've got to move with the fashions/Or be outcast') and the energy of the choruses ('Dressed right, for a beach fight'). The lyric helps to bring the kid's dilemma into sharper focus: he's childishly proud of his 'Zoot suit, white jacket with side vents/Five inches long', yet he registers the pitfalls of conformity and his problematic relationship with his parents. This is encapsulated by the final image 'My fried egg makes me sick/ First thing in the morning', where the words mournfully emphasise the banality of the everyday, a sense which is amplified by Townshend's laconic delivery. Note too that the song ends on a downbeat verse (rather than – as in most rock songs – a chorus), with the kid's revulsion from ordinary reality. In contrast, 'Love Reign O'er Me' doesn't really square with the idiom of either the story or the photographs. Townshend uses a poetic diction – note the archaic 'o'er' for 'over' – at odds with the realism of 'Cut My Hair'. Nevertheless, because the song attempts to encapsulate a sense of transcendence and uplift, this shift in register is appropriate. The beach of *Quadrophenia* is not just where Mods fight Rockers, but becomes a place where the individual is reconciled with his environment: 'Only love can make it rain/The way the beach is kissed by the sea'.

Russell's photographs seem to present a bleaker ending to the story. Plate 4.4.38 shows the kid's alienation as he is half-submerged in the beach beside Brighton Pier; Plates 4.4.39–42 isolate him even further by placing him first in the boat on the open sea, and then as a remote figure chasing the tide by two imposing rocks. Like 'Love Reign O'er Me', these photos juxtapose the Mod idiom of the bulk of the record with the sense of an encounter between the more powerful energies of the natural world. There is no clear resolution to *Quadrophenia*: as in the back cover image of the drowned Lambretta, the record leaves the listener with a series of questions. Is it possible to overcome mental illness? Can the kid's aggressive impulses be reined into his need for love? More broadly still, is it ever possible to grow up? This is where the kid's predicament mirrors that of his creators: like the figure on the beach, *Quadrophenia* shows The Who caught between the music and styles which made them famous in the 1960s and their more ambitious work of the 1970s. For both, the image of the sea offers a challenge and a threat.

REFERENCES

Bush, J. (2005) 'The Beach Boys', *All Music Guide*, available at http://www.allmusic.com (Accessed 8 April 2007).

Cohen, S. (1973) *Folk Devils and Moral Panics: The Creation of the Mods and Rockers*, St Albans, Paladin.

Duchen, J. (2006) 'The Who: it's only rock 'n' roll', *The Independent*, 9 October, available at http://enjoyment.independent.co.uk/music/features/article322145.ece (Accessed 9 October 2006).

Kent, M. (2005) 'Two nights at the opera', essay in the booklet accompanying The Who, *Tommy* and *Quadrophenia Live with Special Guests*, 3 DVD set, Warner Music Vision/Rhino.

Rockwell, J. (1992) 'Rock opera' in Sadie, S. (ed.) *The New Grove Dictionary of Opera*, available at *Oxford Music Online*, http://www.oxfordmusiconline.com (Accessed 27 October 2008).

Shuker, R. (1995), *Understanding Popular Music*, London and New York, Routledge.

Shuker, R. (2002), *Popular Music: The Key Concepts*, London and New York, Routledge.

Townshend, P. (2004) 'Introduction' to *Lifehouse Chronicles*, essay in the booklet accompanying 6 CD set, Eel Pie Recording Productions.

The Who (1969) *Tommy*, Track Records (LP).

The Who (1973) *Quadrophenia*, Track Records (LP).

The Who (1996a) *Live at the Isle of Wight Festival 1970*, Sanctuary Records (CD)

The Who (1996b) *Quadrophenia*, Polydor Records (CD).

The Who (2002) *Live at Leeds* (deluxe edition), Polydor Records/Universal (CD).

Wicke, P. (1990) *Rock Music: Culture, Aesthetics and Sociology* (trans. R. Fogg), Cambridge, Cambridge University Press.

FURTHER READING

Harrison, D. (1997) 'After sundown: The Beach Boys' experimental music' in Covach, J.R. and Boone, G.M. (eds) *Understanding Rock*, Oxford, Oxford University Press, pp. 33–57.

Hebdige, D. (1974) *The Style of The Mods*, Birmingham, Centre for Contemporary Cultural Studies, University of Birmingham.

Marsh, D. (1983) *Before I Get Old: The Story of The Who*, London, Plexus.

Moore, A.F. 'The Who' in *Grove Music Online. Oxford Music Online*, http://www.oxfordmusiconline.com (Accessed 27 October 2008).

Williams, P. (1997) *Brian Wilson & The Beach Boys: How Deep is the Ocean?*, London, Omnibus Press.

RESOURCES

Reading 4.2

Extract from the *All Music Guide*'s biography of The Beach Boys

Beginning their career as the most popular surf band in the nation, the Beach Boys finally emerged by 1966 as America's pre-eminent pop group, the only act able to challenge (for a brief time) the overarching success of the Beatles with both mainstream listeners and the critical community. From their 1961 debut with the regional hit 'Surfin',' the three Wilson brothers – Brian, Dennis, and Carl – plus cousin Mike Love and friend Al Jardine constructed the most intricate, gorgeous harmonies ever heard from a pop band. With Brian's studio proficiency growing by leaps and bounds during the mid-'60s, the Beach Boys also proved to be one of the best-produced groups of the '60s, exemplified by their 1966 peak with the *Pet Sounds* LP and the number one single 'Good Vibrations.' Though Brian's escalating drug use and obsessive desire to trump the Beatles (by recording the perfect LP statement) eventually led to a nervous breakdown after he heard *Sgt. Pepper's Lonely Hearts Club Band*, the group soldiered on long into the 1970s and '80s, with Brian only an inconsistent participant. The band's post-1966 material is often maligned (if it's recognized at all), but the truth is the Beach Boys continued to make great music well into the '70s. Displayed best on 1970's *Sunflower*, each member revealed individual talents never fully developed during the mid-'60s – Carl became a solid, distinctive producer and Brian's replacement as nominal bandleader, Mike continued to provide a visual focus as the frontman for live shows, and Dennis developed his own notable songwriting talents. Though legal wranglings and marginal oldies tours during the '90s often obscured what made the Beach Boys great, the band's unerring ability to surf the waves of commercial success and artistic development during the '60s made them America's first, best rock band.

The origins of the group lie in Hawthorne, CA, a southern suburb of Los Angeles situated close to the Pacific coast. The three sons of a part-time song plugger and occasionally abusive father, Brian, Dennis, and Carl grew up just a few miles from the ocean – though only Dennis had any interest in surfing itself. The three often harmonized together as youths, spurred on by Brian's fascination with '50s vocal acts like the Four Freshmen and the Hi-Lo's. Their cousin Mike Love often joined in on the impromptu sessions, and the group gained a fifth with the addition of Brian's high-school football teammate, Al Jardine. His parents helped rent instruments (with Brian on bass, Carl on guitar, Dennis on drums) and studio time to record 'Surfin',' a novelty number written by Brian and Mike. The single, initially released in 1961 on Candix and billed to the Pendletones (a musical paraphrase of the popular Pendleton shirt), prompted a little national chart action and gained the renamed Beach Boys a contract with Capitol. The group's negotiator with the label, the Wilsons' father, Murray, also took over as manager for the band. Before the release of any material for Capitol, however, Jardine left the band to attend college in the Midwest. A friend of the Wilsons, David Marks, replaced him.

Finally, in mid-1962 the Beach Boys released their major-label debut, *Surfin' Safari*. The title track, a more accomplished novelty single than its predecessor, hit the Top 20 and helped launch the surf rock craze just beginning to blossom around Southern California (thanks to artists like Dick Dale, Jan & Dean, the Chantays, and dozens more). A similarly themed follow-up, *Surfin' U.S.A.*, hit the Top Ten in early 1963 before Jardine returned from school and resumed his place in the group. By that time, the Beach Boys had recorded their first two albums, a pair of 12-track collections that added a few novelty songs to the hits they were packaged around. Though Capitol policy required the group to work with a studio producer, Brian quickly took over the sessions and began expanding the group's range beyond simple surf rock.

Source: Bush (2005).

Reading 4.3 **Mod lifestyle**

The most significant of Britain's youth cults were the mods of 1962–65. They established new terms for teenage fashion, music, drug use, mobility, exclusion. [...] The mods were arrogant and narcissistic, cynical and tense; they came on like winners, and consumption was, for them, as much a playground as a last resort; the urge was movement – from shop to shop, club to club – speeding on pills, on dance floors, on the latest fashion coup. The mods became, indeed, the 1960s symbol of consumption generally. Mod style was exploited to transform shopping (the rise of the boutique), listening (the rise of pirate radio), and dancing (the triumph of soul music).

Source: S. Frith (1981) *Sound Effects: Youth, Leisure, and the Politics of Rock 'n' Roll*, New York, Pantheon, p. 220.

Reading 4.4 **The Mods and leisure**

What made the Mods different from their contemporaries was not only their taste in music, which focussed on rock'n'roll's rhythm & blues roots and its development in American soul music and, diverging as it did from the commercial Beatlemania of the time, was represented in Britain above all by groups like The Who, The Kinks, the early Rolling Stones, The Small Faces or the Spencer Davis Group. The Mods' hallmarks also included a motorscooter, which had to be an Italian model, a Lambretta TV 175. With its battery of lights, horns and mirrors this recently popularised mode of transport was transformed into an obvious cult object. Fashionable, well-cut suits, the obligatory parkas to wear over them and a neat, short haircut were just as much part of being a Mod as the almost ritual arrangement of their leisure. Next to the scooter an excessive cult of dancing occupied centre stage in a Mod's leisure. The cult led them to spend every free evening in one of the West End music clubs or in the Soho rhythm & blues clubs. At the weekends these evenings would carry on into the early hours of the morning and the Mods countered the inevitable exhaustion of this continual ecstasy of dancing with pharmaceutical stimulants, amphetamines. The core of the Mods was composed of fifteen- to eighteen-year-old teenagers from the East End suburbs or the new housing estates in South London who belonged to a social milieu made up of a section of the working class which was participating, within certain limits, in the increasing prosperity of the consumer society and which had a secure basis for its livelihood. [...] There was nothing particularly special about them except that, with the conspicuous and exotic nature of their leisure behaviour, they provided the social basis for an important branch of British rock music.

Source: Wicke (1990), pp. 76–7.

Reading 4.5   **The Mods and The Who**

Even when, in 1965, The Who released their now famous 'My Generation', it was not an expression of a comprehensive consciousness of belonging to a particular generation, even though this was how it seemed and it was often misunderstood in this way. Yet what is emphasised in the song and what, in live performances, was regularly combined with a spectacular auto-da-fé of instruments and amplifiers – systematically reducing them to firewood – simply corresponded to the self-perception of a small section of British working-class teenagers to whom involvement with rock music had become a cultural process of a quite particular kind. These teenagers called themselves Mods, a term derived from Modernists. The Who seemed to them the very incarnation of their concept of rock music, and they were also the first band to adopt in their overall appearance the pattern of cultural use of music developed by their fans instead of merely providing the musical object of this use. Peter Townshend, the leader and artistic brains of The Who, later admitted this quite frankly in an interview for the American music magazine *Rolling Stone*: 'What the Mods taught us in the band was how to lead by following.'

Source: Wicke (1990), p. 76 (footnotes omitted).

Reading 4.6   *Quadrophenia* **short story**

I had to go to this psychiatrist every week. Every Monday. He never really knew what was wrong with me. He said I wasn't mad or anything. He said there's no such thing as madness. I told him he should try standing in a queue at Brentford football ground on a Saturday morning. I thought it might change his mind. My dad put it another way. He said I changed like the weather. One minute I'd be a tearaway, next minute all soppy and swoony over some bird. Schizophrenia, he called it. Nutty, my mum called it.

It used to be alright at home. My dad would get pissed out of his brain every single night, and when the telly finished he'd storm out of the house like a lunatic to get to the Eel and Pie shop before it closed. He'd come home with enough for an army. I never liked the eels, just the pies and mash, and the liquor. My friend Dave said that eels live on sewage. My dad must be full of it, he used to eat five bleeding cartons of eels a day. I don't think he ever twigged I was doing five cartons of leapers [amphetamines] every day. Each to his own sewage. The rows at home started when I got back from the trouble at Brighton. I'd slept on the beach and me suit was ruined. I really cared about my suit, all my clothes, even though my mother said I didn't care about anything. My mother's terrible when she's had a few Guinesses. Not that she'll ever settle for a few. As soon as I said I was leaving she started rejoicing like the war had just ended. I was a mountain of paranoia. Coming down off leapers isn't much fun. You can put it off by having more just as you start feeling bad, but it only makes it worse in the end. Pills used to make me see things. They used to make me feel great. Like Tarzan. But I think I saw life the way it was. People couldn't hide from me when I was leaping. My shrink used to have a sign on his wall to make you laugh. It said that a paranoiac is a person who has some idea what is really going on. That was me on leapers.

I pissed off after I'd slept off the come-down. I got me suit cleaned at the automat and spent two hours pressing the pissing thing. It never did look quite right. I took my parka as well, in case I had to sleep rough. I got a shitty couple of nights sleep under Hammersmith flyover. There only seems to be about five minutes in the night when there ain't some flash bastard in a sportscar going round and round with his tyres screaming and a police car bell coming up behind. On the second night I saw the posters going up outside the Odeon for a WHO concert. I'd seen them down at Brighton. They were a mod group. Well, mods liked them. They weren't exactly mods but mods did like them. They had a drummer who used to play with his arms waving about in the air like a lunatic. The singer was a tough looking bloke with really good clothes. If I hadn't have seen him near home I would have said his hair was gold. Real gold I mean, like gold paint. The guitar player was a skinny geezer with a big nose who twirled his arm like a windmill. He wrote some good songs about mods, but he didn't quite look like one. The bass player was a laugh. He never did anything. Nothing. He used to smile sometimes, but the smile would only last half a second then it would switch off again. My friend Dave said he smiled a lot more at his sister, they were engaged I think. His bass sounded like a bleeding VC10.

They played Tamla stuff and R & B. They could have been perfect if they'd played Blue Beat as well. I used to know one of them before they got their record in the charts so I went to see them. They were alright. They smashed up so much gear that nobody believed it was real. When they played down the Marquee they used real gear. I used to have a bit of bass drum to prove it. After the show I hung around outside waiting for them to come out. When they did they never bloody well recognised me. I shouted and one of them turned round and said 'How are you doing?' like he remembered me. 'Working?' he said. I hate it when people say that. Course I wasn't working. I was still at fucking school.

Next day I got a job as a dustman. Now I know why people say 'Working?' to one another. Nine quid for a full week's filthy work. They stuffed it, I left after two days with two quid in me pocket. Two of the blokes there were talking about striking for more money, but most of the geezers there had been working for the council for years. They looked upon it as some sort of church. The mayor as the Pope. One bloke has medals for being a war hero and he didn't have the guts to strike for more pay. They were all clean though, after hours.

There's a part of me that hates people. Not the actual people but how useless they are, how stupid. They sit and stew while the whole world gets worse and worse. Wars and battles. People dying of starvation. Old people dying because their kids have got their own kids and they ain't got time. That's what makes me smash things up. My shrink says I ain't mad. He should see me when I'm pissed.

I don't know what clicked inside me, but I got fed up with sleeping under the flyover. The weather was terrible for a start. Two rainy nights and that was it. I really started to fancy going back to Brighton. I still had about two hundred leapers left, kept me company. What was really weird was seeing this bird that I really liked, I even had her on the beach at Brighton. Two in a sleeping bag is really cosy until you're finished. Anyway she was with my mate Dave. Him! She walked right past me after a dance at the Goldhawk. The girl of my best friend and all that. It did me in. It was like the last straw. The real last straw was yet to come, I was so brought down, I smashed me G.S. [scooter] up in the pissing rain. I can't bear to think about it. I walked to the station down the railway tracks, across the river. I felt like throwing myself in front of a train, but I didn't. I took about twenty leapers at once, got a first class ticket to Brighton and set off to my land of my dreams.

I did something on the train. At one point I could swear I was floating about in the carriage, looking down at these two city gents. What was weirdest about it was that I could see myself as well. Must have been the pills again.

Brighton is a fantastic place. The sea is so gorgeous you want to jump into it and sink. When I was there last time there were about two thousand mods driving up and down the promenade on scooters. My scooter's seen the last of Brighton bloody promenade now, I know that. I felt really anonymous then, sort of like I was in an army. But everyone was a mod. Wherever you looked there were mods. Some of them were so well dressed it was sickening. Levi's had only come into fashion about a month before and some people had jeans on that looked like they'd been born wearing them. There was this bloke there that seemed to be the ace face. He was dancing one night in the Aquarium ballroom and everyone was copying him. He kept doing different dances, but everyone would copy it and the whole place would be dancing a dance that he'd only just made up. That's power for you. He was really heavy too, though. When the mods collected in Brighton, the Rockers would turn up too. There were never as many of them, but this geezer once took on two of them at once and beat them. That didn't usually happen I can tell you.

I was in a crowd of kids once chasing three Rockers down Brighton Pier. As it seemed they were going to get caught anyway they stopped and turned to meet their fate. All hundred of these kids I was with stopped dead. I was the first to stop, but the rest ran, so I had to follow. There's nothing uglier than a Rocker. This ace face geezer wouldn't have run. He smashed the glass doors of this hotel too. He was terrific. He had a sawn-off shotgun under his jacket and he'd be kicking at plate-glass and he still looked like he was Fred Astaire reborn. Quite funny, I met him earlier today. He ended up working at the same hotel. But he wasn't the manager.

I never ever felt like I blasphemed. You know, in an old fashioned sense. But I was in a pretty blasphemous mood when I left for Brighton. Brighton cheered me up. But then it let me down. Me folks had let me down, Rock had let me down, women had let me down, work wasn't worth the effort, school isn't even worth mentioning. But I never ever thought I'd feel let down by being a mod. I pinched this boat, first time I'd ever been on a boat at sea. I had another few leapers to keep from coming down and I felt a bit bravado. So I headed for this Rock out off the coast. It was sticking up very jagged, but very peaceful. I didn't know then what I was up to, but I know now.

Schizophrenic! What a laugh. It must be alright to be plain ordinary mad. About halfway over I took a swallow of this Gilbeys gin I'd bought. Booze never did help me much though. On the boat it did me right in, specially on top of the pills and the come-down. Anyway, the sound of the engine turned into this drone, then the drone turned into a sound like pianos or something. Like heavenly choirs or orchestras tuning up. It was really an incredible sound. Like the sort of noise you'd expect to hear in heaven, if there is such a place. I pinched myself and I wasn't really drunk anymore. I was floating. I felt really happy. I must have looked bloody stupid as it happens. I was waving me Gilbeys around in the air and singing in tune with the engine. The sound got better and better, I was nearly delirious when I got to the Rock. I switched off the engine and jumped onto it. When the engine stopped, so did the music. And when that beautiful music stopped, I remembered the come-down I had, I felt sick from the booze, the sea was splashing all over the place and there was thunder in the distance. I remembered why I had come to this bastard Rock.

So that's why I'm here, the bleeding boat drifted off and I'm stuck here in the pissing rain with my life flashing before me. Only it isn't flashing, it's crawling. Slowly. Now it's just the bare bones of what I am.

> A tough guy, a helpless dancer.
> A romantic, is it me for a moment?
> A bloody lunatic, I'll even carry your bags.
> A beggar, a hypocrite, love reign over me.
>
> Schizophrenic? I'm Bleeding Quadrophenic.

(No one in this story is meant to represent anyone either living or dead, particularly not the Mum and Dad. Our Mums and Dads are all very nice and live in bungalows which we bought for them in the Outer Hebrides.)

Source: Pete Townshend in the CD booklet of The Who (1996b).

4.7 *BHAJI ON THE BEACH*

Clive Baldwin

INTRODUCTION: BLACKPOOL AND THE SEASIDE

In this section we are going to look at *Bhaji on the Beach* (1993). This was director Gurinder Chadha's first feature film; you may be familiar with it, or you may have seen one of her later films, *What's Cooking?* (2000), *Bend It Like Beckham* (2002), *Bride and Prejudice* (2004), or *Angus, Thongs and Perfect Snogging* (2008). The screenplay was co-written by Chadha with Meera Syal, who has a highly successful career as actor, novelist and writer for the stage and television. During this course you have already studied two plays and looked at other pieces of film, and here you will be taking a further step by considering one of the most common and popular forms of dramatic representation: the feature film. *Bhaji on the Beach* will be discussed both in relation to the themes of the seaside that you have already encountered and as a particular representation of contemporary British identity and culture.

Activity

For this activity, you will need the set DVD, Bhaji on the Beach.

You should begin by getting a sense of the overall story of the film. There are two ways to do this. You could simply watch the whole film, which will take about an hour and a half, or you could watch four key sequences in conjunction with the summary printed in the Media notes. If you choose the latter route, I think you should allow an hour or so. (Note that the DVD of the film has optional subtitles that may be helpful.)

As you consider the film, focus on the following questions:

1   How does the representation of Blackpool fit with, or challenge, impressions of the seaside resort that you may have gained from earlier discussions in this book?

2   Blackpool might be considered the epitome of the English seaside resort, and the film shows us its beach, donkey rides, pier, and so on, but can you find aspects of the setting that refer to different cultures?

Discussion

1   To some extent, this is a personal response. I think that the film echoes the expectation that Blackpool is a destination where people can enjoy themselves and get away from the cares of the everyday world. In many respects the film's representation of Blackpool is exactly what you would expect in terms of such images as the Tower, the beach, the amusements, the pier, and so on.

Perhaps there is another element to this. Watching a film – until you become an OU student! – is a leisure activity and therefore might be expected to be pleasurable. *Bhaji on the Beach* has strongly comic elements and these are likely to be entertaining for the viewer, so there are some parallels between the viewer of the film and the women's enjoyment of their leisure.

Yet the women's outing is certainly not a simple escape from the everyday into the adult playground of Blackpool. For some of them, troubles, in the form of men, pursue them there and disrupt the day in various ways.

This, then, is one dimension of complexity in the film – what might be regarded as a tension between the expectation of a straightforward enjoyment of leisure and the reality that such escape may either be impossible or merely transient.

2   The film draws attention to the 'exotic' aspects of Blackpool. For instance, one of the women – Rekha – exclaims 'Bombay!' on first sight of the Golden Mile. Other examples I noticed were the photographer dressed in a turban who takes photos of visitors holding a python, and the camel race side-show with the supervisor dressed as an Arab. In this, the film draws attention to connections with Britain's colonial past. The Englishness with which we might associate Blackpool is therefore shown to be less straightforward than it might first appear. What I also note is that the tone of the film is playful in this representation of the cultural diversity of the Blackpool experience.

Figure 4.33   The women's group on the bus, from the film *Bhaji on the Beach*. Photo source: BFI. 'By permission of ITN Source'. Left to right, sitting: Rekha, Pushpa, Hashida, Ginder; standing: Ladhu, Amrik, Simi, Madhu, Asha.

WHAT KIND OF FILM?

A useful question to ask in considering *Bhaji on the Beach* is what sort of film it is and therefore what meanings it might have for an audience. Chadha is a successful director and she sees herself as 'more of a populist filmmaker' than involved with experimental film-making, and regards her films as 'part of the mainstream [...] but at the same time subverting and playing with it' (Koshy, 1996, p. 156).

One aspect of this playfulness and subversion may be seen in the film's juxtaposition of cultural elements. In an interview with June Givanni published in 1993, Chadha discusses this in terms of bringing together the aesthetics of Indian cinema and British cinema:

> Some of that aesthetic formation takes place in the editing, particularly the Indian elements because they depend on a different quirkier editing style. The music and sound effects also add another dimension which allows you to expand and enhance certain emotions or themes in conjunction with the pictures. It is during the editing that the film finally takes on the many layers of meaning beyond the main narrative. I always have a great time mixing codes and subverting the expected image of black people on the screen.
>
> In *Bhaji* what I found emerging (although it was always in my subconscious) is the pull between a very British film on the one hand and being quite Indian on the other and that pull is present in every single scene, in every single character, every single frame of the film. I'm pleased that we have been able to bring that tension and dynamism into the film. We as black people live with this duality – this pull – every day of our lives but it's also the force that feeds me as a film-maker.
>
> (Givanni, 1993)

I shall return to this 'duality', but for now I want to pull out Chadha's reference to music and consider the use of the song 'Summer Holiday' in the film, thinking about the way it invokes both the 'British' and the 'Indian' that Chadha talks about. The song was originally recorded by the British singer Cliff Richard for a film of the same title released in 1963. Its use in *Bhaji on the Beach* invokes multiple associations. In the first place it is sung in **Punjabi** and in this it foregrounds the cultural implications of these Asian women indulging in their seaside visit.

The song also associates the film with a particular genre, the road movie. In *Summer Holiday* Cliff Richard and his associates drive a red London double-decker Routemaster bus (another prime sign of Englishness) around Europe. Narratives based on journeys have long been established as powerful ways of exploring aspects of our experience of the world, and the road movie derives from these. As a film genre, it was established in the period after the Second World War when the widespread availability of cars in America increased mobility. The road movie may also be a way of providing a different perspective on a culture. In suggesting four possible endings for the road movie, the online reference source Wikipedia offers a thought-provoking approach:

- Having met with triumph at their ultimate destination, the protagonist(s) returns home, wiser for their experiences.

- At the end of the journey, the protagonist(s) finds a new home at their destination.

- The journey continues endlessly. In such cases, the last shot of the film is almost always the driver's point of view of a lonely highway at night.

- Having realised that, as a result of their journey, they can never go home, the protagonist(s) either chooses death or is killed.

(http://en.wikipedia.org/wiki/Road_movie)

You might find this an interesting way of thinking about the film, but *Bhaji on the Beach* isn't a simple 'road movie': you might think of it also as a comedy, or as having elements of melodrama. In these allusions, you can see Chadha playing with the expectations the viewer may have of particular film genres.

Activity
You should allow about twenty minutes to watch the DVD Video 'Interview with Gurinder Chadha'.

Sholay (1975) is one of the most popular Bollywood films. It is referred to by Gurinder Chadha in the interview on the DVD Video.

The playfulness I have just discussed is picked up by Gurinder Chadha in an interview that you can find on the DVD Video 'Interview with Gurinder Chadha'. This interview was specially recorded for the course and covers a number of other topics. For example, she talks about going to the beach herself as a child, and what films she watched as she grew up. You will also discover that she and Meera Syal, her fellow scriptwriter, thought they would change the world by dealing with two controversial themes. The longest section in the interview is about Chadha's sense of identity and the significance of identity in the film. You might note her comments about how Simi expresses her identity through her choice of clothes and consider Chadha's own style in Figure 4.34. Gurinder Chadha is a very engaging and clear speaker, so this might be a good moment to break off from your reading and discover what the director of the film herself thinks about its themes. You may prefer to press on, but you are certainly advised to watch the interview at some point if you are discussing the film in your final assignment.

IDENTITIES

Let's move on to consider the characters and the plot of the film. I have argued that the film depicts the day trip to Blackpool as more than simple leisurely enjoyment and that the English seaside as experienced at Blackpool juxtaposes diverse cultural elements. So how does the film present the experience of the Asian women from Birmingham?

Figure 4.34   Gurinder Chadha, 1989. Unknown photographer. Photo: BFI.

One way of approaching this question is through the notion of cultural identity. We have already touched on this in considering Blackpool itself. While Blackpool might have a case for claiming to be *the* English seaside resort, entwined in the entertainment on offer are elements from beyond England – elements that derive from England's colonial past. The title of the film itself foregrounds these cultural inter-relationships, referring to the traditional English beach picnic (and possibly memories of the unpleasant combination of sand and sandwiches) and introducing one of the most common Indian snacks. Thus the women themselves bring a new set of cultural interactions to Blackpool. One example of this is Pushpa's reaction to eating chips – she pulls a face but then decides they are much more tasty sprinkled with some spices. Another example is the joke involving the two young Indian teenagers, Ladhu and Madhu, who take up with the teenage cowboys serving burgers.

If you look at Oxford Reference Online, which is available through the course website, you should find a discussion of the term 'hybridity' in *A Dictionary of Sociology*.

One term that has been used in recent thinking about these sorts of cultural encounter is 'hybridity', and this is a word that Gurinder Chadha uses in the interview. The notion of hybridity had negative connotations in the colonial period, when Europeans believed it was essential to ensure the 'purity' of 'races' and cultures, and the 'hybrid' meant a sullying of that purity. Recently, changed attitudes to 'race' and culture have turned 'hybridity' into a more positive term, suggesting creative cultural interaction and change. It could be argued that *Bhaji on the Beach* can be seen from this perspective, and that the film demonstrates how a vibrant contemporary British culture has been created from diverse cultural exchanges. However, while the exchanges in Blackpool noted above are light-hearted representations of mingling cultural identities, the film also draws attention to the tensions that may arise for individuals who are trying to negotiate their way through what may be conflicting cultural demands in contemporary Britain.

Here, for example, is the writer Hanif Kureshi (b. 1954) describing such conflicts of identity in 1986:

> I was born in London of an English mother and a Pakistani father. My father, who lives in London, came to England from Bombay in 1947 to be educated by the old colonial power. He married here and never went back to India. [...]

> In the mid-1960s, Pakistanis were a risible subject in England, derided on television and exploited by politicians. They had the worst jobs, they were uncomfortable in England, some of them had difficulties with the language. They were despised and out of place.

> From the start I tried to deny my Pakistani self. I was ashamed. It was a curse and I wanted to be rid of it. I wanted to be like everybody else. [...] At school, one teacher always spoke to me in a 'Peter Sellers' Indian accent. [Peter Sellers (1925–1980) was an English comedy actor.] Another refused to call me by my name, calling me Pakistani Pete instead. [...]

> [Kureshi goes on to describe a visit to Pakistan when he is older.] I was having a little identity crisis. I'd been greeted so warmly in Pakistan, I felt so excited by what I saw, and so at home with all my uncles, I wondered if I were not better off here than there. And when I said, with a little unnoticed irony, that I was an Englishman, people laughed. They fell about. Why would anyone with a brown face, Muslim name and a large well-known family in Pakistan want to lay claim to that cold little decrepit island off Europe where you always had to spell your name? Strangely, anti-British remarks made me feel patriotic, although I only felt patriotic when I was away from England.

But I couldn't allow myself to feel too Pakistani. I didn't want to give in to that falsity, that sentimentality. [...] I couldn't rightfully lay claim to either place.

(Kureshi, 1996, pp. 73, 81)

Activity

On the DVD of Bhaji on the Beach, *Scene 7 starts at 33 min. 54 sec.*

Kureshi's description of his inner conflicts chimes with Chadha's reference to living with 'duality'. Bearing this in mind, turn again to the film and find Scene 7, 'News travels fast', on the DVD. Watch the events on the beach. How would you describe the events and what they show about the relationships within the group?

Discussion

The scene begins with playful splashing in the water, a donkey ride, beach games, etc., but ends with a blazing row as it is revealed that Hashida is pregnant by her 'black' boyfriend, Oliver. The women are initially shown as united in their pleasure in the English seaside and what it offers. However, differing attitudes to Ginder's rejection of her husband and his family and to Hashida's relationship reveal a generational divide. This divide is not simply one of age but of experience, as the older women look back to India as their source of correct behaviour while the younger women, born in the UK, have to negotiate the contradictory demands of their families and of their own expectations, which have been influenced by contemporary English culture. Suddenly their relationship with the typical Englishness of the seaside becomes symptomatic of their fraught negotiation of identity in contemporary Britain. This is further emphasised in the later café scene, during which first Pushpa and then Bina are racially abused by the owner; they in turn name Hashida a whore; and Hashida reacts aggressively to all of them.

It is worth noting the power of food as a sign of cultural difference. The conflict in the café arises because the women are eating Indian food and because their behaviour breaks the convention that you do not eat your own food in an English café. The women show their difference in these two respects, and for the café owner this seems to justify her aggression.

There is not space here to review the development of what is generally called British multicultural society since the Second World War, but I do want to note that intercultural relationships in Britain are continually changing. For example, at the time of writing in 2008, there is a particular attention to religious difference and the social integration of Muslims. The sociologist Stuart Hall, a Professor Emeritus at the Open University, has written extensively about such changes. For example, in 'New ethnicities' (originally published in 1987) he writes about a shift in black cultural politics around that time. He identifies a first phase that was

the moment when the term 'black' was coined as a way of referencing the common experience of racism and marginalisation in Britain and came to provide the organising category of a new politics of resistance, among groups and communities with, in fact, very different histories, traditions and ethnic identities.

(Hall, 1996 [1987], p. 163)

Hall then goes on to the second phase, which, he emphasises, is not a simple replacement of the first: 'What is at issue here is the recognition of the extraordinary diversity of subjective positions, social experiences, and cultural identities which compose the category "black"' (Hall, 1996 [1987], p. 166).

This is how Chadha herself describes this change:

> what I am is a product of a second-generation black community. I became involved with filmmaking at a time when there were several Afro-Caribbean black film workshops in Britain. They had set up with money from [the television company] Channel 4 and the British Film Institute to start making films that were going to challenge the way black people were represented in mainstream film, and to also find new ways to tell stories about the black community.

> Now up until that point, we had found a lot of value in calling ourselves 'black,' because we sons and daughters of migrants in Britain had found it empowering to categorise ourselves under that united label, and in the struggles on the street and against the state, the term 'black' was very powerful; of course, it had connections with the black movement in the States. Then there came a point within the artistic community where 'black' was too limited as a way to talk about all the subcultural contexts within it.

> (Koshy, 1996, p. 152)

Bhaji on the Beach explores these 'subcultural contexts' by showing differences in attitudes between British Asians and Afro-Caribbeans, between men and women, and between the generations. At the same time, the café scene reminds the audience that beyond such subcultural differences, black people in Britain often remain subjected to racist attitudes.

TRIUMPH AND RESOLUTION?

On the DVD of Bhaji on the Beach, *Scene 15 starts at 1 hr 23 min. 16 sec.*

The final scenes of the film focus on the marital dispute between Ginder and Ranjit, and their conflict over their son Amrik. The sequence begins with scenes in Manhattan's Bar, where the women have arranged to meet up before their return (Scene 15, 'Manhattan's Bar', on the DVD). The film shows the performance of the male strippers at the club and this draws our attention to a further aspect of cultural identity: different expectations of women's and men's sexuality. The performance is also the occasion for revealing the evidence of Ginder's physical abuse by Ranjit and makes clear that her flight to a women's refuge was not undertaken lightly.

Figure 4.35   Hashida and her boyfriend Oliver discuss their future, from the film *Bhaji on the Beach*. Photo: UMBI Films/Channel 4/the Kobal Collection. By permission of ITN Source.

Activity   As a final activity, I want you to use the ideas we have been considering about diverse cultural identities to analyse the end of the film. Here are two questions:

1   How do the events in the final scenes and the arrival of Ranjit and his brothers affect the viewer's perception of the women as a group?

2   One possible ending for road movies is that the protagonists are triumphant at their ultimate destination, and return home, wiser for their experiences. Would you see this as an accurate description of the end of *Bhaji on the Beach*?

Discussion   1   I would say that there is a shift in emphasis. The film has foregrounded issues of ethnic identity and different generational perspectives; now the focal point is the interconnection between **gender** and culture. The first revelation is Ginder's bruising, and the second is the violent behaviour of Ranjit and his brother, Balbir. Up until this point the older women have tended to be suspicious of Ginder and to regard her as failing to conform to culturally appropriate female or wifely behaviour. The scenes outside the club shift the focus onto a demonstration of masculinity that not only asserts its authority but uses force to do so. The older women are shocked by Ranjit's violence and Asha physically intervenes. So the generational divisions between the women dissolve and there is the suggestion that within contemporary British culture there may be strong shared interests between all women.

2   The women return home on the bus having defeated Ranjit, and with Oliver apparently committed to a relationship with Hashida. This seems to be both triumph and wisdom gained.

Figure 4.36   Ranjit and his brothers, Balbir and Manjit, from the film *Bhaji on the Beach*. Photo: Channel 4 Films/Ronald Grant Archive. By permission of ITN Source. The title on the photograph refers to a German version of the film.

However, I would like to suggest that while the various plot lines appear to be resolved, it could be argued that the film leaves open the complex issues of gender and cultural identity that have been presented to the viewer as part of life in a multicultural society.

How in the end does the film represent the women's relationship to the dominant British culture? It is conventional to argue that such articulations of a different cultural perspective have altered our perceptions of what Englishness might be. This is undoubtedly true. However, it is also the case that the resolution of Ginder and Ranjit's conflict takes place on a rainy English summer evening, not in the light of the Blackpool Illuminations but unobserved under the pier in darkness. Do you think this is significant?

I should like to end with a final thought about the seaside. The shore marks the border between the solid land and the fluid sea. The seaside is therefore a liminal space – a threshold – where people may move from one element to another. If you consider the seaside in these terms, it might seem a particularly appropriate space for the women in the film whose identities are not clearly fixed, but subject to negotiation and renegotiation in contemporary Britain.

REFERENCES

Givanni, J. (1993) 'Blackpool's Bhaji: Gurinder Chadha interviewed', *Black Film Bulletin*, vol. 1, no. 1 (spring), p. 10.

Hall, S. (1996 [1987]) 'New ethnicities' in Baker Jr., H.A., Diawara, M. and Lindeborg, R.H. (eds) *Black British Cultural Studies: A Reader*, Chicago, Chicago University Press, pp. 163–72.

Koshy, S. (1996) 'Turning color: a conversation with Gurinder Chadha', *Transition*, no. 72, pp. 148–61.

Kureshi, H. (1996) 'The rainbow sign' in Kureshi, *My Beautiful Laundrette and Other Writings*, London, Faber & Faber, pp. 71–102.

Wikipedia entry on 'Road movie', available at http://en.wikipedia.org/wiki/Road_movie (Accessed 11 November 2007).

FURTHER READING

Bhattacharyya, G. and Gabriel, J. (1994) 'Gurinder Chadha and the *apna* generation: Black British film in the 1990s', *Third Text*, vol. 27 (summer), pp. 55–63.

Malik, S. (1996) 'Beyond "The cinema of duty"? The pleasures of hybridity: Black British film of the 1980s and 1990s', in Higson, A. (ed.) *Dissolving Views: Key Writings on British Cinema*, London, Cassell, pp. 202–15.

RESOURCES

Media notes

Notes on *Bhaji on the Beach*

Principal characters

Ginder: wife of Ranjit and mother of Amrik

Amrik: Ginder's son

Ranjit: Ginder's husband

Balbir: Ranjit's violent brother

Manjit: Ranjit's sympathetic brother

Hashida: prospective medical student, who is pregnant

Oliver: Hashida's boyfriend

Asha: shopkeeper/mother, who has visions

Simi: runs the Saheli centre, a women's refuge

Pushpa: older woman

Ladhu: teenage girl

Madhu: teenage girl, Ladhu's sister, particularly interested in boys

Bina: Asha's friend

Rekha: visiting from Bombay and away from her businessman husband

Ambrose Waddington: stalwart of Blackpool theatre who takes up with Asha

Key sequences

In order to get a sense of the overall story of film, you could watch the following key sequences in conjunction with the plot summary. The summary shows where each sequence appears in the film. The total running time of the sequences is about forty minutes.

Sequence	Description	DVD Scene
1	Asha's newsagent's shop and the Hindu gods	Scene 1 (from opening credits to 2 min. 49 sec.)
2	Picnic on Blackpool beach	Scene 7 (from 33 min. 54 sec. to 42 min. 53 sec.)
3	Blackpool scenes	Scene 10 (from 53 min. 26 sec. to 1 hr 6 min. 33 sec.)
4	In the Manhattan bar and under the pier	Scene 15 (from 1 hr 23 min. 16 sec. to 1 hr 35 min. 52 sec.)

Plot summary

Sequence 1   The film opens in Birmingham. It focuses on Asha, who is a principal character with her own sub-plot. In the opening of the film we are shown Asha's visions, which are a recurrent element of her experience – in this case she sees visions of Hindu gods. These are interspersed with scenes of her with her husband and children. The beginning of the film presents us with the context in which Asha – and, by implication, the other characters – lives, juxtaposing a variety of cultural images. This variety, it is suggested, is for Asha in fact a set of conflicting demands on her which leave her confused.

Ginder in the Saheli women's refuge. She is reading a letter and looking concerned. She is then shown with her son, Amrik, dressed as Batman and asking to see his father. She tells him they are going to the seaside for the day.

Ranjit in his bedroom with an empty cot. His brother, Manjit, comes in and asks whether there is any news in the letter he has received. Ranjit angrily sends him away.

Street scene in suburban Birmingham – semi-detached houses. Ladhu and Madhu's mother is talking to the teenage boy next door. Ladhu and Madhu come out ready for the trip to Blackpool and their mother observes that he is a lovely boy, but they mock him and her.

The kitchen and dining room in Ranjit's house at breakfast time. Ranjit's mother is berating him for Ginder's behaviour and her request for a divorce – this will cause social embarrassment. The information about the divorce suggests the content of the letters received by Ranjit and Ginder that morning. Ranjit's father tells him to bring back Ginder and their grandson. He asks Manjit to go with Ranjit, but their brother Balbir intervenes, saying that he will take charge as he is the eldest.

At Asha's shop. Ranjit arrives and it is made apparent that he is related to her. He asks her whether she knows anything of Ginder; she doesn't but shows her sympathies are with him, calling him a 'Poor boy'. Asha is ready to go to Blackpool and calls her neighbour, Pushpa, to come along. Pushpa has the shop next door and her husband is attempting to clear off a large swastika daubed on the shutters.

Ginder at the refuge, holding the letter and speaking on the phone to her mother. Her mother is telling her to try again, and when Ginder tells her that the divorce has already gone through, the connection is cut. Ginder goes upstairs with Amrik, and Simi arrives. Simi runs the centre and is organising the trip to Blackpool. Ginder shows the letter to Simi, who responds that she has turned a corner. However, Ginder is clearly disturbed by the letter and the call to her mother. She is debating whether to go to Blackpool but she agrees that Amrik needs to get out.

Hashida is at home in the bathroom, just discovering she is pregnant from the test she has done. She then tries to get on the phone to Oliver, her lover, who is in student accommodation, but is called away by her mother before she can speak to him. Over breakfast Hashida's parents are discussing the fact that she is going to university to read medicine. Hashida has retreated to her room and is weeping when Simi arrives to pick her up for the trip to Blackpool. Hashida tells Simi what has happened and asks her to give her a lift to tell Oliver, but Simi is doubtful, saying that Oliver is 'not exactly Mr Reliable'. Hashida gets in the car with Simi, Ginder and Amrik, who asks if they are going to pick up his father.

Rekha, in western dress with a short skirt, arrives at the Saheli centre in a taxi. Bina, Asha's friend, also arrives, followed by Asha and Pushpa. It becomes evident that Asha has invited Rekha, who is on a visit to England from Bombay. Hashida is dropped off at Oliver's student accommodation.

Hashida is in Oliver's room. In their conversation it becomes apparent that their relationship has had to be kept secret from Hashida's parents and Oliver accuses her of always doing what pleases them. He claims that the relationship has been nothing but 'hassle' and Hashida walks out, saying she will have to sort things out herself.

Simi arrives late at the Saheli centre and the women all get in the minibus. Ginder says hello in a friendly manner to Asha, who coldly tells her that she should ring her husband. Simi welcomes the women onto the bus, telling them that it is not often they can escape from patriarchy and the double yoke of sexism and racism. The older women exchange doubtful glances. As Simi drives off, Hashida arrives and gets on the bus. As they drive away, 'Summer Holiday' is played for the first time, and continues as they drive up the M6.

The scene is a small commercial kitchen and Balbir is physically threatening Ginder's uncle and demanding to know where Ginder is. Ranjit intervenes and tries a softer approach, but Balbir is impatient and seizes him again. He succeeds in obtaining the address of the refuge.

On the minibus, and the older women are sharing their negative assessment of Ginder, expressing concern for the respective families. Asha has a melodramatic vision, this time of Ranjit's family at a meal with Ginder behaving in a slovenly way and Ranjit's mother having what appears to be a heart attack.

The previous scene dissolves into a scene of the refuge with Balbir harassing the women and children there and destroying property. One of the women tells them of the trip to Blackpool. It is at this point that Manjit reveals a more sympathetic character, stepping in between Balbir and the women and apologising for his behaviour.

The women in the minibus are 'mooned' by some young white men in another minibus. Ginder tells Hashida that she gave up the chance to go to college to get married, saying that Hashida wouldn't be so stupid, but she also celebrates having had her son.

The student accommodation. Oliver is with his friend Joe, who tells Oliver that he should be pleased Hashida has gone.

The minibus stops at the motorway services. Ranjit and his brothers set off up the M6. There is a scene in the women's toilets, where Hashida is talking in a cubicle to Simi about her pregnancy – a conversation that Ladhu and Madhu overhear. After the girls have spoken to Hashida about what they have heard, they leave and Asha appears from another cubicle. Hashida phones Oliver, but the conversation breaks down as in the background Joe prompts Oliver to end communication. As Hashida and Simi come out of the building at the services they are harassed by two of the young men who had 'mooned' them on the M6. When they brush them off, an aggressive incident ensues with the group of young men gesturing at the minibus and throwing beer cans at it.

Oliver calls on his father and tells him that Hashida is pregnant. Oliver's father assumes that they will get married and expresses concern because he knows that Oliver will not be welcomed by Hashida's family. Oliver responds that he will not marry as the relationship is over, but his father asks if he is going to abandon Hashida when she is pregnant, saying that is not how he has brought him up. So his father makes Oliver feel he has a moral responsibility for Hashida.

On the minibus, Asha has another vision, informed by her new knowledge about Hashida: Hashida turns up at a religious ceremony with her parents, with dyed orange hair, dressed in a provocative red dress, obviously pregnant and smoking.

Oliver arrives at Hashida's parents' house and asks where she is. Oliver introduces himself as a friend of hers from college but her parents are uneasy about this unexpected visitor. However, they tell Oliver where she has gone and he sets off to Blackpool on his motorbike, carrying a spare helmet.

Ranjit has stopped at the motorway services and is talking to Manjit, who is trying to persuade him that he cannot force Ginder to return, especially as the courts are involved. It becomes apparent from this exchange that while Ranjit has blamed Ginder for their marital problems and protests his innocence, Manjit does not believe the official family account. Balbir returns and tells Manjit that every time he talks, his wife 'jumps out'.

The women in the minibus are singing a traditional song as they approach Blackpool.

Sequence 2   Blackpool and the picnic on the beach. The sequence ends with Ambrose, the theatrical Englishman, rescuing Asha from the sea.

In a Blackpool pub. Hashida is weeping and talking to Ladhu: she has realised that she can no longer keep her pregnancy secret from her parents. Madhu has got changed and is putting on make-up. The cowboys turn up and buy Ladhu and Madhu a drink. It turns out that

Ranjit and his brothers are in the same pub. While Ranjit and Manjit are talking, Balbir is chatting up a young woman. Ranjit reveals that he is going to try to get hold of Amrik in the expectation that Ginder will then come home after him. Balbir finds Ladhu and Madhu in the pub and realises that Ginder must be around.

Ambrose has helped Asha buy some shoes and he is shown outside hobnobbing with some theatrical friends who are dressed as sharks – Ambrose lives for the theatre and his acting. Simi talks to Asha, who may be slightly embarrassed about being seen with Ambrose and is feeling guilty about revealing Hashida's pregnancy. Simi suggests that she talks to Ginder, who is nearby. Manjit arrives, following Ladhu and Madhu, but when he sees Ginder he steers Ranjit and Balbir off in another direction. Asha says to Ginder that perhaps she could intervene with the two families. Ginder refuses the offer, but Asha gives Ginder the money to have her hair done.

Ladhu and Madhu are following Hashida, who is going to a clinic to find out about an abortion. Hashida tries again to phone Oliver, but he is on his motorbike approaching Blackpool.

Sequence 3   Various scenes in Blackpool

Asha is walking in the public gardens with Ambrose. It turns out that the previous year Ambrose's wife 'turned feminist' and went off with her agent Mandy. Asha then has another fantasy in which Ambrose is an Indian and is pursuing her. The vision is spoiled when she wakes up drenched by the garden sprinklers.

Ladhu and Madhu are saying goodbye to their cowboys. Hashida is having a consultation about abortion and Oliver arrives in Blackpool. They are both shown wandering about, but Oliver cannot find her. However, he meets Simi, who tells him that if he wants Hashida he must be everything to her: family and community.

Ambrose shows Asha the theatre. He is affectionate but she has another vision of a deity who reminds her of her duty, although she asks, 'What about me?' She then has a vision of her husband and tells Ambrose she must go back to her group.

Ranjit and his brothers bump into Asha, and he asks her to help him. She abruptly abandons Ambrose.

Simi and Oliver are looking for Hashida. He sees a Mervyn Peake exhibition and surmises that Hashida may be there – what she is truly interested in is art, not medicine. He finds her and there is the beginning of a reconciliation.

Ladhu is berating Madhu for her dalliance with the cowboy, asking why she is going for the 'white prats' – Madhu answers that it's because the 'brown prats' are doing it with the white girls.

Manhattan Bar. The group gradually reassembles. Meanwhile, out on the seafront, Oliver and Hashida are talking things through and Hashida tells him she will have the baby and go to college. He responds that they will do it together but with no sneaking around. They kiss and, as they do so, the Illuminations are turned on. Simi arrives at the Manhattan. The male strippers – the Sons of Liberty – are announced. Asha brings Ranjit to the Manhattan so he can speak to Ginder. Pushpa is brought up to dance with the strippers in a scene that amuses her friends but she finds humiliating.

Sequence 4   Ranjit and his brothers wait outside the Manhattan, having discovered from Asha that Ginder is there. Ranjit's pursuit of Ginder and Amrik is concluded under the pier in the dark.

GLOSSARY

angle of vision   the implied line along which an imagined viewer looks into the represented space of a painting.

ataraxia   an ancient Greek word meaning tranquillity. Epicurus identified pleasure with a state of tranquillity. He thought that achieving this state was the objective of human life.

axonometric   a term used to describe an architectural plan in which vertical lines are rendered vertically and lines on the ground plane (e.g. wall lines) are drawn at either 45 or 135 degrees to the horizontal.

black-face minstrels   a form of musical entertainment that emerged in the USA in the nineteenth century and became more widely popular. It involved (usually) white performers stereotypically blackening their faces to perform what were then perceived as traditional 'black' songs.

brass instruments   the family of musical instruments that includes the trumpet, trombone, tuba and cornet. Oddly, not all brass instruments are made of brass. The factor that defines the species is the way the sound is produced. In brass instruments the sound is always produced by the player's lips, which vibrate in the 'mouthpiece' of the instrument.

charabanc   from the French 'char à bancs' (carriage with benches), in Britain the term denotes an open-topped motorbus commonly used for outings during the first half of the twentieth century.

communards   members of the 1871 Paris Commune.

costume painting   pictures of people and episodes from the past – a past that was often romanticised or used to introduce moralising content into art.

Druid   a member of a religious movement associated with pre-Roman Celtic spirituality.

Epicureanism   a philosophical school of thought following Epicurus, a moral and natural philosopher of the late fourth century BCE.

ethics (or **moral philosophy**)   the branch of philosophy that concerns how people ought to conduct their lives, and how they ought to behave towards each other.

eudaimonia   an ancient Greek word which is usually translated as 'well-being', 'flourishing' or 'happiness'. Greek philosophers agreed that *eudaimonia* is the objective of human life, but disagreed about what it is. Aristotle took *eudaimonia* to be a life of virtuous and rational activity, supplemented by good health, moderate wealth and friendship. Epicurus identified *eudaimonia* with pleasure, which he took to be a state of tranquillity (***ataraxia***).

falsetto   treble vocal register which can be produced by the adult male voice.

feedback   in music, the whining sound created when part of the electronic signal produced by an electric guitar played at high volume is fed back to the guitar through the amplifier.

forum   a central public space or square in a Roman town.

gender   in analysing the different status of men and women in Western societies, feminist theory of the 1970s emphasised a distinction between 'sex', to refer to biological differences between men and women, and 'gender', to refer to culturally produced differences. This distinction is still commonly used, but the notion of straightforward male and female biological identities has been questioned.

Industrial Revolution   conventionally, the period of British history from the later eighteenth to the early nineteenth centuries when the basis of the economy shifted from agriculture to manufacturing. This term is sometimes challenged by historians who believe (i) that it obscures the importance of much earlier cultural, economic and technological changes; or (ii) that it underestimates the continuities between the agricultural and the industrial economies; or (iii) that 'revolution' is an inappropriate label for processes that took a century and perhaps more to work though the economy.

lido   an open-air public swimming pool, and associated facilities. Lidos became popular in the early twentieth century. The name comes from Venice's famous bathing beach.

megalith   literally 'large stone', usually referring to a stone erected as part of an ancient construction, such as Stonehenge.

menhir   this term is derived from a Breton word to refer to a large stone, erected singly or in arrangement with others in an ancient construction.

metaphysics   the branch of philosophy that is concerned with what kinds of thing exist and how they relate to each other. Examples of metaphysical questions include: could there be time travel? Is the mind the same thing as the brain? Do living things have functions?

middle eight   part of a song which is not a verse or a chorus; it typically comes towards or just after the middle of a song, and may or may not last eight bars.

mosaic   an artistic medium that uses small pieces of differently coloured stones, usually cut into cubes and placed side by side to form a pattern.

Motown music   a style of **soul music** that was produced in Detroit, Michigan, USA in the 1960s (Motown is a derivative of Detroit's nickname, 'Motor-town', because it was the centre of the US car industry). Motown songs included the use of tambourine along with drums, and a 'call and response' singing style that originated in gospel music.

negotium   a Latin term, meaning literally 'not leisure'. This could cover business activities, political duties or public service.

new town   a planned urban development that may be an entirely new settlement built from scratch, or a planned extension to an existing one.

otium   a Latin term, meaning leisure, implying time away from the obligations covered by *negotium*, and an opportunity for intellectual and creative pursuits.

outro   an ending to a song. It sometimes has lyrics or words but is usually just music.

Padjamers   a term originally applied to the artisans and small farmers who trekked each year from inland Lancashire to the coast, seeking benefit from the supposed health-giving properties of seawater, at the time of the August spring tides (unusually high tides occurring at the time of a full or new moon). This time was known as Bathing Sunday. A contemporary chronicle of Blackpool implies that the term is a corruption of 'Padihamites', Padiham being a small town near Burnley in Lancashire.

Pagan   a member of a religion centred on the celebration of nature.

percussion instruments   the family of musical instruments where sound is produced by one part of the instrument striking against another. Thus drums and cymbals are percussion instruments, as is the piano (because the sound is made by tiny 'hammers' striking the strings).

pierrot troupe   a group of musical entertainers, taking their name from Pierrot, a stock character of English and French theatre. From the 1920s to the 1940s, pierrot troupes presented open-air shows in resort towns, consisting of songs, dances and comic sketches.

Pop Art   a visual artistic movement that emerged in the late 1950s in Britain and the United States. It is characterised by themes and techniques drawn from popular mass culture, such as advertising and comic books.

popular medicine   medicine practised without doctors in the eighteenth and nineteenth centuries. Popular medicine was adopted by patients who could not afford medical treatment, and by those who shunned orthodox forms of medicine. It was also used as a complement to professional care.

portico   a colonnade, or range of columns at the front or side of a building.

Punjabi (Panjabi)   the language spoken by 50 million people in the Punjab (a region of north-west India and Pakistan). It is one of the fifteen languages recognised by the Indian Constitution.

rock music   a broad label for the huge array of musical styles that evolved out of 1950s' rock'n'roll. Rock is often considered to carry more weight than pop, and has connotations of integrity and sincerity.

rhythm & blues   a musical genre combining jazz, gospel and blues influences. The music usually consists of a melody, a rhythm section and filler.

Romano-British   relating to Britain during the Roman period.

Rosicrucian Order   an influential esoteric movement, claiming roots dating back to medieval times.

sacro-idyllic   a term used to describe the depiction of a landscape that includes idealised rural scenes and shrines.

Salon   a large state-sponsored exhibition held in Paris, with the admission of works controlled by a jury of Academicians. Before the development of the commercial gallery system, this was the main opportunity for artists to show their work. It was very popular with the French public. For the 1841 exhibition, one million visitors were recorded.

Ska music   a musical style, originating from Jamaica in the late 1950s, that combines calypso, jazz and **rhythm & blues**.

soul music   a genre that combines **rhythm & blues** and gospel music, originating in the late 1950s in the United States.

subculture   a social group distinguished from the dominant society by its own structures, rules, style of dress and musical taste.

texture   in music, the method by which different lines of music are woven together.

thought experiment   in a thought experiment, we are invited to imagine a hypothetical situation – sometimes of an improbable or fantastical kind – and to consider our reactions to it. Philosophers and scientists devise thought experiments to test specific claims.

timbre   the quality, or 'colour', of a musical note or sound that distinguishes, say, a flute and a trumpet even if both are playing notes at the same pitch and volume.

verse/chorus structure   a musical structure in which the two elements (verse and chorus) are repeated in that order. The melodies of the verse and chorus are constant on each occurrence as are the words of the chorus. However, each verse has different words. 'Oh, I do like to be beside the Seaside' is an example of the verse/chorus form, which is used in various musical styles.

Wakes Week   originally a pagan festival, during the **Industrial Revolution** the Wakes became an annual summer break for mill-workers. At first these breaks were associated with travelling fairs, but in the railway era the workers themselves began to travel, and each mill town became identified with taking a break over a particular summer week during the seaside holiday season.

woodwind instruments   the family of musical instruments that includes the flute, clarinet, bassoon and oboe. Not all woodwind instruments are made of wood: most flutes are made of metal and the saxophone is also a woodwind instrument.

ACKNOWLEDGEMENTS

Grateful acknowledgement is made to the following sources for permission to reproduce material in this book.

Chapter 3

Radice, B. (transl and ed.) (1969) 'Book 1, letter 6: to Cornelius Tacitus', 'Book 2, letter 17: to Gallus', and 'Book 9, letter 36: to Fuscus Salinator' in *The Letters of the Younger Pliny* (revised edn), Harmondsworth, Penguin. Copyright © Betty Radice, 1963, 1969. Reproduced by permission of Penguin Ltd.

Chapter 4, Section 4.6

Bush, J. (2005) 'The Beach Boys', *All Music Guide*, All Music Guide LLC/Macrovision Solutions Corp.

Quadrophenia liner notes (1973), Fabulous Music Ltd.

Every effort has been made to contact copyright holders. If any have been inadvertently overlooked the publishers will be pleased to make the necessary arrangements at the first opportunity.

INDEX

Page numbers in **bold** refer to figures.